The Scottish Novel Since the Seventies

THE SCOTTISH NOVEL SINCE THE SEVENTIES: NEW VISIONS, OLD DREAMS

Edited by
Gavin Wallace
and
Randall Stevenson

Edinburgh University Press

Edinburgh University Press Ltd
22 George Square, Edinburgh

Typeset in Linotron Garamond 3 by
Photoprint, Torquay, and
printed in Great Britain by
Hartnoll Ltd, Bodmin

A CIP record for this book is available
from the British Library.

ISBN 0 7486 0415 4

The Publisher wishes to acknowledge
subsidy from the Scottish Arts Council
towards the publication of this volume.

Contents

Acknowledgements

The editors would like to thank Douglas Gifford, whose encyclopaedic knowledge of the Scottish novel was generously put at our disposal in the early stages of planning this book and helped in determining its overall shape. We are also grateful to Vivian Bone of Edinburgh University Press for her encouragement, advice and, above all, forbearance throughout the inevitable difficulties in bringing this large and complex project to fruition. Finally, we owe a considerable debt of gratitude to Pauline Jones and Sarah Carpenter, without whose support the book could not have been completed.

Gavin Wallace
Randall Stevenson

Introduction

Gavin Wallace

It has become commonplace to observe that the past two decades have proved the most productive and challenging period in Scottish literary culture since the Scottish Renaissance of the 1920s and 1930s. Indeed, the profusion and eclecticism of creative talent across all genres and all three of the nation's languages has led some to speak not simply of revival, but of a new – perhaps even more 'real' – Scottish Renaissance.[1] Such declarations of confidence have also been made possible through equally major achievements in literary criticism, scholarship and Scottish cultural studies throughout the same period which have restored the long-eroded intellectual context in which past cultural achievements can be satisfactorily retrieved and appraised, present trends reflected, and future developments fostered and encouraged. To these concentric circles of creative and intellectual flowering can be added a third: the dynamic rejuvenation of the Scottish publishing industry which, a little over ten years ago, few would have dreamt was possible.

So thorough have these achievements proved that few, other than the most eccentric, would now gainsay the category of 'the Scottish novel' as a distinctive literary force or as a viable critical concept. The days when a *Sunday Times* reviewer could applaud George Mackay Brown's *Greenvoe* as a novel in 'the great tradition of English social realism' seem long distant; echoes of the time when understandable extremes of apology and defence seemed prerequisite critical reflexes for protecting Scotland's claim to cultural autonomy against the forces of assimilation to an English or British continuum. Objective, confident debate, both critical and popular, about Scottish fiction has flourished as the laments which dominated the early 1980s for traditions immured in ignorance and neglect – unpublished, unread, untaught – have faded.

The thriving literature connoted by a 'new renaissance', however, continues to mirror a country where political aspirations remain thwarted in the face of social and economic blights if anything more grimly intractable than those reflected by Scottish writers sixty years ago. There is a sense in which Scottish fiction prospers in inverse proportion to the difficulties of the cultural and political situation which it confronts. This is the diagnosis with which Francis Russell Hart opened his survey of the Scottish novel in 1978, when he considered 'the haunting possibility that Scottish culture has features inimical to the novel'; a situation which he nevertheless suggested 'may be not just inevitable but healthy'.[2] If he is right, the recent rude health of Scottish fiction might be taken to indicate that the recent life of the country itself must have been not just 'inimical' but also fruitfully unendurable. The period since 1970 is likely to be seen with hindsight as a phase in which the Scottish novel flourished with a maturity and consistency reminiscent of the heyday of Galt, Scott and Hogg in the nineteenth century or Gibbon, Gunn, McColla, Linklater and Mitchison in the twentieth, producing reputations of an analogous stature and influence which have extended well beyond the native. This is not to imply that levels of attainment within Scottish poetry and drama of the same period have been in any way secondary, either in terms of quality or quantity. In fact, much of the 'renaissance' in fiction can be directly attributed to continuing innovation in the other two genres, in which many fine writers have sought to extend the potential of Scotland's complex linguistic inheritance and cultural identity as a means of confronting, and highlighting, urgent sociocultural and aesthetic issues.

It is significant, too, that while Scottish poetry in the late twentieth century remains dominated to a large extent by the distinguished achievements of Sorley MacLean, Norman MacCaig and Edwin Morgan – poets who, in radically different ways, reveal tangible creative links with the still-potent legacy of MacDiarmid – there are no equivalent writers of fiction (with the possible exception of Naomi Mitchison) who would declare a similar sense of allegiance and continuity with the central novels of the 1930s which MacDiarmid so undervalued. Novelists of subsequent decades have, if anything, written in increasing opposition to Renaissance preoccupations with myth, archaism and symbolic ancestral historicism. Yet perhaps it is possible to detect a subtle process of reconciliation here. Those equally potent Renaissance themes of language, nation and community have continually resurfaced – albeit with a new and ironic urban emphasis – in Scottish poetry and drama since the 1960s. Most contemporary novelists have clearly profited from the new creative possibilities opened up to them by the explorations of phonetics, ironic juxtapositions of standard English and Scots, and linguistic subversion in the work of Tom Leonard, Liz Lochhead and Edwin Morgan.

Demythologising is a process which often operates simply by fashioning new myths from the rubble of the old which, once inscribed, can prove equally monolithic monuments. In this way, the novelists of the 1950s and 1960s challenged the Renaissance epic-mythic impulse by means of a deliberate preoccupation with cynical and deterministic urban realism – a world from which the would-be artist fled in recoil from the absence of fulfilment and failures of idealism. The battlegrounds were left to that stubborn survivor, the 'hard man' – brutalised in the struggle against social injustice and industrial decline; sustained by loyalties to community, class and proletarian culture. These writers' vision was not of the symbolically organic Scotland of 1930s novels – the dear green place – but the alternative 'myth' of an organism far from whole and, moreover, no longer worth reviving. The myth of a barren Scotland was to assume an all-too-literal, and painfully accurate, relevance following the apparent stifling of hopes for an autonomous Scottish political culture, and cultural politics, with the devolution debacle of 1979, a date likely to live on as a prominent point of fracture in Scottish letters, unless the shock-waves of the similar reversal of 1992 emerge as an even more deeply-felt rupture.

The intellectual wasteland to which many believed Scotland had been reduced in 1979 was, however, not barren for long – if, in fact, it ever had been. The late 1970s and early 1980s witnessed the beginnings of a third and infinitely more radical phase in twentieth-century Scottish literature, in which fiction was to prove especially fertile ground. A movement of fictional innovation, led by the Glasgow writers Alasdair Gray and James Kelman, suddenly emerged, indebted to the parameters of working-class urban realism established in the preceding decades, but simultaneously transcending them. What had come to be felt as the stultifying restriction of a defeatist realism was redefined and redeemed by awareness of movements within a wider experimental context, such as the French *nouveau roman* or postmodernism and metafiction.

The considerable impact of this bold enlargement of Scottish creative potential remains symbolised by the publication in 1981 of Alasdair Gray's novel *Lanark*, whose still-reverberating effects on Scottish literature can be likened to earlier enduring literary landmarks like *A Drunk Man Looks at the Thistle* (1926) and *Sunset Song* (1932). Here was an epic, formally adventurous, thematically profound novel synthesising realism and fantasy, in ways made familiar by – and with much of the dexterity of – writers such as Borges, Marquez, Rushdie, Grass, Pynchon et al.; yet remaining wholly faithful to a specifically Scottish tradition. And to Scottish places, or one place in particular: Gray's science-fictional and naturalistic projection of Glasgow/Unthank marked a culmination of the creative nucleus which Glasgow, and the urban west of Scotland, had provided for novelists for much of the century, as well as providing new points of departure. The author's almost Joycean treatment of locality led some critics to suggest that perhaps the Scottish novel at last had something resembling its *Ulysses*. Complemented on the visual plane by his powerful graphics and artwork, Gray's novel detonated a cultural time-bomb which had been ticking away patiently for years, even if many believed after 1979 that the mechanism had seized up for good. London publishers were jolted into a better-informed awareness of Scottish writing, becoming eager to seize on the commercial promise of a rejuvenated literary tradition that might conform to the dictates of a new and lucrative 'fashion': a marketable efflorescence of the Scottish imagination.

Much more importantly, the tenacity and vision of their infinitely smaller and poorer Scottish equivalents, often operating against impossible financial odds, flourished in the dual policy of producing affordable, quality reprints of classic texts – which had, shamefully, long languished in unavailability – alongside a steady stream of equally affordable new works and voices from a new generation of authors. In less then a decade, Scotland has restored much of its once-powerful publishing industry, though on a far from financially-secure basis. That it has succeeded, despite these limitations, in fostering an innovative eclecticism and flexibility in its products is all the more remarkable, a confidence which singles out the publishing scene in Scotland as one of the liveliest and most challenging anywhere.

At the same time much more than this has been achieved. Alongside the continuity with twentieth-century precedents revealed in a still-productive older generation – Naomi Mitchison, George Mackay Brown, Iain Crichton Smith, Robin Jenkins – the impact of Gray and Kelman on Scottish fiction has been succeeded by several new reputations, new œuvres and new stylistic and thematic priorities all identifiably 'native' within Scotland's wide range of cultural groupings, but by no means confined to Scotland in terms either of reputation or relevance. The Scottish novel has several new contours of achievement to chart as a tradition which continues to reconcile, synthesise and juxtapose new visions with old dreams; old visions with new nightmares. Traditional ideologies have been thoroughly adapted, challenged and opposed, to the extent that many of the old dreams, too, of literary criticism in Scotland no longer guarantee a good night's sleep but instead a rude awakening in a reconfigured country, alert in ways it has never been before to issues of past political and historical experience; to the limitations in its myths of dualism; to alternative representations of linguistic fissure; to ossified stereotypes of community, class and gender.

Given the confident upsurge in Scottish studies in the same period – which cannot be separated from the simultaneous tide of new creativity – the fact that the critical establishment has found it difficult to keep up is testimony to the exhilarating pace at which writing in Scotland seems to be developing. Discovering, mapping and evaluating a tradition and a literary history so long marginalised has furthermore sapped a disproportionate amount of intellectual energy, and obliged researchers and scholars to look too long towards the past. One result is that at the beginning of the 1990s there are no more than two book-length studies of twentieth-century Scottish fiction which examine the work of contemporary novelists: Francis Russell Hart's *The Scottish Novel: A Critical Survey* (1978) and Isobel Murray and Bob Tait's *Ten Modern Scottish Novels* (1984).[3] Hart's concluding chapter fleetingly considers the fiction of the early 1970s, while Murray and Tait select their works from a period of fifty years and conclude, tantalisingly, with 1981 and Gray's *Lanark*. It is not to criticise these valuable works to point out that, in the absence of revision and challenge, isolated interpretations can assume an authority disproportionate to their actual relevance. Much of the still-scanty critical attention which Scottish fiction attracts, too, still exists in less than coherent form: in magazines and journals, reviews, initiatives such as the Aberdeen University Press *History of Scottish Literature*, and brief analyses of fictional trends within larger projects such as single-volume literary histories.

The huge potential for a new critical focus on existing interpretations, and the urgent need for extending them to cover the prodigious developments of recent years, provides the motivation behind this collection. The aim is twofold: to assess the diversity within the achievements and preoccupations of Scottish fiction since the 1970s, and to provide a forum for the corresponding range of critical perspectives which has begun to emerge during the same period as contrasting, often conflicting interpretative responses to the Scottish novel. Each chapter offers independent critical assessment of its topic, but all share the intention to clarify the relationship between the present intellectual and cultural context and past traditions, especially where those older shared beliefs have been conspicuously rejected or challenged. The contributors give proper recognition, where appropriate, to related achievements within other genres (the short story in particular) and within other cultures.

The chapters themselves have been divided into three thematic sections which provide a partly chronological, partly conceptual framework offering coherence to the material under discussion and to the various critical methodologies and ideas which pertain in Scotland. Part I examines Robin Jenkins, Iain Crichton Smith, Muriel Spark, William McIlvanney and George Mackay Brown as writers who have been productive since the 1950s and 1960s, assessing the implications of continuity and change in their fiction and their relationship with contemporary writing. Part II traces developments in 'the Glasgow novel', and addresses the impact of the wave of experiment and innovation in James Kelman, Alasdair Gray, Iain Banks and Janice Galloway, considering their creative potential and limitations. Part III offers new interpretations of contemporary novelists by examining the challenges to 'Scottishness' presented in the work of prominent Anglo-Scottish novelists; the shared preoccupations in fiction by women writers; the reflection of Scotland's political ideologies in fiction as they compare with analogous concerns in the Welsh novel; the relationship between media analysis and fiction criticism; and the prevalence of the themes of breakdown and damaged identity. The book concludes with a comprehensive bibliography of Scottish fiction, from 1970 to the present, which includes the work both of the authors under discussion and of those who lie outwith the scope of the chapters themselves.

By its very nature, the book cannot hope to be inclusive, and several obvious omissions have regrettably had to be made. Restrictions of space have made it impossible to include essays on several important writers who deserve book-length studies in themselves, such as Naomi Mitchison. Similarly, critical parameters have remained necessarily narrower than the editors would have wished, so that areas of cultural production crying out for detailed attention, such as the continuing solidity and success of Scottish popular fiction – still much underrated in its significance and misrepresented in terms of quality – have been left untouched as too substantial in themselves to risk incorporating in minimal form for the sake of tokenistic comprehensiveness.

A multi-author project of this kind cannot pretend to be definitive either. A chorus of opinion has been favoured precisely to illustrate the fact that, by its very political and cultural nature, Scotland has produced and continues to produce a complex literature which accords with conflicting conceptions of what precisely constitutes 'Scottishness', let alone nationality. It is for the reader of the novels discussed and of the discussions here to decide to what extent the chorus sings in harmony, and how far they reflect a culture in which the dissonant duets of duality may at last be giving way to a healthier polyphony. If this book provides a reference point for ongoing analysis and debate, and offers some encouragement to the many urgent projects in the field as yet unwritten, then it will have served its purpose.

NOTES

1. Douglas Gifford, 'At Last – The Real Scottish Literary Renaissance?', *Books in Scotland* 34, 1990, pp. 1–4.
2. Francis Russell Hart, *The Scottish Novel: A Critical Survey* (London: John Murray, 1978), Preface, p. viii.
3. Much valuable work in the field has been produced outwith Scotland, notably Manfred Malzahn's *Aspects of Identity: The Contemporary Scottish Novel (1978–1981) as National Self-Expression* (Frankfurt am Main: Peter Lang, 1984).

Part I

CONTINUITIES

One

Disruptions: The Later Fiction of Robin Jenkins

Glenda Norquay

Robin Jenkins is a 'difficult' novelist. Although now a respected, even venerable, figure on the Scottish literary scene, with over twenty novels to his name, he is nevertheless still not a 'popular' writer outside the country; nor has his fiction become any easier with age. Part of the problem with Jenkins's work is that he is not even 'difficult' in the conventional sense. His novels are, in fact, deceptively straightforward: not for him the elaborate fiction-games of postmodernism, the problematising of language, the manipulations of time, the questioning of character. Nor are his subjects at all avant-garde: although his fictions pose challenging questions in their uncompromising exploration of moral issues, they do not offer the unflinching dissections of modern life to be found in other recent Scottish writing. He seems several generations and worlds away from the work of Alasdair Gray, James Kelman or Janice Galloway. And yet, even in his early writings, his work seemed unlike that of his contemporaries, who also explored the experiences of Scottish working-class life that so frequently drew Jenkins. He is a writer primarily interested in creating scenarios which represent a testing of values, a questioning of moral codes, and which reveal the conflicts and contradictions inherent in any organisation of human society. In so doing, he never permits complacency: all his fictions present an unsettling experience for the reader in their radical questioning of moral categories, in their refusal to accept compromise, in their reliance on irony as a dominant mode of thought, and, increasingly, in their willingness to expose the contradictions of Scottish identity. In this respect, a more accurate description of his writing might be 'disruptive' rather than difficult. I am going to argue that the challenges always present in his work, operating as a force for disruption, emerge more sharply in the period since 1979, although the fiction produced since then is also clearly continuous with his previous concerns. I also want to suggest that there has recently been a bifurcation of interest and approaches in his writing: this divides the four novels published since 1979, and reveals how Jenkins has both built upon and diverged from his early works.

In Jenkins's writing, the idea of disruption has several implications. Reading one of his novels can be a disruptive experience: in the moral issues they explore, there is no compromise, and the willingness to shock – present in the early novels through his probing of innocence and goodness – comes again to the fore in *Just Duffy* (1988), with its depiction of a young boy declaring war on the world in an attempt to bring his local community face to face with its own inhumanity. His most recently published work, *Poverty Castle* (1991), by depicting a writer unable to write a book with a positive conclusion, serves as an ironic comment on his own inability to settle for the comfortable and comforting. Increasingly, too, in the later works his explorations of the intractable have taken him into an examination of a specifically Scottish experience and structure of feeling. At its most obvious in *Fergus Lamont* (1979), with its parodic yet tragic depiction of a search for Scottish identity, this concern with dissecting a nation's sense of itself and its history is also evident in *The Awakening of George Darroch* (1985). Taking as its focus the Great Disruption of 1843, the novel explores an event which still presents a challenge in its relationship between Scottish religious feeling and the desire for self-determination. The idea of disruption may also be applied to the form and structure of Jenkins's novels, and it is here that the tension between continuity and innovation is most evident. In many ways, his work can be linked with writers of the 1950s and 1960s who were using the realist novel to explore the experience of Scottish urban and working-class life; but throughout Jenkins's fiction, and most particularly in recent works, the desire to unsettle the reader has significance for the literary strategies adopted. The shift between the perspectives of characters (as in *Just Duffy*), the juxtaposition of different forms of writing (noticeable in *Fergus Lamont*, and an intrinsic part of *Poverty Castle*), and the concealing of motivation at the most crucial points (teasingly used in *The Awakening of George Darroch*), combine to produce a reading experience which shares aspects of the 'defamiliarisation' process to be found in the work of more recent Scottish writers.

Just Duffy (1988) and *Poverty Castle* (1991) are in many ways building on the themes of his earlier novels. In the 1970s, Jenkins published several novels, *A Toast to the Lord* (1972), *A Figure of Fun* (1974) and *A*

Would-be Saint (1978), in which a central character, with a particularly extreme moral stance, is set against his or her society. In each case, the novel considers both the extent to which society might wish to exclude those who adhere too rigorously to the very ideals it wishes to uphold, and the possibility that if an individual occupies such an absolute position of goodness, he or she becomes so incomprehensible to those around them that they are treated with hostility and dislike. Enacting this set of dichotomies in the novels involves the creation of situations full of moral ambiguity, with the text positioning the reader in such a way that no guidelines are given as to our response. Even the narrative perspective itself is slyly shifting and frequently contradictory. *A Would-be Saint* shows this theme of inaccessible goodness, and its necessary literary correlative of narrative ambiguity and reader bafflement, at its most complex. In this novel, the central character, Gavin, aspiring to such goodness, not only becomes an outcast from a society suspicious of his motives, uncomprehending of his values, but also appears to move out of the narrative's grasp, an increasingly enigmatic figure, with the reader denied access to his thoughts. In many ways, this novel can be seen as the most intense exploration of 'ruinous goodness' in Jenkins's œuvre. In *Poverty Castle* and *Just Duffy*, while he returns to this theme, and in particular to the world of children that so fascinated him in his earlier novels, the intensity is less, the concerns broader. Throughout his writing career, Jenkins has been particularly engaged by the possibilities that lie in using the world of a child – or an innocent of some other kind, as in *The Cone-Gatherers* (1955), his most famous work – to confront social hypocrisy and to expose the contradictory nature of moral expectations. In both novels, he returns to this theme, drawing upon its possibilities of shocking an audience, and structuring the book in such a way that the position of the reader too becomes ambiguous and uncomfortable.

This desire to shock and disrupt is at its most obvious in *Just Duffy*. Like earlier novels, such as *A Would-be Saint* and *The Cone-Gatherers*, *Just Duffy* has as its central character an ambiguous figure who could be either saint or fool, a teenager who believes that 'the greatest favour you can do people is to force them to face the truth about themselves'.[1] The novel allows the reader to see the workings of his mind to a certain extent, but much of the writing explores the reactions of those around him as they attempt to make sense of his actions when he 'declares war on society'. Thematically, then, Jenkins's earlier concern with impossible idealism is foregrounded in an extreme manner. Typically, too, for Jenkins, the novel itself opens with an uncomfortable moment:

'When I come back,' she said, 'there could be big changes.'

> Her dressing-gown fell open, revealing her plump white breasts. She knew he hated her to expose herself to him, so she did it often. She had never forgiven him for being born sixteen years ago.
>
> 'There would be no place for you, Duffy. That's what I mean.'
>
> She pretended to speak sadly, but her lips, mauve with lipstick, were pleased. Like everybody else she thought her selfishness was a secret known only to herself. (*JD*, 7)

This scene, between a mother and son, immediately signals its own transgressive nature, indicating the way in which the novel as a whole seeks to question and to defamiliarise what might be seen as 'normal' in relationships. What is also typical of Jenkins's style throughout his writing career, but even more evident here, is the immediate moral comment, the ruthless exposure of hypocrisy and the almost palpable dislike of the mother's self-interest and cruelty. Duffy, of course, is set up in opposition to the kind of society which encourages such behaviour; but, characteristically of Jenkins, his attempt to discover some way of purging society, his belief in 'truth' and the need to confront people with it, is treated with equal irony. At one point in the novel, he is told he is 'not human': this fascination with the irony of people being at their least 'human' when they are most clearly aspiring to the ideals of humanity echoes Jenkins's concerns elsewhere. In this novel, however, the narrative voice is even more explicit than usual in setting out the nature of the dilemma, and the shifts from one character's perspective to another, which keep the reader in a constant state of moral confusion, are more disconcerting. No sooner has the text led us into the interior of Duffy's mind, where his actions seem rational, even exemplary, than we are encouraged to view him from an external perspective, from which the possibility that he is seriously disturbed appears equally convincing.

Jenkins obviously expected the novel to shock and unsettle: 'It can't be popular. Duffy shows a prodigious disgust of humanity. At times he is almost paralysed with this terrible disgust. It's a feeling most of us have at one time, though in a lesser degree, unless we want to take things easy from a moral point of view.'[2] Clearly, this novel can be seen as part of his enterprise to prevent things being 'easy from a moral point of view'. And yet, while *Just Duffy* seems an angry book, the world that is attacked is not recognisably contemporary, and the elements of moral allegory, present in earlier novels, prevent this from becoming a fully-engaged analysis of contemporary society. Instead, it is the character of Duffy that is problematised, rather than the society of which he is a product. While Jenkins may not be attempting that representation of a slice of Scottish life to be found in the fiction of his contemporaries, the novel's unusual theme, of an individual standing against the whole of his society, might seem to encourage social analysis. Instead, the focus on Duffy's isolation seems to prevent either an examination of the character as social product or a full critique of society as damaging to the individual. The novel attempts a complex negotiation between the social and the metaphysical, but positions the reader between the two in a way that certainly avoids complacency but also appears in some ways to hinder understanding of the issues.

In certain respects, *Poverty Castle* resembles *Just Duffy*: it too makes explicit some previously unacknowledged elements which have sustained Jenkins's work. By far the most 'metafictional' of his novels, this book moves between the story of a dying novelist, requested by his wife to write at least one pleasant novel which affirms a faith in humanity, and the 'novel' itself which he is trying to finish. 'He had always hoped that in his old age he would be able to write a novel that would be a celebration of goodness, without any need of irony'.[3] Serving, then, as an ironic comment on the impossibility of writing a book that does 'make things easy', the plot of the novel-within-a-novel follows the lives of a family of three young girls who take over an almost-ruined house on a Scottish island. The family have inherited money, so there is no financial worry; they are close and loving and talented. The fiction flirts throughout with the possibility that if events were to turn against them their goodness would become much more problematic; but as the story is left incomplete, with the author dying just before the end, this eventuality is not put to the final test. But again, as with *Just Duffy*, the isolated world of the novel lacks a sense of contemporary relevance, and [illegible] have a curiously archaic feel. It would seem here, too, that the novel, although creating all kinds of disruptive experiences for the reader, leaves us unsure as to the direction in which our anxieties should be engaged: are we to explore fundamentals of morality, to question fictional techniques, or to focus on a critique of the society represented in the novel? Or does the cause for concern lie elsewhere? The text, pulling in various directions, offers little resolution to the contradictions which it raises.

Both novels, then, might be said to create an expectation of social analysis which is not fully sustained, as the fictions fall back on questions of metaphysics and morality familiar from Jenkins's other novels. What does emerge more strongly than in previous works is Jenkins's own ironic attitude, possibly even dissatisfaction, with the role of books themselves, and with the ways in which fiction-making in general, and the realist novel in particular, lulls the reader into a false sense of security and comfort. In *Just Duffy*, one of the first actions of the eponymous hero, having declared war on humankind, is to steal into the public library, with a motley crew of helpers, and to tear one page from the middle of each book. When the crime is discovered before the readers take out the books, Duffy is disappointed:

> There would be no shocks for the readers of the books. They would not suddenly be jolted from the world of make-believe into the world of reality. They would not be forced to face the truth about themselves. (*JD*, 108)

These words, of course, could be taken as a description of Jenkins's own writing career: his attempts to refuse to allow the reader to settle; his sudden shifts in perspective; changes of sympathy; refusal to compromise. And Duffy's second attempt to provoke – breaking into a church and dabbing excrement on the page of every Bible – is likewise an image of Jenkins's writing: he wants us to be confronted by our own stench, by an awareness of human physicality, with the juxtaposition of body and morality – and to experience disgust. The desire to disrupt plays, therefore, a powerful, if unfocused, part in the structure and theme of each novel.

Both *Just Duffy* and *Poverty Castle* work reflexively, offering fascinating comments on Jenkins's writing career: the former provides a symbolic image of the writer's own battle with glib moral categories and facile social codes, while the latter foregrounds the novelist's anxiety that an optimistic story is in itself a betrayal of the human condition. As such, the two novels may be read as a form of retrospective analysis of the writer's work. In their subject matter, however, they show little development from earlier works; it is in the two novels published before them – *Fergus Lamont* and *The Awakening of George Darroch* – that Jenkins is at his most experimental and complex. It is in those works, too, that his fictional techniques are deployed in such a way that the scope of his enquiries extends beyond the metaphysical and acquires a political and national dimension, allowing the techniques of disruption to work towards a more focused end.

Although the formal characteristics of *Fergus Lamont* are not particularly innovative in fictional terms, they represent a new direction for the writer. Using a first-person narrative, retrospective but with interspersed flashes forward into the time of writing, Jenkins adopts a less linear, more spatial approach to narrative. His thematic concerns likewise broaden out: Fergus is an old man, living in squalor, sitting in a public library writing his memoirs, but he has also been 'a Scottish soldier', has had pretensions to the aristocracy, was known as a fine figure of a man who always wore a kilt, and at one stage became a recluse, living on a Hebridean island with a pipe-smoking Celtic goddess called Kirstie. Fergus thus occupies a central position within several powerful Scottish myths, and represents an ironic commentary on the structuring of a Scottish identity within certain social and historical contexts. Typically, the story that Fergus tells could be read either as one of hypocritical self-justification for some reprehensible actions or of a hard-headed realism, mixed with good intentions, surviving in difficult circumstances. *Fergus Lamont* was the most explicit of Jenkins's novels to date in its linking of moral ambiguity with a specifically Scottish context. We are told, for example, that Fergus's grandfather, who cuts himself off from his daughter because of her lifestyle, refusing even to go to her funeral, both displayed 'atrocious callousness' and 'compelled most people to think of him as a Christian of formidable and magnificent staunchness'.[4] This is connected in the novel with the self-destructiveness of Scottish morality: in attempting to create a national identity by clinging to a fierce and unforgiving Calvinist morality, Scotland annihilates its own capacity to love, to forgive, to grow. Yet the novel also reveals how the other side of this stern Scottishness, the sentimentality that attaches so much significance to the wearing of the kilt, that invests a small island with mythic power and that glorifies all things Scottish, is equally unproductive, permitting various kinds of social and emotional exploitation.

Jenkins also goes further in this novel in exploring the implications of his own bleak moral perspective in literary terms, for Fergus is a poet, and the tensions of Scottish identity are given a powerful pertinence for his position as a writer. Talking to an ex-teacher, once a writer and as near to a friend as Fergus gets, he is told

> You could never have written such good poetry if you had been able to think things out to their nihilistic conclusion. Then you would have to remain silent. Like me. (*FL*, 290)

In a way, this seems to sum up Jenkins's dilemma: because of the intractability of moral questions, and the apparently insoluble contradictions of Scottish identity, built as it is upon so many oppositions, the writer is suspicious of anything that hints of compromise, of anything in fiction that seems to offer a neat pattern. Instead, his writing seeks to establish its own dynamic – to keep moving its perspective, to keep the reader working at the contradictions rather than expecting answers, to deny stability or security. Although this could also be said of Jenkins's previous works, in *Fergus Lamont* it is the historical and political context of the situations which gives the novel its sharpness, as the specifically Scottish parameters of the moral dilemmas are brought into focus. If there is no stability offered to the reader, it is because the particular cast of mind being explored is one which itself is established through the series of contradictory and frequently self-destructive codes and myths which make up this thing called Scottish identity.

If *Fergus Lamont* offers an exploration of oppositions within the Scottish psyche, the intersections of morality and nationality are addressed even more directly in *The Awakening of George Darroch*. In all his writings, Jenkins explores issues of morality, apparently fascinated with absolutes of good and evil, and in this respect his work offers a direct engagement with the impact and role of Calvinism in Scotland. With his interest in religious hypocrisy, which Calvinism's emphasis on the Elect and the Damned might seem to encourage, there are obvious connections in Jenkins's concerns with the work of other Scottish writers, most notably Burns, Hogg and Stevenson. A central contradiction within Scottish mythologising, however, is the extent to which elements of its Protestant history have been ignored at the expense of a romantic celebration of Catholicism: Mary Queen of Scots and the Jacobite rebellions form the subject matter of many narratives, whereas the Covenanters, clearly central to Scottish history and consciousness, have been largely forgotten in the nation's fiction-making. The Great Disruption of 1843, an event at which a group of Scottish ministers walked out of the General Assembly in protest at state interference in the Church, and which led to the establishment of the Free Church, has been even more obviously denied the attention in story and fable which it appears to merit. By taking the Disruption as his subject matter in *The Awakening of George Darroch*, Jenkins makes his interest in the Scottish Church itself, as an institutional example of Scotland's moral and social contradictions, more explicit than in any of his other novels, and the subject allows him to explore connections between a nation's morality, its cast of mind and its concept of nationhood.

Jenkins himself is well aware that he is treading on neglected ground. In the foreword to the novel, he reminds us that

> history has dismissed in a few dry lines an event that took place in Scotland and was considered by those who played a part in it as the most momentous in the history of their country since the Reformation.

Implicitly acknowledging that the event is not only reduced to a few lines by historical accounts but also largely neglected by fiction, Jenkins's novel is a brave departure for the writer: his only historical novel to date, but also a foray into an almost untouched area of Scottish experience. Yet, in some ways, it is an obvious novel for him to write: a culmination of his concern with human idealism in conjunction with human self-interest, and with the extent to which a particular religious history and struggle for national identity have shaped a country's sense of itself. The events of the Great Disruption offer a fascinating intersection of personal and political dilemmas, a juxtaposition of spiritual and economic concerns. The ministers involved are, after all, not simply choosing a course of action in line with their beliefs, but are also determining their livelihoods: to leave the Established Church also means giving up their church, their status, their stipend, their home. In many cases, they would also lose most of their congregation. Whatever action they take involves a certain amount of self-justification – or self-deception.

Characteristically, Jenkins's way into the subject is to centre the issues around one problematic figure. George Darroch is a type familiar from other novels, such as *The Changeling, A Toast to the Lord* and *A Would-be Saint*: the apparently innocent idealist who, in his search for 'goodness', inflicts thoughtless cruelty on those around him, and who himself appears unsure about his own motivations and desires. Darroch, for example, sees it as wicked to abstain from 'loving' his wife, even though he knows another childbirth will kill her. He is a man who believes that 'people left to themselves could not be trusted to act sensibly. They acted selfishly, greedily, callously and cruelly, as well as stupidly.'[5] And, while devout in the extreme, the narrative reveals again and again the practical workings of his mind which get in the way of his much-proclaimed spirituality:

> Though he had prayed thousands of times, Darroch still did not find prayer simple; there could be so many complications. To begin with there was always the problem of whether to speak aloud or inwardly. Whether God himself had a preference was impossible to discover but for the person praying it could matter a great deal, since there could be circumstances in which, try as he might, he would not be able to keep out of his voice a girn of complaint or a whine of self-pity. (*AGD*, 82)

A typical feature of Jenkin's writing here is that strange mixture of a real involvement in the dilemma which confronts the character, trivial as it may be, with a narrative hostility – a despising of the character – which emerges in the language of the last few words. Likewise, when the narrative comments on the excessive, almost foolish, nature of Darroch's deeds of kindness – 'In all this bountifulness his sons saw an element of conceit. He was as foppish in his good deeds as his dress' (*AGD*, 16) – the reader is left with the uncomfortable feeling that we are intended both to be suspicious of Darroch's self-glorification and also to condemn the sons for their narrow-minded reading of his actions. Most damningly, Darroch is described as being like all the other Evangelicals, in that he is unable to laugh at himself: 'George always took him literally. Irony was a way of laughing at yourself. That was something George and all the other Evangelicals never did'. (*AGD*, 64). To be without irony is a serious deficiency in the novel, for that itself is the mode through which the text operates. The author's view of life, as it emerges in his writing, might be described as deeply ironic, aware of the high ambitions which humankind has for itself, but also of the deeply-flawed nature of morality which inevitably leads his characters to fall short of their ambitions. Yet, even when they fall short, the narrative is wary of condemning the aspirations themselves. This condemnation of George's lack of irony ensures that the tone of the narrative is directly opposed to the cast of mind of its central character – a tension which again works to disrupt the security of the narrative and activate the reader through the juxtaposition of contradictory discourses.

The subject matter too presents the reader with 'difficult' issues. In the course of the novel, Darroch's wife dies, he is left with a large family and a meagre income, fantasising about various sexual liaisons that might be open to him in his new state as a widower, and he is then offered a wealthy new parish, with much greater prestige – but only if he remains within the Established Church. In exploring this scenario, the writer not only depicts the conflicting motives of a man who realises that in his innocence may lie the seeds of worldly success, and that in adopting an isolated position for the sake of his principles he may further his status and reputation, but also reveals the inability of Darroch's friends, family and parishioners to reach any definite interpretation about the worth and significance of his actions. The subject of the Disruption, then, provides an ideal forum for the continued examination of human behaviour found in earlier novels, and again prevents the reader from assuming any easy moral position.

This novel, however, like *Fergus Lamont*, also embraces a wider and more specifically social concern which permits an exploration of spiritual endeavours within a set of specific material and historical circumstances. Set in the 1840s, a decade of political disruptions, the novel presents issues of Christian morality within a wider ideological framework, as the emergence of an early form of socialism, preached by various disreputable characters whom George encounters, is shown to present an increasingly viable alternative to the Church. Darroch is shown to favour making miners Christian and thus enhancing the reputation of the Church among the poor, but he increasingly worries about socialism – which in some senses he endorses – as a rival for the people's attention:

> The Church was right in fighting for spiritual independence, but when this was won what use would be made of it? Would the new free Church set an example to the old Church, still a servant of the State, and to the whole nation, of courage, compassion, self-sacrifice, and love, for Christ's sake? If it did not the future would deservedly belong to men like Taylor who would set up a just social order, from which God was excluded. (*AGD*, 131)

While he may have sympathy with such people as the itinerant radical, Taylor, he later describes a struggle which has begun in the country

> between Taylor and his kind on the one hand, and ministers of the Gospel, such as ourselves on the other, for the minds and souls, not only of the poverty-stricken and degraded masses, but also of those intelligent and educated members of society who consider it unjust and unchristian that some men should have much more than they need while others have much less. (*AGD*, 229–30)

Again, there is considerable irony within the narrative at Darroch's expense, for, while he makes this speech, he is still considering the possibility of accepting the offer of a new parish. Present in his mind too is the thought that in making this declaration he will impress the Church leaders with his integrity:

> He saw no reason why, with the Lord's help, he himself should not become as dominant as Dr Chalmers or Dr Cook in the councils of the Church, with a bolder message to proclaim. (*AGD*, 223)

In this conflict of interests and of systems of belief, however, the novel also indicates that even the highest ideals, socialist or Christian, are inevitably tainted by the opportunism, self-interest and power-seeking of those who advocate them.

Our reading of Darroch's character oscillates between seeing in him an admirable refusal to compromise and seeing an overweening arrogance and self-aggrandisement. As with his other novels, but even more noticeably here perhaps, because so much is at stake, Jenkins prevents the reader from settling for any one account or understanding of Darroch's motivation. The novel forces us constantly to re-evaluate not only characters and situations, but also whole systems of belief. Even at the moment when George Darroch is shown as arriving at some sense of his different selves – the lustful sinner, the friend of the poor, the opportunist and the good father – there is a hint of self-indulgence in his perceptions: 'he lay, in a state of delicious suspension . . .' (*AGD*, 246). Once again, it would seem that narrative accounts are inadequate in detailing the complexity of the individual mind as it responds to conflicting social and moral demands. When the novel reaches its climax, the moment at which George Darroch will make his decision, the apparent impossibility of comprehending motivations becomes evident; the narrative perspective seems to recede from the character, leaving the reader in even more doubt as to his thoughts. The scene in the General Assembly itself is presented through the viewpoint of Darroch's two sons, neither of whom wholly understands their father and who cannot agree on the significance of his actions. Is their father unable to resist the moment of self-glorification that would come from following the dissenting leaders out of the assembly, or is he genuinely committed to the cause, and willing to sacrifice everything – including the future prosperity of the family – to it? One son, Arthur, views his father with 'pride and anxiety'; the other, James, is much harsher, watching with dismay and anger:

> He knew what had happened: given the best opportunity of his life to show off his father had not been able to resist it. For the sake of a minute's vanity he had sentenced his family to years of hardship. (*AGD*, 266)

Denied access to Darroch himself, the reader is no wiser.

In criticising his father, however, James offers an analogy with the character of his country, which serves to extend the impact of Jenkins's subject matter in the novel:

> What they had seen was a demonstration of the disastrous divisiveness of the Scottish nation, which had kept it materially and spiritually improverished in the past and was still doing so today. (*AGD*, 267)

At this point, the novel makes clear those connections between individual morality and a set of specific social and historical circumstances contributing to the structures of Scottish life and Scottish identity, which had previously been hinted at in Jenkins's work. *The Awakening of George Darroch* represents an acknowledgement of those factors which construct for Jenkins's characters the frequently contradictory and potentially destructive codes by which they operate, but extends the significance of that tension into a political analysis of a whole country's history. And, as with *Fergus Lamont*, in this novel, disruption is presented as inherent in the subject matter as well as a characteristic of the form.

In conclusion, Jenkins's recent writing can be seen as both a continuation and a development of his previous work, but in both respects maintaining a disruptive character which is distinctively his own. In *Just Duffy* and *Poverty Castle*, the disruptive nature of the work lies in the moral questions and the unsettling effect which his shifts in narrative perspective and sympathy have on the reader, but these elements build on features of his earlier works. In returning to the theme of children which has so fascinated him, the writer is also covering familiar ground. Yet here, in a sense, may be found the limitations of these works. The children about whom Jenkins writes could be said to belong to an earlier world; even in *Just Duffy*, with its attempt to create a gang of hoodlums, the children themselves seem curiously innocent: they rarely swear, their sexual knowledge is obscure and even their acts of violence contain a moral intensity. In some respects, then, this is a world that has stayed the same for Jenkins; and, while the fictional techniques may still have the power to unsettle, the subjects which are intended to 'shock' in *Just Duffy* appear curiously innocuous. Where *Poverty Castle* and *Just Duffy* are at their most valuable is in the insights which they offer on the writer's attitude to, and anxieties about, the process of making fictions.

In *Fergus Lamont* and *The Awakening of George Darroch*, however, there may be seen real innovation: in those novels, Jenkins has discovered, through their very different subjects, a means of exploring issues of principle, self-image and compromise in relation to both the individual and the nation. And in those novels, the disruption for the reader leads to a full engagement with genuinely problematic questions. If his novels address the question of how an individual responds when caught in the tension between impossibly high ideals of morality and the contradictory demands of a society which prioritises self-interest and advancement yet resents success, they also increasingly move towards a recognition of similar tensions within the situation of Scotland itself. In *Poverty Castle*, Scotland is described as 'a country in some ways grand and noble but in other ways small-minded and poverty-stricken' (*PC*, 133); in the novels where Jenkins allows himself to explore a Scottish cast of mind, to acknowledge the historical and political elements which help to create the moral dichotomies on which he focuses in his other fiction, a genuine development and innovation in his writing may be found. 'Disruptions' in the reading create a focus on genuinely intractable social, moral and political questions that are of a peculiarly Scottish dimension. And it is in the same novels that he makes a positive and necessary contribution to the questions of Scottish identity that writers younger than him continue to explore. If writers such as Gray and Kelman appear more assured in placing such concerns at the centre of their fictions, it may be that they are more confident of their implied audience, its interests and its receptiveness to their experimentation. Nevertheless, it could be argued that it is in these recalcitrant texts of Jenkins, initially reassuring but profoundly unsettling, that the reader is led to confront the complexities of a Scottish sense of self and to recognise the progressive effects of disruption.

NOTES

1. Robin Jenkins, *Just Duffy* (Edinburgh: Canongate Publishing, 1988), p. 33. Subsequent references are to this edition.
2. Unpublished interview with Robin Jenkins, in Glenda Norquay, 'Moral Absolutism in the Novels of Robert Louis Stevenson, Robin Jenkins and Muriel Spark: Challenges to Realism', PhD thesis, University of Edinburgh, 1985.
3. Robin Jenkins, *Poverty Castle* (Nairn: Balnain Books, 1991), p. 7. Subsequent references are to this edition.
4. Robin Jenkins, *Fergus Lamont* (Edinburgh: Canongate Publishing, 1979; reprinted Edinburgh: Canongate Classics, 1990), p. 27. Subsequent references are to the first edition.
5. Robin Jenkins, *The Awakening of George Darroch* (Glasgow: Waterfront Communications, 1985), p. 88. Subsequent references are to this editon.

FURTHER READING

Binding, Paul, 'Ambivalent Patriot: The Fiction of Robin Jenkins' in *New Edinburgh Review* 53, 1981, pp. 20–2.

Burgess, Moira, 'Robin Jenkins: A Novelist of Scotland' in *Library Review* 22, no 8, 1970, pp. 409–12.

Malzahn, Manfred, *Aspects of Identity: The Contemporary Scottish Novel (1978–1981) as National Self-Expression* (Frankfurt am Main: Peter Lang, 1984).

Morgan, Edwin, 'The Novels of Robin Jenkins' in *The Listener*, 12 July 1973, pp. 58–9, reprinted in *Essays* (Cheadle Hulme: Carcanet, 1974).

Murray, Isobel and Tait, Bob, *Ten Modern Scottish Novels* (Aberdeen: Aberdeen University Press, 1984), pp. 194–218.

Norquay, Glenda, 'Four Novelists of the 1950s and 1960s' in *The History of Scottish Literature*, Volume 4: *The Twentieth Century* (Aberdeen: Aberdeen University Press, 1987), pp. 259–76.

Norquay, G., Sellin, B. and Gifford, D., 'Robin Jenkins: Special Feature' in *Cencrastus* no 24, Autumn 1986.

Sellin, Bernard, 'Actualité de Robin Jenkins: *Fergus Lamont*', (Congrès SAES Amiens: 1982).

Two

Bleeding from All that's Best: The Fiction of Iain Crichton Smith

Douglas Gifford

> God may not be beautiful, but you
> suffer a local wound. You bleed to death
> from all that's best, your active anima.
>
> (*Deer on the High Hills*, 1962)

This, taken from one of Crichton Smith's most elusive and ambitious poems, and six years before *Consider the Lilies* (1968), reminds us that Crichton Smith had been a poet for fifteen years before attempting fiction, and that the basic and polarised dichotomies underlying his work were established in important volumes like *Thistles and Roses* (1961), *The Law and the Grace* (1965) and *The Permanent Island* (1965). It is well worthwhile for readers of the fiction to approach *Consider the Lilies*, especially, via some of these earlier poems – in particular the earlier 'Old Woman' explorations of maternal bigotry and senility: 'Statement by a Responsible Spinster', 'Home' and 'She Teaches Lear'. Indeed, 'Old Woman', from *The Law and the Grace* could be taken as a poetic expression of everything that Mrs Scott of *Lilies* stands for – the only difference of content lying in the lack of absolution in the poem, as opposed to the novel's epiphanies, which allow Crichton Smith to forgive and understand what the poem condemns. Crichton Smith's fiction is about suffering, atonement and absolution.

Arguably, Crichton Smith is essentially a poet. His fiction can often appear naive and ill-expressed in its redundancies; its attempts at worldly ease, which too often betray an awkward unease with the street and modern society; its heavy traditional narrative structures. It would be wrong, however, to see the fiction as secondary, despite Crichton Smith's recent statement that 'I'm more naturally a poet than a novelist . . . Their gifts are essentially different'.[1] Writers are not their own best witnesses. Crichton Smith has worked in both genres so close to the cutting edge of his own experience that it may well be easier for the reader to perceive the complementary nature of poetry and fiction and the important way that the fiction reflects in extended fashion, in a way denied to the poetry, on the ironies and intricacies of human situations more boldly treated in the poetry. In addition, the fiction seems also to perform for Crichton Smith a therapeutic and exorcistic function, humanising early painful experience and insights. Here, one must tread warily; the abundant autobiographical material woven into virtually all the fiction could easily tempt the reader towards a biographically-based interpretation of the development of the fiction which supposed a correlation between Crichton Smith's own acknowledged breakdowns and recoveries, and the oscillation in his fiction between negation and affirmation.[2] A single major theme dominates all the fiction, whether it be in short story or novel length, and whether apparently close to or distant from Crichton Smith's own experience.

This can be found most representatively in the collection of short stories *The Black and the Red* (1973), which is divided into two parts. In the first are stories of the pointlessness and absurdity of death, irredeemable loneliness at parties, in railway stations (a recurrent image of transience throughout all the fiction), even at weddings, and certainly, as in the poignant account of an exile's return to his island, 'An American Sky', in the recognition that leaving the island means losing both where one has left and where one is going. The first part shows 'black' as the characteristic of modern materialism, the negativity of fragmented society, as well as of traditional rural Scottish narrow-mindedness and bigotry, the theme of Crichton Smith's Lewis- and village-based fiction. But with the final, title story of this part, the volume turns to 'red': the colour of life and risk-taking liberation, as well as blood. 'The Black and the Red' has the confessional quality of *The Last Summer* (1969) and its related fictions; indeed, it takes up from *The Last Summer*'s ending in which 'Malcolm' sailed from Lewis, his own emigration and Highland Clearance. Landing in Kyle and going to an unnamed city (which is recognisable as Aberdeen) opens 'The Black and the Red'. 'Black' is the colour of much of the rest of the story – the disappointing grey lecturers, the city suicides and tragedies (the suicide note: 'I am tired of being drained of my blood'), the shadowy advances of the tutor, cerebral, arid, sexually in limbo, as well as black childhood memories of summer days in bed due to TB, and the mother's black letters about church squabbles at home – all summarise Part I's metaphoric statement that mean-spirited introversion, egotistical intellectuality, religious bigotry and apprehensive fearfulness about living are ubiquitous and life-denying. It would be glib to argue that Part II reverses polarities, allowing 'red' and optimism to dominate: 'In Church', 'The Return' and 'Through the Desert' are nightmares of distorted religion, endless wasteland and unhappy return. But somehow these darkest stories become contexts for affirmation, just as in Edwin Muir's 'The Labyrinth' it is the claustrophobic maze which sweeps its victim to its enemy, the lovely world. Like Muir – with whom, in terms of recurrent oscillation between solipsism and release, Crichton Smith has many affinities – Crichton Smith is beginning to assert that without the black, the red is impossible. Indeed, Crichton Smith goes further as he develops this dualism, this Manichean inextricability. 'Red' life in these stories can be aggressive, ferocious, selfish, even though it is natural and free; and, as in many other poems and stories, black – colour of the simple woman in church, of death – can possess a dignity, just as scholarship and respect for classical tradition are not always grey and arid. Balance and harmony are all, though it has to be said that, throughout his work as a whole, Crichton Smith is hardly consistent about where the balance should be poised.

'The Black and the Red' reflects the process by which polarities are reversed. Kenneth (Malcolm's successor) changes metaphysical places with George, red-haired, vital, and Malcolm's opposite; the story may overstate its red-black imagery, but the reversal is clear. Colour, life and fiery Fiona claim Kenneth, and, like Mrs Scott in *Consider the Lilies*, he breaks down in order to regenerate and be refashioned in positive relation to life. Thus, Part I touches bottom and rises; Part II, through portrayals of moments of ultimate darkness in mental disintegration, wartime horror, or more mundane disillusion ('A Day in the Life Of', 'The Crater' and 'The Professor and the Comics' respectively), widens the previously narrow scope of the stories from pseudo-autobiographical and domestic Scottish to explore the minds of women, soldiers, professors – people other than the author. This dualism of approach and perspective is central to all the fiction. This chapter will examine how this dualism operates in the most personal and confessional of Crichton Smith's fiction, concluding with an examination of both his first and his most recent novel as oblique explorations of personal crises and dilemmas central to his work.

The 'confessional' novels begin with *The Last Summer* (1969) and continue with *My Last Duchess* (1971), *Goodbye, Mr Dixon* (1974), *The Hermit* (novella among stories, 1977), *On The Island* (1979; interdependent stories forming a novel, much as Gunn's *Young Art and Old Hector* (1942)), *A Field Full of Folk* (1982), *The Search* (1983), *Mr Trill in Hades* (novella among short stories, 1984), *In the Middle of the Wood* (1987) and *The Dream* (1990). Add a crucial short story, 'Murdo', from *Murdo and Other Stories* (1981), and the recurrent autobiographically-rooted situations of the less personal stories, and this asserts itself as the core of his output. Broadly, they trace the development of Crichton Smith's deepest relations with himself, his family, his village (whether in Lewis or Argyllshire), his island and mainland, the Scottish Lowlands and the world at large. The movement is in the chronological order stated, outwards and away from the peculiarly isolated environment of Bayble, his original home. In *Towards the Human* (1986) and other autobiographical pieces,[3] Crichton Smith has stressed how unplaced and unrelated to Scotland and the world this village and island bareness was – and here, surely, is the root of that lack of mythology so striking in his poetry and fiction. In direct contrast to writers of the Scottish Renaissance such as Gunn and Gibbon, and later writers such as Naomi Mitchison or Mackay Brown, there is no anthropomorphic or legendary continuum in Crichton Smith's work. No standing stones carry a message to sensitive moderns – just the opposite in novels like *The Last Summer*, where they are simply there, devoid of relevance, just as, in 'At the Party' in *The Black and the Red*, the songs of the Highlands are shown as irrelevant and absurd in a Lowland context, or, as late as *The Dream*, drunken traditionalism is exposed as banal self-indulgence. No Chris Guthries or Finn MacHamishes for Crichton Smith[4] – as with MacCaig, myth is suspect and ultimately dishonest, distracting from attention to the complexity of the immediate.

These novels chart two kinds of development. On one level, they are concerned with Smith's reaction to village, island values, Gaelic heritage and relations between Lowland and Highland, with an attendant progressive exorcism of Calvinist repression. On another level, they transcend such local considerations in order to examine abstract and cultural issues, placeless and timeless: the place of classical literature and history in contemporary anti-canonical culture, the value of metaphor, poetry and Art, the nature of freedom and duty, and finally the questionable validity of any of these issues in the face of chaos and existential flux. Both levels are present in all the novels, but it is useful to distinguish between those which express Crichton Smith's native dilemma primarily, and those which express his recurrent anxieties about social morality, Art and the validity of experience.

In many novels, these levels are interdependent. *The Last Summer* is the crisis period for Malcolm, eighteen, sixth-year pupil in Stornoway. Shadows of Mrs Scott fall about him: his mother's anxious disapproval of his football, his friends, of almost everything but his study for a bursary. The village tugs at his loyalty through its claim on him for the football team – so too does the school. Local Sheila competes with cool and sophisticated Janet, an archetypal Crichton Smith character, akin to the golden girls of the poetry who effortlessly radiate their beauty and influence around them. The novel builds to the climax of a choice of loyalties which is that of the claim of Home against that of Away, that of community against wider attractions – in microcosm, the challenge to be repeated again and again, of the native and vernacular against the imperialist and centralised. It is presented with gentle understanding and a simplicity of structure which belies the skill and poetry underlying it.

Although one can argue that this novel is primarily about island issues, these already show themselves to be harbingers of flux. Malcolm faces timeless problems of duty and loyalty, brought to a head for him through the machinations of Ronnie (another archetypal figure), who is the representative of casual morality, selfish power, cool detachment from the world's failures and ordinariness. Crichton Smith had used the Janet and Ronnie types in the poem 'She Teaches Lear' to allow a spinster teacher to explore *Lear*, herself and her timid addiction to duty, and the much older Western concept of 'lear': knowledge, social obligations, public wisdom and morality. Here, central to the book, is a similar classroom discussion of another definitive Western text, Virgil's *Aeneid*. Now Malcolm is the focus for self-discovery, rather than the teacher. Ronnie sees Virgil's presentation of Aeneas and the gods as naive, and sardonically denigrates the function of conscience and human love in the poem. He instigates a debate on whether duty in the poem is to human feeling or to 'bigger' claims, to Dido or to Rome. Malcolm is of course for Dido, and Ronnie [illegible] to ensnare Malcolm in a game for his amusement. 'The power that corrupts, that power to excess / The beautiful quite naturally possess . . .': Auden's expression of ordinary masochism in the face of the beautiful, unscrupulous and powerful fascinates Crichton Smith as well as Malcolm, reading it now for the first time. Thus, Crichton Smith has Malcolm cope with home issues and recognise – without solving – wider and more metaphysical challenges. Locally, he solves the dilemma posed by Ronnie (to play football for the school or to go out with Janet) *and* his school-village dilemma by withdrawing from both issues – and leaving the island. But is this real resolution, or running away? As yet, Crichton Smith leaves the rival claims of freedom open; the novel is concerned mainly with places and people that form or deform us.

It is useful to follow the confessional fiction down through the village- and island-centred novels, always remembering that these share all the wider moral concerns of the other confessional fiction. But the concern with origin and tradition is such a dark strand through the work that it is indeed almost 'the Black' of Crichton Smith's Black-and-Red symbolic opposition, and worth recognising as distinct in its roots, if merging with wider issues later. We have observed the setting-up of this polarity in *The Black and the Red*, some four years after *The Last Summer*; there, home issues were specifically set against those of the far-flung worlds of emigrant and exile. *The Village* (1976), *The Hermit* and *On the Island*, short stories appearing between 1976 and 1979, all show Crichton Smith further working out his tortuous feelings of love and hate for small island (and mainland 'islanded') communities. *The Village* is a black book of grotesque characters, incidents and dark poetic reflections. Hypocrite ministers, manipulative children, vicious teachers, brooding melancholics, pious mothers, foolish policemen dominate these fragments of what appear – from their recurrence throughout Crichton Smith's work – to be mainly memories. There is humour, but it is always painful – for example, in the *Murdo*-like story 'The Ghost', where the author meets the ghost of a writer of Highland Kailyard plays who upbraids him for his 'depressing morality'. The author concludes that

> a light anecdote or two might distract my two or three agonised readers wherever they are, scattered on the surface of this hilarious tortured globe. Even the one who reads my work back to front in Cambodia.[5]

The overall impression of Crichton Smith's response to his background now is one of muted horror at the introspection, the false piety, the wasted lives. 'The Painter' sums this up: two village enemies finally fight – shockingly, in a vicious dance of death with scythes as weapons. A painter, detached, witnesses and records. However, one should note that the teller of the tale drives out such callousness in dismay. Crichton Smith, it seems, is both the painter, detached, and the despiser of his own detachment. There is just the glimmer of a new attitude in 'The Red Door', where, predictably, the mysteriously-painted red door is a new sign of hope and humanity. And perhaps all the negative feeling is summed up in a powerful piece which, significantly, Crichton Smith will extend to become a novella in *The Hermit*. In both the short story, 'The Existence of the Hermit', and the novella, the figure of the hermit is one of Crichton Smith's most disturbingly poetic. In both, the self-sufficiency of the silent, mysterious figure acts as catalyst within the neighbouring village. He is an innocent scapegoat who reminds observers that they lack his integrity. They make him the repository of their deficiencies, their malice, their lost chances and wasted lives. The novella is a dramatic monologue, with 'Holy Willie' overtones. The retired headmaster, sterile and lonely within the travesty of community, effects the banishing of the harmless hermit, and this eviction carries something of the symbolism of the 'internal clearances' of *Consider the Lilies*.

The Hermit also marks a turning point in Crichton Smith's relationship with island and community. Beyond this study of village blackness are nine stories from the wider world: as in *The Black and the Red*, the volume manifests the division at the heart of the fiction. In the context of viewing native tradition, 'The Brothers' is a poetic and significant retelling of the biblical story of Joseph and his brothers. A writer who has left the Highlands for the city despises the Gaelic world – 'that placid and unchanging world which knows nothing of Kafka or Proust' – and comes back to his typing, to find the Joseph story expressed not in his chosen English, but in Gaelic, 'rougher and more passionate', and seeming to argue 'that Joseph had abandoned his land for another land and that in doing so he had betrayed his own'. The writer admits to negative aspects in himself which have been hindering his story. In a series of weird events, his denied heritage reasserts itself; in a night of virtual breakdown, his attitudes are reversed, and he accepts the Gaelic version with its claim that Joseph was a traitor. An epiphany and a rediscovery have taken place which seem important for Crichton Smith's coming to terms with exile and alienation: in *A Field Full of Folk* (1982) and *The Dream* (1990), the two following novels most concerned with the theme, the attitude to village and community is, if never unquestioning or entirely favourable, accepting and recognising that nowhere is any better. Perhaps *On the Island*, the [illegible] year-old Iain Lewis, helped the transition, for the apparently simple view of village and landscape through the eyes of the child belies the significance of these minor, cumulative ephiphanies. Iain conquers his fear of the pier steps; he suddenly perceives and pities his mother's dignified poverty; he sees through the vision of a blind man; he is arrested by the enormity of winter landscape; he makes the transition from village school to Stornoway. Such art is deceptively understated. As in Gunn's *Young Art*, or the opening sequences of Edwin Muir's *An Autobiography* (1954), these moments have a crucial significance for future character and development; they are the future life, with its agenda, in microcosm. By going back to moments of early maturation, of moral discovery of the limits of self and world, the middle-aged Iain comes to an important stage of forgiveness of the distance between himself, village and island.

When we next grapple with the small community – this time in Argyllshire – in *A Field Full of Folk*, there is a shaped patterning whose purpose can only be described as to reveal a kind of grace – not Calvinist, or even religious, but transcendental all the same – in the village. Reverend Peter Murchison has lost his faith; everywhere he looks, he sees images of predators, seeing parishioners as snakes, buzzards, scavengers; while a crab of cancerous spiritual unease eats away within him. He feels his instinctive liberalism being distorted by a kind of collective unconscious, dark and mean, of the villagers, and refuses the church hall to youngsters for dancing. Hatred and gossip seem all; an old man nurses hatred of Germans, another hates children; eccentric old Annie (a wonderful Murdo-related creation, with crazy and unintentional fun in her gunfire, opinionated ramblings on Buddhism and the Bible) mirrors his disbelief in the manner of Scott's parodic fools; and each seems so separated from any other that the only tie seems to be their common negativism. All this is summed up in young Chrissie Murray's abandonment of her family, taking only a tinny radio, for a lover in Glasgow. The minister genuinely does not know whether to admire her for having the red courage to leave the black village, or to see her decision as symptomatic. But Chrissie returns, the prodigal daughter, and the village reveals a deeper tact and kindliness than could have been expected. Through her decision and her re-acceptance, Peter is led to transformation. In a moment which carries simultaneous reminders of the ending of Woolf's *To The Lighthouse* (1927) and Muir's 'One Foot in Eden', Peter sees his community with the villagers on this 'supremely imperfect and perfect earth':

> At moments we are touched by the crown of grace . . . And he had a vision of the people of the world, the fireman, the doctor, the lifeboatman, the minister. He saw tenement doors being broken down by axes, and the half-dead receiving tea from extended hands. He saw at night the lifeboat heading out to sea . . . and he saw the village itself as a subtle structure like a spider's web on a summer's day, the spider existing on the justice of heaven.[6]

This is an epiphany paralleled in the confession, more intimate and courageous than ever before, of *In the Middle of the Wood*, which, like *The Dream*, pulls together the two strands of the confessional fiction. We should, before considering them, go back now to trace the other strand, that which is mainly concerned with more abstract issues of the relationship between Art and life, language and reality, freedom and duty. These may be 'abstract' issues, but Crichton Smith's presentation of them is harrowing and deeply personal.

Three earlier novels can be grouped together: *My Last Duchess*, *Goodbye, Mr Dixon* and *An End to Autumn* (1978). All show a lonely, sensitive and idealistic protagonist (lecturer, would-be writer and teacher respectively) whose experience (northern university education, doubts concerning audience, schoolteaching in a West Highland town by the sea) partly reflects Crichton Smith's own. The first centres on loss. Life-loving Lorna has taken her paintings and left; Mark Simmons is too remote, detached from actuality. The title, as so often in Crichton Smith's work, indicates through an archetypal literary text the meaning of the situation before us: like Robert Browning's Ferrara, Mark is at first incapable of realising how he has tortured Lorna. The novel is his growth to self-realisation, and the rawness of feeling, together with representation of so much of Crichton Smith's own experience, suggest that Crichton Smith would not deny the closeness to his own therapeutic process. Black and red imagery throughout this and the later novels show that we are dealing with issues related to those deep-rooted in Crichton Smith's island background – though now, as in *Goodbye, Mr Dixon* and *An End to Autumn*, the issues are placed in a much wider context. And we should here note a habit of presentation which Crichton Smith shares with other modern Scottish writers like Jenkins, Friel, and Elspeth Davie. *Place* is undefined in terms of names or recognisable local characteristics, beyond the very broadest. It is as though the writer deliberately wants a general implication to arise from his agent's actions, together with a limbo-like flatness of atmosphere like Fergus Lamont or Mr Alfred, Crichton Smith's protagonists *are* in limbo, in a conflict of loyalties and a paralysis of will. Crichton Smith allows his lost innocents more hope, however, than these other novelists. Mark is allowed to come back from virtual breakdown to end the novel in a doorway – a stage of possiblity that one feels instinctively is close to where Crichton Smith felt himself to be. Similarly, in *Goodbye, Mr Dixon*, Tom Spence rejects his doppelgänger, the mannered, well-to-do aesthete who writes after the manner of Henry James, the role model who exists only in his mind. He is saved by the actuality of love with the teacher Ann, who pulls him into Life. 'Stepping out into the flux', is how it is described; again, one recalls Woolf and the ending of *Mrs Dalloway* (1925), when Peter Walsh looks at human relations and asks 'What is this terror? what is this ecstasy?'

A more explicit literary framework, that of Eliot's *Waste Land*, underlies *An End to Autumn*, where the schoolteacher Tom Mallow and his wife Vera are prematurely in autumn in their relationship – arid, childless, if well-to-do in their pretty seaside town. It takes the intrusion of three different types of women (Tom's dependent mother, the earthy Irish and vulgar Mrs Murphy, and a lesbian teacher) to force a crisis which makes Tom and Vera claw their way back to actuality and survival as a couple. Literature, lifestyle, crosswords and dolls are nothing compared to 'the terrifying multiplicity of the world, its trivial inanity'; and, in a fire-ceremony which purges their arid past, Tom and Vera (now pregnant) rediscover a vulnerable spring. But *An End to Autumn* has a 'literary' feel about it; the Eliot apparatus is intrusive and heavy, purely imagined and intellectual experience lacking the personal agony of earlier work. Tom and Vera's solution was not to be Crichton Smith's: in handling the breakdown which Crichton Smith himself has publicly revealed, *Murdo and Other Stories* both indicates the agony and suggests what is to be Crichton Smith's most effective mode of moving forwards. As a whole, the collection has the variety of the earlier *Survival Without Error* (1970), with the full range of Crichton Smith's lonely, unhappy survivors living off memories and self-delusions – until error or accident precipitates them through what Bertrand Russell called the 'thinly-cooled crust of lava' which keeps us from the burning. The earlier volume had stories on the edge of control, such as 'Je t'aime' or 'The Idiot and the Professor', but *Murdo* darkens these considerably, so that the bleakness of the title story 'Survival Without Error', with its account of narrow-minded self-justification, becomes the grotesque and well-nigh surreal horror of 'The Missionary', which tells of total breakdown of insulation through self-righteous belief.

Where *Survival* has delightful zaniness and bubbling absurdist fun in 'On the Island', the story 'Murdo' is at once among Crichton Smith's most hilarious and most horrifying. Murdo is all Crichton Smith's stresses and agonising tied together in self-parody, in his letters to Dante and the prime minister, or to the papers to tell them that Calvin is still alive; in his shouts to the sky of earth-shaking inspirations like 'MacBrayne's Boats', 'Betelgeuse' or 'Neil Munro'; or in his discussions (while wearing a red nose) with neighbour Mrs McLeod about the weather or murders in caravans and the importance of neighbours. Mrs McLeod thinks him mad, and wife Janet patiently suffers, until Murdo's father dies. About this time, Crichton Smith had his darkest hour, a nervous breakdown in which he feared he would never write again, that all the world was in conspiracy against him. Yet, paradoxically, the eccentric Murdo, in a version of Dostoevsky's 'If the fool persists in his folly he will be wise', indicates Crichton Smith's salvation, which has much in common with the later strategies of Jenkins and with the work of a range of modern Scottish novelists, going back to Linklater and *Magnus Merriman* (1934) and forwards to writers as diverse as Spark and Kennaway, Friel and Gray. Scottish fiction since *The Man of Feeling*

(1771) and *Waverley* (1814) has frequently had recourse to the presentation of a central figure who is a kind of 'holy fool' – naive, romantic, quixotic, yet unsuccessful in love and public action – a peculiarly Scottish beast whose paralysis is engendered by the clash of past moral education with present scepticism, of categorical imperatives with existential despair. The Scottish writer from an authoritarian and religious pedigree finds release through self-parody and grotesque self-debasement, and a transformation takes place in which the concept of grace is altered to allow a more human face. Note the multiplicity of novels and poems in modern Scottish literature with the word 'grace' – always qualified – in their titles, Crichton Smith's included. In this new dispensation, as MacCaig finds in 'Culag Pier', 'Grace is hilarity'. From now on, Crichton Smith, in pulling himself back to a new balance, will remember Murdo and find a new perspective on himself.

His next novel was *A Field Full of Folk*, discussed above in terms of his relations with his past upbringing. It can now be seen as highly significant in telling of loss of faith in life and hard redemption of hope. Equally revealing is *The Search*, which followed. Set in Australia (Crichton Smith had had an appointment as writer at the University of Canberra), it is about Trevor Grierson's quest for his long-estranged brother, Norman. Once again, a literary motif creates thematic subtext: Trevor is studying Stevenson, and the brothers Ballantrae resonate throughout his own search. But once again, the literary parallel somewhat obscures the real search – for Trevor himself. Encapsulated in the cocoon of the bus which carries him endlessly in his quest across the limbo-like plains, Trevor becomes increasingly aware of the alien quality of this hard country of hard pragmatists and dispossessed natives, and discovers himself amid the poetry of dream time and the flux of a country of exiles. Exiles, he finds, are ubiquitous in the contemporary world. For Crichton Smith, Australia provided the knowledge that there were many, many ways of being an exile, and that his Trevor was hardly unique, writer and academic though he might be. There is also a further, personal movement forward, reconciling Crichton Smith to loss – and an acceptance of relationships with the future rather than the past.

The novella *Mr Trill in Hades* (1984) continues the process of rearranging the past. Percipient readers of Crichton Smith will realise that Mr Trill crops up several times, from the classics teacher of early novels to the killer of an obnoxious pupil in 'Murder Without Pain' in *Survival Without Error*. He is a persona for Crichton Smith, representing not the whole man but the Murdo-style parodic distortion which enables self-caricature and release. Trill can kill where Crichton Smith cannot. Moreover, Trill is the focus for that major debate in Crichton Smith's mind concerning the validity of the study of classical civilisation. Trill's trip to the underworld is wonderfully reductive of all his former heroes. For here is the real, arrogant and swollen-headed Achilles, the real, petulant Helen – the golden people, the proud hunter of the poetry ('She Teaches Lear') seen as they probably were. Here is the pain of Dido, and the truth of Orpheus, so demented by romantic enquirers that he deliberately looked at Eurydice because he could not take her ideal goodness. Is there a comic comment on Crichton Smith's own descent to the shades, and a very personal statement in Trill's decision to forsake the comfort of a kind of civil-service job in Hades (teaching?) for rebirth as a city newsvendor, shouting delightedly about births and deaths?

The Tenement (1985) could well be assessed as short stories, conveniently if rather laboriously linked by the device (employed in 1978 by Elspeth Davie in *Climbers on a Stair*) of making the building which houses the random lives the central character, which crumbles and sweats through change. Familiar figures appear – drunks and old ladies, defeated dreamers, in contrast with those willing to take risks with life. Trevor Porter is here the link with Crichton Smith. And we should note now the significance of Crichton Smith's choice of names for his protagonists. 'Trill' was his running sign for ascetic academicism, with its association of highbrow music and slightly ridiculous and effeminate birdsong; but, in the other main recurrent persona of the alienated writer/teacher who wants to be in touch with life but cannot because of spurious literary values, Crichton Smith chooses a set of linked names. Mark Simmons, Drew Dixon, Tom Mallow, Trevor Grierson, Ralph Simmons, Trevor Porter are most un-Gaelic, and carry deliberately strong associations with southern English society and culture. Why? We find the answer in *The Search*, as the lost brother Norman, reunited with the searcher, says he is glad to see him:

> 'God knows', he said to his wife, 'why my mother called him Trevor. It's not a Scottish name. She saw it in a book, I think . . .'[7]

These are names from an alien world, and they hint at the false values of those who possess them, removing them from the red world of life. Trevor Porter of *The Tenement* 'must move out of the middle of the dark wood'; his flat is his dead self, his remoteness and addiction to literature dehumanising. He must begin again.

In the Middle of the Wood is Crichton Smith's culminating account of this process, repeated much more dramatically in the life of Ralph Simmons, a married West Highland writer. Crichton Smith weaves a

Murdo-strand through his account. Ralph is Murdo over the edge, and part of the novel's intensity comes from the way in which Crichton Smith makes us smile wryly at the surreal idiocy of Ralph's delusions – that Linda has hired the taxi-driver to kill him, that his hospital is peopled by hired actors to induce total breakdown in him, that the entire outside world is his enemy. *Hamlet* is the literary parallel here, except that (like Muir's account in his *Autobiography* of how he was, as a child, slowly allowed release from his spiritual imprisonment) the novel is deeply affirmative in the manner of *A Field Full of Folk*; it is the cathartic equivalent for Crichton Smith's dilemma in the world of ideas.

The Dream is a kind of coda, fusing together issues of Island and the issues of Ideas. It is somehow a more relaxed and solid novel entirely. Martin is a lecturer in Gaelic at Glasgow University, and the very naming, throughout, of solid places such as Byres Road is new for Crichton Smith. So too is the orientation of the protagonists, for it is Martin who has the dream of going back, rejecting academia for real work, saving the culture of the island. Jean has suffered the island's blackness terribly as an orphan, and the novel is their struggle. The satire on phoney Gaeldom is sustained and powerful, yet relaxed in presentation and full of recognisable realities of character and situation. In this novel, Crichton Smith finally cuts his affiliations to his island, and at the same time accepts that his world of study and culture must negotiate at a 'table of reality' with the claims of wife and the society which feeds him. It is the end of a long struggle for Crichton Smith himself, one which started even before he left his island; and it has been a struggle won through enduring the necessary suffering, transmuting it to repeated versions in fiction, and indeed 'bleeding from all that's best', admitting that the process of healing involved further wounding, again and again.

This account so far leaves out two major novels: *Consider the Lilies*, and his latest, *An Honourable Death* (1992). These seem to be atypical of Crichton Smith's work, though both centre on the recurrent issues of the rest of the fiction. But the presentation is vastly different. The appearance of *Consider the Lilies* as a novel about the Highland Clearances led critics into confused responses – some seeing it as 'a timeless comment on officialdom'; some, like John Prebble, seeing it as giving eviction 'a burning immediacy'; some seeing the central figure as an 'evocation of the humanity and goodness of an old woman'. But Mrs Scott has many very inhumane qualities, having forced her husband and her son from her because of her cold religiosity; Crichton Smith emphasises that his main subject is 'internal clearance, the eviction of fun and love from the hearts of the Highlanders'.

Consider the Lilies is in fact very close to Crichton Smith's 'confessional' fiction. No-one who has read the 'old woman' poems can fail to see how Mrs Scott shares personal history and qualities with Crichton Smith's own mother, whose relationship with him left such a powerful impression and confusion of response. Indeed, the very fact that the fiction opens with this study of an archetypal island woman tells us that its function is to be a mixture of atonement and self-recognition. Here, Crichton Smith allows the mother-figure the epiphany that one suspects his own in real life never achieved. Mrs Scott (and the name also tells us that she stands for wider reference than merely to Crichton Smith's island situation) is to an extent eponymous, representing black Scottish religious belief through the ages. Crichton Smith thus places his own situation into a context where he is only one of countless to suffer repression. An old story is retold, but one which has continued during his own childhood. And through this story of real clearance, the other story of internal clearance of love and joy is told – and forgiven. Again, the patterning of *The Black and the Red* is followed – that of initial black emphasis, pivoting around a central agony or breakdown, which allows redemptive bleeding, productive pain. The first half of the novel is a series of flashbacks to bleak moments of failure for Mrs Scott – with her son, who is straining to be free; with her husband, who left to find life as a soldier; with her own rooted blackness, the agony of seeing her own mother go mad with religion. These personal defeats are paralleled with a series of present failures, as she fails to gain help from church elder, from minister or any of the authorities.

Central to the novel is her crossing of bridges, as central as for Stephen in Joyce's *Portrait*. There, aridity turned towards life; here, through breakdown at perceiving that her ideals were rotten (embodied in the savage actuality and symbol of the dead sheep, boiling with maggots), and through a series of redemptive layers of sleep and dream, Mrs Scott finds in the home of her previous arch-enemy, the freethinker, a new beginning. She discovers love letters – which may be fiction; and in these, and in her attempt to tell stories to the stonemason's children, she discovers creativity, imagination, empathy and perhaps even Art. The theme of real clearance is rather downgraded by the end; where Mrs Scott will go is secondary to the fact that she will be going as a new woman, released. She bleeds, but from all that's best for her – cleansing herself of the black bile repressed for so long – and, in seeing her grope towards self-expression in her story of the imprisoned witch at the end, we are indeed seeing her 'active anima' in redemptive action. It is simultaneously a cleansing for Crichton Smith, in his own time; for the Highlands, in that anger about history is expressed and shaped; and for Scotland's dark Calvinist inheritance.

This first novel disguised deeply personal material as fiction about an old woman; the latest is the only other to depart so far from Crichton Smith himself as protagonist. What led Crichton Smith to choose such a different character from himself as Hector MacDonald of Imperial Britain as the quintessential 'Fighting Mac'? Again, we must realise that there is a strand of identification. Essential deep loneliness, a yearning for classical order and mathematical coolness, combined with an abiding sense of alienation from the reality of things – these are the qualities which Crichton Smith imagines underlie the public persona of Hector. It is true that the topic allows Crichton Smith to deliver himself of deeply-felt ironic comment on the strangeness of dispossessed tribes killing dispossessed tribes for the benefit of Lowland Britain, and to perceive ironies in the juxtapositioning of the army's contempt for the language of its troops (Gaelic) with its contempt for the languages it encounters across the world. It is also true (although this appeared more prominently in the first, short-story version, 'The True Story of Sir Hector MacDonald', in *Selected Stories* (1990) that the sheer randomness of events struck Crichton Smith forcibly; that Picasso as a young man might have passed the suicidal Hector in a Paris street, this Inverness draper who became hero of Omdurman. But isn't the juxtapositioning of Picasso and this 'flawed lonely man' another, more public and more complex, presentation of the Black and Red? What Crichton Smith finds in MacDonald is sensitivity distorted, an extrapolated version of the loneliness and uneasiness in relation to English culture that he has always felt. MacDonald, it is repeatedly emphasised, is an outsider, an alien amid officers, a man caught between his past and his present. Is it 'there but for the grace'? What is less convincing, unfortunately, is Crichton Smith's presentation of the story of a man who must surely have suffered huge passions and attacks of sensuality to betray his office and his life – there just is not the empathy for that banked-up, Hyde-like appetite which makes MacDonald such an archetypal Victorian. Crichton Smith treats sexuality with a taste and sensitivity relevant to his teachers and writers; but that very tact and limitation has no chance of letting us see into MacDonald's fiery emotional and sexual heart. His homosexuality is always peripheral, and almost accidental; an afterthought, when duty is done. This latest novel does confirm, however, that from first to last, Crichton Smith's fiction – for immense better and occasional worse – is about his search for himself amid black backgrounds and terrifying, hilarious worlds.

NOTES

1. 'To Hell and Back Again' (interview with Alan Taylor), *Spectrum, Scotland on Sunday*, 22 March 1992, p. 37.
2. See Douglas Gifford, 'The True Dialectic: The Fiction and Poetry of Iain Crichton Smith', *Chapman* 34, February 1983, pp. 39–46; '*Deer on the High Hills*: The Elusiveness of Language in the Poetry of Iain Crichton Smith', in Derick Thomson, ed., *Gaelic and Scots in Harmony*, University of Glasgow, 1988, pp. 149–63.
3. *Towards the Human: Selected Essays* (Edinburgh: MacDonald, 1986); 'Between Sea and Moor' in Maurice Lindsay, ed., *As I Remember* (London: Robert Hale, 1979), pp. 107–22.
4. The heroine and hero of Lewis Grassic Gibbon's *A Scots Quair* (1932–4) and Neil Gunn's *The Silver Darlings* (1941) respectively.
5. Iain Crichton Smith, *The Village* (Inverness: Club Leabhar, 1976), p. 31.
6. Iain Crichton Smith, *A Field Full of Folk* (London: Gollancz, 1982), p. 141.
7. Iain Crichton Smith, *The Search* (London: Gollancz, 1983), p. 180.

FURTHER READING

Lindsay, Frederic, 'Disputed Angels: The Poetry of Iain Crichton Smith', *Akros* 36 (December 1977), 15–26.

Lines Review 29 (1969), entire issue.

Macintyre, Lorn, 'Poet in Bourgeois Land: Interview with Iain Crichton Smith', *Scottish International* (September 1971), 22–7.

Morgan, Edwin, 'The Raging and the Grace: Some Notes on the Poetry of Iain Crichton Smith', *Lines Review* 21 (Summer 1965); in his *Essays* (Cheadle: Carcanet, 1974), 222–31.

National Book League, *Iain Crichton Smith* (Glasgow, 1979), Writers in Brief, no 8.

Tait, Bob, 'Love and Death in Space', *Scottish International* 5 (October 1972), 28–9.

Iain Crichton Smith also writes in Gaelic; these works are not included in this bibliography. He has also written plays.

Three

The Deliberate Cunning of Muriel Spark

Ian Rankin

Throughout the mid- and late 1960s, Muriel Spark sought contemporaneity: a rejection perhaps of the popular success of *The Prime of Miss Jean Brodie* (1961) and *The Girls of Slender Means* (1963), which had been praised in turn for their protrayal of the 1930s and 1940s.

So, *The Mandelbaum Gate* (1965) tackled the Arab/Israeli conflict, while *The Public Image* (1968) cast a cynical eye on the contemporary film industry. By 1970, Spark seemed to have redefined the goal of her books, what their themes and concerns were to be, and, as importantly, how they were to be written. Her early novels, despite their often macabre subject matter, were classed as comedies, but from *Brodie* through to *The Public Image* that comedy had been whittled away, and by the time of *The Driver's Seat* (1970) there is precious little to smile about.

The shift in Spark's [illegible] seems to be from what might be termed a peculiarly secular Catholicism to Christian Absurdism. A character in her 1973 novel *The Hothouse by the East River* says: 'There's only one area of conflict left and that's between absurdity and intelligence', while Spark herself, in a 1970 interview, admits: 'I don't believe in good and evil so much any more. . . . Now, there is only absurdity and intelligence.'[1] This idea is fleshed out in a speech given the same year to the American Academy of Arts and Letters, a speech explaining the task Spark sets herself in the 1970s.

Spark begins the speech (published as 'The Desegregation of Art') by stating the importance, the primacy even of literature as an artistic form. But it should not be 'a special department set aside for the entertainment and delight of the sophisticated minority' – it should be desegregated.[2] 'Ineffective literature,' she says, 'must go', but in a Platonic twist this means that

> good things, when they begin no longer to apply, also must go: the art and the literature of sentiment and emotion, however beautiful in itself, however striking in its depiction of actuality, has to go. It cheats us into a sense of involvement with life and society, but in reality it is a segregated activity. In its place I advocate the arts of satire and of ridicule. And I see no other living art form for the future.

Spark would like to see in all forms of the arts 'a less impulsive generosity . . . and a more deliberate cunning, a more derisive undermining of what is wrong', for 'the art of ridicule . . . can penetrate to the marrow. It can leave a salutary scar. It is unnerving. It can paralyze its object.'

Spark continues:

> The only effective art of our particular time is the satirical, the harsh and witty, the ironic and derisive. Because we have come to a moment in history when we are surrounded on all sides and oppressed by the absurd . . . The art of ridicule is an art that everyone can share in some degree, given the world that we have. . . . The rhetoric of our times should persuade us to contemplate the ridiculous nature of the reality before us, and teach us to mock it.

The absurd first gains prominence in *The Mandelbaum Gate* whose pivotal scene concerns the trial of Adolf Eichmann, head of the Jewish Section of Hitler's SS. Spark herself attended the trial, and her heroine finds the atmosphere to be like 'one that the anti-novelists induce . . . repetition, boredom, despair, going nowhere for nothing, all of which conditions are enclosed in a tight, unbreakable statement of the times at hand'.[3] Spark in the 1970s produces several of these tight, unbreakable statements, using as her central theme the absurdity of 'the times at hand'.

Spark is a Catholic convert for whom God is 'absolutely irrational', but for whom too 'if we don't believe, there *is* an absurdity there too'.[4] She has said that the theme of her novel *The Only Problem* (1984) might be 'absurdity', and has termed herself an 'anarchist'.[5] From early in her career, she was aware of the theories and writings of authors such as Alain Robbe-Grillet and Samuel Beckett, recalling in a 1971 interview that 'in the early 1950s, there was no Robbe-Grillet, and scarcely anyone had heard of Beckett. Hardly anyone was trying to write novels with the compression and obliqueness I was aiming at.'[6]

In all of this, Spark comes over as a serious-minded, intellectual novelist, a far cry from the 'sparkling' author of 'entertainments' who seems to appear in book reviews. Anthony Burgess correctly observes of one novel: 'Mrs Spark constructs and writes as she always did – with great cunning and economy. She sometimes appears frivolous but is in reality very profound'.[7] In recent years, Spark has learned how to combine her profundity with a great level of 'entertainment', so that her books appear less serious in intent than in fact they are. *The Driver's Seat*, however, though fascinating, has nothing frivolous about it, even on the surface.

As early as 1961, Spark was championing Alain Robbe-Grillet, at a time when only two of his novels were available in English translations.[8] *The Driver's Seat* is both a homage to Robbe-Grillet's technique and a rejection of the philosophy of the *nouveau roman*. For Robbe-Grillet, the world is 'neither meaningful nor absurd. It quite simply *is*.'[9] For Spark, however, the world is both meaningful *and* absurd: meaningful because there is a divine (if 'irrational') pattern behind it; absurd because we choose to live and die as though this were not the case. 'Knots,' says Barbara Vaughan in *The Mandelbaum Gate*, 'were not necessarily created to be untied', nor can God's ironies always be explained. Spark's characters may feel bewildered by the world, but their creator never lacks purpose. Her narrators have been said to express 'a disturbing authority whose patterns are not easy to understand', and it is the fact that this 'authority' exists for Spark which differentiates her from other practitioners of the absurd. For Spark, it is *we* who are absurd in God's eyes, not the world which is absurd in ours. The subject of *The Driver's Seat* is the non-contingency, the determinism of this world.

The Driver's Seat, like Robbe-Grillet's *The Erasers*, deals with the day leading up to a murder. The twist is that Lise, the apparent victim, actually spends her last day on earth searching for someone to kill her. Just as Annabel in *The Public Image* becomes [illegible] of her own fate, so Lise tries to take the 'driving seat' of her destiny. She dresses brightly, talks loudly and shrilly, and carries a lurid paperback, begging to be noticed by her 'type' and by the world at large. Her efforts, however, are clumsy, and she is mistaken at first for 'a temptress in the old-fashioned style'. According to Alan Bold, Lise 'assumes the driver's seat to proclaim that in a deterministic universe she will nevertheless choose her own destiny':[10] the central irony of *The Driver's Seat* is that she does not actually succeed. Her eventual killer, a partially rehabilitated sex offender, was in the seat next to her on the morning flight – placed there determinedly by the author. And though Lise wants death, not sex, her murderer will and does have both. In those final moments, Lise is no longer in control.

The Driver's Seat, one of Spark's shortest novels, is also one of her most successful. In a 1984 interview, she called it her 'most classic novel and the most satisfactory. The construction seems to me the most complete.'[11] It is interesting that Spark stresses 'construction' here, for critics have attacked her 1970s novels for being more concerned with technique than with character. Certainly, these books have the look of experiments; there is something of the laboratory about them. Spark finds that the sparer her language becomes, the more information can be transmitted to the reader at the level of deep structure. The implied becomes crucial.

Not to Disturb (1971) is an Ortonesque black comedy combining outrageous statements with deadpan delivery. Three people are ensconced in the library of a Swiss stately home, and are not to be disturbed. The servants know that something dreadful is about to happen. Indeed, so sure are they that they have already sold their stories to the media, and are now negotiating film rights and other deals.

Not to Disturb, like *The Driver's Seat* before it and the two novels following it, is narrated in that most urgent and contemporary of tenses, the present. In *Not to Disturb*, Spark is again interested in determinism and (so-called) free will. Locked in the library together, the Baron, Baroness and friend may seem to be in charge of their collective fate, but it is clear that strings are being pulled, with the butler Lister acting as a minor deity ordained by the author. 'What's done is about to be done,' says Lister, 'and the future has come to pass', the ill-fated trio having 'placed themselves within the realm of predestination'.[12] This seems not so much an echo of Calvin as a pointer that the occupants of the library were unwittingly manoeuvred into their present situation by Lister and the servants.

Spark's fiction has always made use of fakery, blackmailers and charlatans. All three are prominent in *Not to Disturb*, with Spark most definitely on the side of the plot-makers and truth-twisters. It comes as little surprise when the only possible hazard in Lister's way – a couple who are hanging around the grounds of the house – is erased by a bolt of lightning (a veritable act of God and of author-as-God), the couple having been mere 'extras' (*ND*, 86). As far back as Spark's first novel *The Comforters*, a character vanished into thin air whenever she was no longer needed, the author showing the character to be merely a device.

Spark's experimental novels of the early 1970s do owe a debt to her first two books, published in the 1950s. These were wary investigations into the form and techniques of the novel genre by someone who had, until asked by a publisher to write a novel, thought of the form as 'third-rate'. Spark has said that she wrote *The Comforters* 'to sort of make it all right with myself to write a novel', and her books after 'The

Desegregation of Art' seem attempts to do the same thing, to ensure that the novel form can still do what Spark wants it to do.[13]

Some of the younger servants in *Not to Disturb* dance to a record by 'The Far-Fetchers' – the author again showing her hand. *The Hothouse by the East River* (1973), one of Spark's most far-fetched stories and one of her most allusive, took eight years to write, including time spent reshaping it in the present tense. The level of reworking and the time involved are unusual in Spark, who admits to starting with a novel-title, writing it on the front of an exercise-book (always bought from Thin's Bookshop in Edinburgh), turning the page, and starting to write. She says she never really knows how a story or its characters will develop, never has a synopsis, and does little revision.[14]

Hothouse is a very personal book, though in matters of technique it is determinedly experimental. Set in New York, where Spark lived for a time in the 1960s, it is the story of Elsa, whose shadow falls the wrong way, and of her husband Paul. During the war, Elsa and Paul worked in England, putting out propaganda broadcasts to Germany. In New York, characters from this period come to 'haunt' Paul especially.

In World War Two, Spark herself worked for British Intelligence: 'we were supposed to be a German radio station, broadcasting subversive material to their troops'.[15] This period of her life proved crucial to the writing career that followed. Spark often uses forgeries and fakes in her novels, and she deals, not always flatteringly, with creators of fiction. Throughout *The Driver's Seat*, Lise will not tell the truth when a lie will suffice, while in both *Not to Disturb* and *The Public Image* Spark paraphrases an old Italian saying: 'It's not true, but that's not to say that it isn't right'.

Spark is self-conscious about the fact that she uses *fiction* as a means of telling a 'kind of truth'. In *Hothouse*, 'reality' is the lie, the fiction, for Paul and Elsa are dead, and have been since a bomb hit their train-carriage in 1944. Spark's satirical technique here is that of inversion: the dead are haunted by reality, just as in *Not to Disturb* mourning preceded death, and in *The Driver's Seat* a victim hunted her killer.

Hothouse also comprises Spark's most sustained attack on the contemporary abuse of language, on the use of words to distort meaning rather than to clarify, and it is also a detailed exploration of ambiguity. When a character says something is 'not real', the reader must understand the phrase in its fullest meaning, since the novel's main characters truly are not real. Many passages show a Beckettian concern with the gap between language and reality, together with a similarly Beckettian relish of puns and linguistic play. *Hothouse* poses several important questions. What is reality? Can it ever adequately be conveyed by language? Are novels suitable vehicles for an exploration of reality and meaning?

Like Beckett, Robbe-Grillet and others, Spark attempts to define for herself the conception of reality which a writer brings to the modern world. Finding God 'irrational', and that we are 'surrounded on all sides by the absurd', Spark seems to suggest that absurdity is a condition of existence. This being the belief, the use of the absurd in novels needs no justification, for the absurd *is* reality. Like *The Comforters* – and equally important to the period in which it was written – *Hothouse* is a metafiction, making the reader '*participate* in the aesthetic and philosophical problems the writing of fiction presents, by embodying them directly in the narrative'.[16] In the end, it suffers because the plot lacks motive: the question of *why* and *how* these ghosts come to be inhabiting New York is never answered, and only later in her fiction does Spark stress that motive is not really important.

Spark's most memorable characters – Jean Brodie, Lister and the eponymous *Abbess of Crewe* (1974) – are mythologisers and fiction-makers on a grand scale. Spark looked at the Watergate cover-up, and decided to set similar events in a British nunnery, complete with buggings, revelations, consequent cover-ups, and the editing and erasure of tapes. Spark's concerns and techniques are familiar: blackmail, the use and abuse of language, media manipulation. She shows that language can be used as a falsifier more readily than it can be used as a force for truth. The nuns speak in contemporary American idiom: people get 'laid' or have been 'screwing', while the Abbess herself says of one particular plan to twist the facts: 'I don't see that scenario'.

Spark herself has denied that *Abbess* is merely about Watergate, and the novel's central concern seems rather to be with class. In one scene, Alexandra, the Abbess-to-be, makes a speech to the nuns telling them she will appeal to their 'higher instincts' – and then goes on to appeal to their basic snobbery.[17] Certainly, there is a distinction in the nunnery between mere wealth and aristocracy of mind. Many nuns brought fortunes to the abbey, while Alexandra brought nothing but 'her noble birth and shrewd spirit', and throughout the book taste seems an issue; things are in 'poison bad taste', or are 'common' or 'ugly'. Alexandra, on the other hand, is 'lofty', 'tall', 'splendid' and 'straight'. She is also very like Lister: both are able organisers of chaos because remote from it. They are myth-makers, controllers of people and of rhetoric (as was Jean Brodie), and as such they are images of the novelist.

'A good scenario,' says the Abbess, 'need not be plausible, only hypnotic, like all good art.' *The Takeover* (1976) is full of good scenarios.

'Appearances *are* reality,' says one character, Hubert Mallindaine. He should know: he sells off his benefactress's antiques and replaces them with copies. He then sets himself up at the head of a pagan church, all of this in 1973–4, in the midst of oil hikes and economic crisis, years which saw 'a sea-change in the nature of reality'.[18] Idolatry is at the heart of *The Takeover*; people have put their faith in material wealth, and even priests attend Mallindaine's rites. Personality cults and the evil resulting from them prove a recurrent concern in Spark's fiction. Hubert, though, is a time villain. By the end of the book, he is able to exclaim: 'I haven't done so badly', while his benefactress has been financially ruined but is on her way to recovering – through resorting to kidnap – some of her fortune.

The Takeover is Spark's most anarchic novel. Everyone seems to be cheating, lying, breaking the law. Priests are 'terrorists', while Watergate appeals to 'everyone's latent anarchism' (*T*, 54). Moreover, almost nothing is what it seems – burial plots and kitchen steps are in reality safe deposit boxes, chairs and paintings are copied, and people pretend that their real jewels are paste in an attempt to trick potential thieves. Hubert the self-faker is another of Spark's 'types' of the novelist, and, as Michael Wood puts it, 'no writer of fiction . . . can feel truly ill-disposed toward confidence men'.[19]

The Takeover is Spark's longest novel since *Mandelbaum Gate*. Allan Massie describes it as 'a far looser and more genial work than the novellas'.[20] The problem with the book is that Spark 'tells' rather than 'shows', as though she is not confident that her techniques, honed through the course of the previous short books, really are working. *The Takeover* is a more traditionally-told tale than anything preceding it in the 1970s, and it signals a change of direction in Spark: a shift from forthright experiment.

Territorial Rights (1979) again features essential Spark ingredients: blackmail, terrorism, 'skeletons in the closet' and notions of reality. Again, it is a 'genial work', a tale of bed-hopping and wartime plots, set in present-day Italy. At one point, a character in Venice phones Anthea Leaver in Birmingham to relate the complex interrelationships taking place in the city: 'It may seem far-fetched to you, Anthea, but here everything is stark realism. This is Italy.'[21]

Throughout the novel, Anthea uses as bedtime reading a 'kitchen-sink drama', and the 'stark realism' of events in Italy (actually, to the reader, absurd farce) contrasts sharply with the 'realism' of Anthea's novel. There are echoes here of Spark's 1971 *Observer* interview: 'I might claim to be the opposite of C. P. Snow in every possible way. He thinks he's a realist: I think *I'm* a realist and he's a complete fantasist.'[22]

In *Territorial Rights* and in *The Takeover*, Spark's themes and concerns seem as ever, but over the course of these two books she makes a conscious effort to move away from recondite theorising and chronological difficulties. In effect, she is aiming for accessibility – the accessibility she enjoyed with her novels of the 1960s, but now tempered by the lessons of the early 1970s. In 'The Desegregation of Art', she had said that art should above all 'entertain'. Whatever the strengths of a novel like *The Hothouse by the East River*, entertainment was not much in evidence. Spark will still aim for ridicule, will still invoke 'a sense of the absurd', but her touch becomes lighter.

In *Loitering With Intent* (1981), her first first-person narrative since *Robinson*, Spark appears (note the word) to allow a lot of her own voice and personality to obtrude into the text. The main character, Fleur Talbot, is writing her first novel in the London of 1949. She takes a job with the 'Autobiographical Association', run by Sir Quentin Oliver. Fleur's job is to add interest to the memoirs of the Association's members. In other words, she is to write lies about them.[23] When one member complains about a fictionalised scene, another praises its 'stark realism'.[24] This echoes the telephone conversation in *Territorial Rights*, but here the 'stark realism' is in fact the result of Fleur's imagination. Spark is again in ironic mode: stark realism is a contrivance, and mundane truth is dispensable when the maintaining of interest is at stake. Or, put another way, 'realism' is relative: apparent reportage (diaries, memoirs, news reports) can be fictive, while fiction itself can tell the truth – Fleur's own first-person 'memoirs' are, after all, fiction too. This is the essence of what Spark in 1971 called 'the ridiculous nature of the reality before us'.

Sir Quentin uses the faked memoirs to exert power over members of his circle, turning it into another personality cult. Why he does this is not made clear and does not seem important. At one point, Fleur says of her own novels: 'I didn't go in for motives, I never have' (*LWI*, 161). Interestingly, January Marlow (in *Robinson*) and Barbara Vaughan say similar things, Barbara refusing to believe that 'people should tear themselves to bits about their motives' (*The Mandelbaum Gate*, p. 161), while January says: 'I see no call to tear myself to bits over motives'.[25] There is much of Spark in all three characters, and much of her point of view, too. For Spark, the motivation behind any action is less important than the effect it has on those involved.

What makes *Loitering* such a success is that Spark's overriding themes, her concern with appearance, reality, truth and fiction, are included in a narrative which fully engages and involves the reader (as first-person narratives, apparently frank and confiding, often do). Fleur successfully defends herself against the charge that novelists 'wriggle out of real life', not by arguing that the novelist *does* participate in real life, but by implying that real life is more of an artifice than is art itself. The novelist 'loiters with intent', this being also, of course, a criminal act: Spark as ever acknowledges the darker side of the creative impulse.

For *The Only Problem*, Spark stretches just as far back into her past, the novel containing verbatim quotes from a 1955 Spark essay on the Book of Job.[26] The 'only problem' of the title is the question of suffering: how can the Creator condone the suffering of the world? It is a question pondered by wealthy Harvey Gotham, who has retired to France to write a monograph on Job. However, 'comforters' soon intrude, Harvey's wife becomes a suspected terrorist, the media term him a 'guru', and the police take an interest.

Harvey's own suffering is interior: the suffering of the religious intellect when faced with modern-day horrors, no matter how banal those horrors might appear to the secular mind. There is more meditation than plot in *The Only Problem*; Spark has called it 'an analytical book' with 'absurdity' and God's irrationality as its themes.[27] What Spark is saying, as Gabriel Josipovici sees it, is that the book 'demonstrates the continual tiny triumphs of questions over answers'.[28] We are back to not pulling ourselves to bits over motives and acknowledging that knots were not necessarily created to be untied.

The Only Problem is full of instances of appearances belying reality. Harvey is misquoted by the press, policemen look like businessmen or priests, and a maidservant turns out to be a policewoman.[29] Harvey is rueful when the newspapers misquote him, but then Spark has never [illegible] the media as a carrier of 'truth'. Perhaps she still feels hurt that Derek Stanford, her lover and collaborator in the 1950s, later wrote what she considers to be 'lies' about her, and also sold a collection of her old love letters (which a dealer promptly tried to sell back to Spark). Certainly, in the interval between *Loitering With Intent* and *A Far Cry From Kensington* (1988), Spark seems to have grown much sourer regarding 1950s London.

Set in Kensington in 1954 and 1955, *Far Cry* concerns a period in the life of Mrs Hawkins, who works in publishing and speaks her mind. The phrase most often in her mind is '*pisseur de copie*', which she applies to writer *manqué* Hector Bartlett. A Polish immigrant, Wanda Podolak, drowns herself, and it comes to light that she had received anonymous letters and calls, faked newspaper cuttings and equally faked photographs. The line is traced to Bartlett, though nothing is ever made of it. Meanwhile, Bartlett, who has befriended a famous writer, Emma Loy, years later tries to do her 'a lot of damage' by writing 'pathetic inventions' about her.[30]

It is assumed that Bartlett was blackmailing Wanda into operating a 'Radionics Box' as a power of evil, Radionics being one of the many pseudo-sciences around in London after the war. As Mrs Hawkins puts it: 'There was an upsurge of interest in the supernatural in those years, probably as a result of the uncontemplatable events which had blackened the previous decade' (*FC*, 103–4). Or, to paraphrase one commentator, when people stop believing in religion, they do not believe in nothing; they believe in *any*thing.

Far Cry is a slight work, good on period detail, purposely naive in outlook, but lacking deeper resonance. Bartlett is oafish, but it is hard to visualise him as 'evil' or as a force for the absurd. His sole punishment is ridicule by Mrs Hawkins, a punishment laid down in 'The Desegregation of Art', and the fitting punishment of an ironic, post-Auschwitz God.

In *Symposium* (1990), Margaret Murchie is fed up being a magnet for tragedy and strives to be an active perpetrator of evil. Three times in her life, people close to her have been murdered, have drowned or have simply disappeared. Now, having pursued a rich husband, she looks to her mad Uncle Magnus for help in disposing of her millionairess mother-in-law.

With its array of Catholics, butlers, bachelors, charlatans, nuns, malign plotters and the super-rich, its self-reflexive asides and prolepses, and its passing biblical quotes and mentions of Venice, *Symposium* comprises a veritable compendium of its author's concerns. It also brings the reader back to 'The Desegregation of Art' and *The Driver's Seat*. Margaret wishes, in Uncle Magnus's phrase, to 'perpetrate evil'.[31] Spark, however, said in 1970 that she 'doesn't believe in good and evil so much any more', and in *Symposium* Margaret is not allowed to carry through her plan. Instead, a member of a 'random gang' disposes of the mother-in-law. The question begs: how random is random? Margaret, battling against determinism, loses, begging comparison with Lise who wished actively to be a victim, while Margaret is fed up of being a passive 'carrier of disaster' (*S*, 143).

Symposium is Spark's most obviously Scottish novel for some time, with its references to Calvinism, the Border Ballads and *Jekyll and Hyde*, and its scenes played out in St Andrews and Perthshire. There is also more than a whiff of Hogg's *Justified Sinner* about Margaret's thinking: since she is damned to be a carrier of death, why not actively murder someone? Spark's Scottishness over the course of her œuvre is, however, difficult to assess. In almost every novel, there are oblique references to

Scotland. These may comprise no more than the mention of a Church of Scotland minister turned Arab guerrilla (*The Mandelbaum Gate*, pp. 100, 105), or of an anti-sex drug being tested in Edinburgh (*Not to Disturb*, p. 51). A character may have Scottish roots and recite Border Ballads (*Territorial Rights*) or may attend an inverted version of Barrie's *Peter Pan* (*Hothouse*). In some cases, Spark is making a joke at her birthplace's expense. In other cases, such as with *Peter Pan*, there is deeper meaning (the ghosts in *Hothouse* never grow old, and Elsa's shadow has been stitched back on the wrong way).

Spark left Scotland in 1937 (aged nineteen) and has not returned for any great length of time since. She says of her birthplace Edinburgh that it 'bred within me the conditions of exiledom', yet praises the city's 'spirit of democracy and anarchy', and she agrees that it has 'influenced her way of thinking'.[32] Edinburgh to her 'means rationalism. Believing in a strong difference between right and wrong', while she explains her coolly detached author's stance in terms of her education: 'There couldn't be anything better than a Presbyterian school to teach detachment. I was taught that truth is totally separate and on its own, not a matter of opinion. One thing that the Scots do know is the difference between truth and fiction.'[33] The difference between truth and fiction, of course, is Spark's central theme. She exposes those who would 'doctor' the truth or treat it with malign intent – blackmailers, fakers, certain corners of the media – pointing out that they manipulate the truth for selfish reasons, while the novelist does not.

One critic has noted that Spark's strong female characters may be 'shadows of the strong Scottish women she knew as a child', while Spark herself, talking about her schooldays, acknowledges a debt to Robert Louis Stevenson, the Old Testament and the Border Ballads.[34] Derek Stanford recalls that 'there lay embedded in her memory the rock-like form of the Border Ballads. . . . I sometimes think that Scotland has accounted for more in Miss Spark's imagination than any other factors in her experience.'[35] Edinburgh's 'rationalism' and 'detachment' lend scepticism to Spark's outlook, colouring her Catholicism and the moral content of her books.

Spark is often asked whether she regards herself as a 'Scottish writer', and her replies are usually wary: 'I am certainly a writer of Scottish formation and of course I think of myself as such. I think to describe myself as a "Scottish Writer" might be ambiguous as one wouldn't know if "Scottish" applied to the writer or the writing.'[36] She is, however, a Scottish writer in both senses of the term, and what make her so are her particular dualisms. Here is a profound writer who says that she does not like to say things 'too seriously', a Christian with a belief in the absurd, a novelist with the mind of a poet. But Spark has also said: 'Edinburgh has always been a European city: its ties are with Europe and not with England'.[37] Edinburgh-born, Muriel Spark has lived in Italy since the 1960s, and is surely the most 'European' writer whom Scotland has produced.

NOTES

1. *The Hothouse by the East River* (Harmondsworth: Penguin, 1975), p. 63; *Guardian*, 30 September 1970, p. 8.
2. Muriel Spark, 'The Desegregation of Art', in *Proceedings of the American Academy of Arts and Letters* (1971), pp. 20–7.
3. *The Mandelbaum Gate* (Harmondsworth: Penguin, 1967), p. 177.
4. Transcript of an interview on BBC Radio Four's *Bookshelf*, 4 November 1984.
5. *Bookshelf* interview: 'The Culture of an Anarchist', *Telegraph Sunday Magazine*, 20 March 1988, pp. 16–20.
6. *Observer Magazine*, 7 November 1971, pp. 73–4. Spark quotes from Beckett's *Waiting for Godot* in *The Mandelbaum Gate* (during the trial scene, p. 180). In his book *Writing and the Body* (Brighton: Harvester, 1982), Gabriel Josipovici mentions Spark in the same breath as Beckett and Borges (p. 92).
7. 'Yellow Eyeballs', *Observer*, 9 September 1984.
8. Elizabeth Jane Howard, 'Writers in the Tense Present', *The Queen*, (219), August 1961.
9. Alain Robbe-Grillet, *Snapshots and Towards a New Novel* (London: Calder, 1965), p. 53.
10. Alan Bold, *Modern Scottish Literature* (London: Longman, 1983), p. 225.
11. *Bookshelf* inteview.
12. *Not to Disturb* (Harmondsworth: Penguin, 1974), pp. 9, 37. Subsequent references are to this edition.
13. Frank Kermode, 'The House of Fiction', in *The Novel Today*, ed. Malcolm Bradbury (Glasgow: Fontana, 1977), pp. 131–5.
14. 'Job Hunting in the Eternal City', *Time*, 16 July 1984.
15. Nicholas Shakespeare, 'Suffering and the Vital Spark', *Times*, 21 November 1983, p. 8.
16. David Lodge, *The Novelist at the Crossroads* (London: Routledge and Kegan Paul, 1971), p. 24.
17. Alexandra's name is certainly a punning reference to the English football league team Crewe Alexandra.
18. *The Takeover* (Harmondsworth: Penguin, 1978), p. 91. Subsequent references are to this edition.
19. Michael Wood, 'Endangered Species', *New York Review of Books*, 11 November 1976, p. 30.
20. Allan Massie, *Muriel Spark* (Edinburgh: Ramsay Head, 1979), p. 85.
21. *Territorial Rights* (London: Macmillan, 1979), p. 161.

22. Op. cit.
23. Spark held a similar job. See Derek Stanford, *Muriel Spark* (London: Centaur, 1963), p. 46.
24. *Loitering With Intent* (London: Bodley Head, 1981), p. 43. Subsequent references are to this edition.
25. *Robinson* (Harmondsworth: Penguin, 1964), p. 167.
26. Muriel Spark, 'The Mystery of Job's Suffering: Jung's New Interpretation Examined', *Church of England Newspaper*, 15 April 1955, p. 7. Cf. *The Only Problem* (London: Bodley Head, 1984), pp. 29, 30.
27. *Bookshelf* interview.
28. 'On the Side of Job', *TLS*, 7 September 1984, p. 989.
29. Spark's first published story dealt with this same theme, ending with a description of the Zambesi River replete with its 'rocks that look like crocodiles and the crocodiles that look like rocks'. See 'The Seraph and the Zambesi', in *Observer Prize Stories* (London: Heinemann, 1952), p. 12.
30. *A Far Cry from Kensington* (London: Constable, 1988), pp. 99, 181. Subsequent references are to this edition.
31. *Symposium* (London: Constable, 1990), p. 144. Subsequent references are to this edition.
32. Muriel Spark, 'Edinburgh-born', *New Statesman* 64 (10 August 1962), p. 180; Conrad Wilson, 'Muriel Spark Prefers to Hide in the South', *Scotsman*, 20 August 1962, p. 4.
33. 'The Culture of an Anarchist'; 'An Elegant Withdrawal from Literary Fuss', *Independent*, 2 August 1989, p. 17. I find a similar detachment in the novels of Allan Massie and Ronald Frame.
34. Victoria Glendinning, 'Talk with Muriel Spark', *New York Times Book Review*, 20 May 1979, pp. 47–8; Muriel Spark, 'How I Became a Novelist', *Books and Bookmen* 7 (November 1961), p. 9; 'The Spiritual Strength Beneath a Stylish Surface', *Sunday Times*, 13 March 1988, pp. [illegible]
35. 'The Early Days of Miss Muriel Spark: Some Prime Recollections', *The Critic*, vol. 20 (April–May, 1962), pp. 49–53. Stanford's 'recollections' should, of course, be treated with caution, but here he seems correct.
36. Bold, op. cit., p. 221.
37. 'The Culture of an Anarchist'.

Four

Class and Being in the Novels of William McIlvanney

Beth Dickson

William McIlvanney has sometimes been dismissed as a lightweight author, but his seven novels and volume of short stories demonstrate a talent richer and more serious than such judgements would lead one to expect. McIlvanney's fiction mirrors important aspects of Scottish life. In particular, the identity of the working class has undergone a number of recent transformations, and his fiction reflects, and reflects on, this historical experience. McIlvanney's writing also marks a transition between the authors of the Scottish Renaissance and the more recent emergence of fiction focused on the bleak, urban realities of the West of Scotland.

In these and other areas, however, his work does raise a number of questions. In writing mainly about working-class experience, is his treatment of violence, and his characterisation of women, sufficiently critical of that experience? Has the modernity of subsequent writing on urban themes superseded his more traditional styles? And what relationship does he establish between his socialist politics and the continental existentialist writing and philosophy which he has consistently pointed out as an influence?

Born into a working-class family in Kilmarnock in 1936, the central feature of his cultural inheritance was a Scottish vision of practical socialism, undistracted by rigid ideology. In *Surviving the Shipwreck* (1991; '*SS*'), McIlvanney writes:

> Scotland has existed for almost 300 years in a uniquely arrived at limbo in which a strongly shared sense of social and cultural values persists without the political means to express itself effectively . . . Here is held in embryo the possiblity of some kind of socialism, a more just way of living with one another.[1]

This analysis of Scotland's position is reminiscent of the work of the writers of the Scottish Renaissance. Neil Gunn, Naomi Mitchison, Eric Linklater and Lewis Grassic Gibbon all saw political change as the basis of a more just and culturally self-confident society. Like these earlier writers, McIlvanney is one of the few contemporary Scottish writers to be actively involved in politics. Though not belonging to any political party, his socialism prompted him to contribute an essay to a book examining the causes of poverty in Scotland, *Scotland: the Real Divide* (1983), edited by Gordon Brown and Robin Cook, now senior figures in the Labour Party.[2] McIlvanney has also been associated with the Scottish Nationalist Party, speaking to its Annual National Conference in 1987 (*SS*, 241–53). This is not to say that McIlvanney was *directly* influenced by Renaissance writers but merely to show that the kind of socialism to which he was heir was a shared inheritance.

However, McIlvanney has always been wary of seeing himself in a Scottish literary tradition and has openly disavowed direct Scottish influences on *Docherty* (1975) in 'A Shield Against the Gorgon' (*SS*, 217–37, 231). McIlvanney was motivated to write because of 'the absence of the life I came from in what was called literature' and because he 'wanted to write a book that would create a kind of literary genealogy for the people I came from, the people whose memorials were parish registers' (*SS*, 223). While it is possible to point to earlier portrayals of industrial working-class experience in the Scottish novel – Edwin Muir's *Poor Tom* (1932), George Blake's *The Shipbuilders* (1935), James Barke's *Major Operation* (1936), J. F. Hendry's *Ferniebrae* (1947) and Edward Gaitens's *The Dance of the Apprentices* (1948) – none of these works was very well known in the 1960s and 1970s and their absence from the autobiographical essays in *Surviving the Shipwreck* suggests that none of them was a work of personal significance for McIlvanney. He was doing something that many Scottish writers have had to do: because of the perceived absence of a literary tradition, he had to start from scratch. In this, he reflects what Douglas Gifford has called the dilemma of the Scottish writer, which is that he exists 'in a literary environment which fails to inform him' and that the Scottish fictional tradition '*is precisely about the writer's repeated sense of there being no tradition*'.[3] The writers to whom McIlvanney points as being influential include Ernest Hemingway and John Steinbeck, with D. H. Lawrence a powerful but negative example.

When *Docherty* was published, it successfully caught critical attention outwith Scotland, winning the Whitbread Prize. McIlvanney built on his two early novels, *Remedy Is None* (1966), which also has a working-class setting, and *A Gift From Nessus* (1968), in which he begins to outline the typical McIlvanney hero in Eddie Cameron. Even though Robin Jenkins had also been using working-class backgrounds since 1950, McIlvanney was perceived as a new, modern voice. Formally, he made no major changes in his technique over the next twenty years. When Alasdair Gray's *Lanark* appeared in 1981, it caused a sea-change in Scottish literature. Gray was the first Scottish writer to couch a vision of the Scottish urban wasteland in the postmodernist idiom, with parallel worlds, disappearing narrators and an eclectic bibliography. In 1982, James Kelman published *Not Not While the Giro*, and his novel *The Busconductor Hines* followed in 1984. In these works, the portrayal of working-class experience in its ferocious bleakness, repetitiveness and hopelessness was unflinching. Did such changes leave McIlvanney behind?

To discover why McIlvanney made the stylistic and thematic choices that he did, we should return to the lodestar of his career: his commitment to working people. It is this identification which decided his typical narrative style, a relaxed naturalism. Both McIlvanney and Kelman have addressed the immediate difficulty which arises with this formal choice: what relation should the author adopt to the consciousness of the character he creates? McIlvanney chooses to *tell* us about the character by using whatever language or level of discourse best reflects what characters experience, even though it is language that such people could not have known or achieved themselves. Kelman is happier to *show* his character's consciousness, using only language which it is likely that a person in that situation would have used.[4] However, it is significant that both writers use third-person narration, assuming the role of guides to a way of living with which, the style implies, their readers are likely to be unfamiliar. The didacticism of earlier writers about the working class is still present, though on a more sophisticated level, in the work of these writers.

With *Docherty*, McIlvanney was faced with the paradox that the book 'was written for people most of whom would never read it' (*SS*, 220). In 'The Courage of our Doubts', McIlvanney explains that he took up the detective story because it was 'a popular form, capable of sustaining "serious" writing' (*SS*, 153–62, 156). *Docherty* was a historical novel, and, after he had written it, McIlvanney found that he wanted to comment on contemporary events. The ease with which he blends contemporary plot with serious reflection was achieved by the detective stories – *Laidlaw* (1977) and *The Papers of Tony Veitch* (1983). Some critics felt that this move was retrograde, but with hindsight it is easy to see that these novels were an integral part of McIlvanney's development as a writer eager to be read by as many people as possible.

As a detective story, *Laidlaw* belongs to a genre which sets up expectations about how the story will proceed. McIlvanney has discussed these expectations in 'The Courage of our Doubts'. He subverts common expectations by introducing the reader to the murderer on page one. Thus the reader knows more than the detective: in a genre where knowledge is all, McIlvanney exploits irony to the full, almost mocking the detective genre itself when Laidlaw is given the last piece of information he needs by Eck Adamson, an alcoholic, who does not know the significance of what he is saying. Laidlaw toasts him: 'To Sherlock Adamson, public benefactor', thus judging the unreality of the genre – the Most Unlikely Person, bodies in the library, intellectual puzzles – against the real difficulties of wresting truth from ignorance.[5]

The great strength of these novels is the imaginative coherence contributed by the perspective of Jack Laidlaw, with his echoes of the hard-bitten, fast-talking Philip Marlowe in Raymond Chandler's fiction. Laidlaw provides the further focus that the third-person narrative of the previous novels sometimes seemed to require. Yet the detective stories are still written in the third person. Though growing in stature, Laidlaw is still 'presented' by the narrator, who has room to take up an attitude towards him if he wants to. It is not until *Strange Loyalties* (1991) that McIlvanney closes down that gap by making the distance between author and character formally invisible – though technically, of course, it still exists – by employing first-person narrative. But in a way, Laidlaw also speaks for himself. The gains in immediacy are real: through Laidlaw, McIlvanney has found his ideal means of commentary, whether distanced or committed.

Another striking feature of McIlvanney's narrative is its inclusiveness. *The Papers of Tony Veitch* begins with the murder of Eck Adamson; Cam Colvin, who was only a name in *Laidlaw*, takes on flesh; John Rhodes reappears. This tendency to transport characters from book to book becomes more marked in McIlvanney's later novels as he tries to hold all his characters together in a unified fictional world. It is a common enough occurrence in detective series to transfer detective and chief villain from one story to the next, but the wholesale transfer of characters in *Walking Wounded* (1989) and *Strange Loyalties* suggests a deeper purpose.

This is linked to McIlvanney's existentialism as well as to his Scottishness. Though some characters are minor and some are major, no character is ever less than that; each character has his own story. This is unlike some areas of English fiction in which characters look at others outside their sphere of knowledge and wonder what they think. In

According to Mark (1984) by Penelope Lively, the main character, a biographer, looks at a bus conductor, certain that his set of cultural references will be different, and presumes that he will know nothing about *art nouveau*. In Scottish literature, bus conductors are not aliens but have entire novels devoted to them.[6] McIlvanney does not use characters merely to show off the difference or superiority of others. He is quite capable at any time of shifting the narrative perspective to some previously uninvolved character. He does this in the description of the party after the fight in *The Big Man* (1985), when the narrative passes from the narrator first to Dan's Thornbank friends, then to Chuck Walker. The latter is a hired thug acting as a bouncer at the party, yet he too is given the chance to pass judgement on Scoular: a judgement that has its own validity, for he sees in Dan, as a weakness, something that is absent in himself – moral scruple. In 'The Sacred Wood Revisited', McIlvanney attacks the assumptions of cultural elitism which seem to him to be implicit in the work of T. S. Eliot (*SS*, 185–204). Instead of literature being for the favoured few who understand the allusions, McIlvanney feels strongly that it should be for all. His inclusive narrative indicates a difference not necessarily between good and bad art but between restricted and open views of humanity.

Thus it is of little value to criticise McIlvanney for traditionalism or for not being a postmodernist. Though in contemporary terms he is technically conservative, within those terms he shows a wealth of innovation intimately related to his subject. He has solved the technical problems which have arisen in his writing, and, in Laidlaw, creates a powerful character perfectly expressing all that he has to say.

Much of what McIlvanney does have to say concerns the working class, often expressing an ambivalent vision of it. Isobel Murray points to this when she suggests that *Docherty* is 'warm, celebratory, witty and uniquely affirmative of the value of Tam Docherty and people like him', yet also 'gloomy and pessimistic . . . Tam Docherty will be defeated: this is inevitable'.[7] The novel gives a historical account of the iron imperatives of poverty and hard work which govern the lives of the High Street community in the early twentieth century. *The Big Man* and *Walking Wounded* bring this account up to date, showing difficulties encountered in the 1980s, particularly the misery of unemployment arising from the erosion of much of Scotland's manufacturing base. Yet the grimness of *Docherty* is offset by the solidarity of family and friends and shared periods of freedom spent poaching, talking, drinking or laughing. West of Scotland humour is quick-witted and frequently reductive. McIlvanney can create it endlessly, as in the Hogmanay scene from *Docherty* or the bus scene in

Remedy is None. In the later books, however, a transformation has taken place in working-class life: there have been material gains but losses in solidarity. McIlvanney accurately observes that the ornate interior decoration of Mrs White's home is her son's way of thanking her for the personal privations that she endured to bring him up. Yet Dan Scoular thinks ordinary people keep big dogs now because they are frightened of each other.

Two aspects of this depiction have disturbed critics: McIlvanney's descriptions of violence and his treatment of female characters. McIlvanney has been sensitive to the criticisms and has addressed them directly in *The Big Man*, which is essentially an exploration of fighting and violence. McIlvanney has argued that, though people object to the depiction of physical violence, the violence of the social structures depicted in his novels does not receive the same criticism, though it is the greater evil. Yet if the violence that society wreaks on its victims is worse, that does not *excuse* personal violence, even if it makes it understandable. In *The Big Man*, McIlvanney has also shown the fight as a means of gaining knowledge. It is a place where words have to stop and where a man has to dig deep into himself to find out who and what he is. Dan discovers a root of anger in him which defies the interpretation of the fight which the crowd holds. He moves towards despair, finding all life intolerably broken. Yet the realisation is enabling, and comes to him in the physical extremities of the fight: arguably, it could not have been achieved any other way. Despite these justifications, it remains true that all McIlvanney's main male characters are angry, hot-blooded, quick-tempered and violent, physically and verbally. McIlvanney's heroes naturally resort to violence to solve their problems. They are so convinced that their way of living is better that they have no hesitation in imposing it by force. The paradox is that, even if their arguments are better, their methods lead to the disintegration, not the affirmation, of the self.

McIlvanney is also aware of the criticism that the women in his books remain remarkably stereotyped. He has written about this in 'Another Six Whiskies, Please, Barman' (*SS*, 100–3). Again in *The Big Man*, in his portrayal of Betty Scoular, McIlvanney shows some skills in portraying her hopes, resentment and growing bitterness at Dan's treatment of her. Though she remains as a meaningful presence, Betty is actually absent for much of the book, which is dominated by the male world of the fight. The other unusual feature of *The Big Man* is the cameo of Dan's mother. Although she seems cheerful and self-giving, in reality she has been hurt by the many small things which Dan's father could have given her but did not. Though outwardly secure, inwardly the marriage had tensions which left her bitter about what she had sacrificed. She is an illuminating contrast with Jenny Docherty. In these chapters in *The Big Man*, McIlvanney makes a valid attempt to see women from their own point of view. However, other parts of his fiction tell a different story: often when women appear in a position of significance, they inhabit a stereotype. Mother figures are working-class heroines: gentle, self-sacrificing and cheerful. Fast Frankie White's mother in *Strange Loyalties* is almost a candidate for sainthood, lying on her deathbed with Laidlaw as a secular priest administering the last rites of her faith in her son, performing a miracle by turning him into a respectable man. Sisters or sister figures like Kate Samson in *Strange Loyalties* are more outspoken. With the exception of Jenny Docherty – who is seen more as a mother than as a wife – wives are poisonous, brittle, materialistic, empty creatures who want to consume their husbands and whose main aim is upward social mobility. They are almost without redeeming features: it is a great mystery why McIlvanney's heroes married the women they did.

Perhaps the character in whom the uncertainty is deepest is Jan, Laidlaw's mistress. She appears only briefly in the first two Laidlaw novels, where she has the usual tasks of providing sex, comfort and understanding for the hero. Jan is an ambivalent figure. Her few appearances make her seem exotic and self-contained. She seems to accept Laidlaw as he is: 'His complexity didn't annoy her' (*L*, 163). After Laidlaw has given her one of his theories, however, Jan decides: 'You had to shut the door eventually on that stuff' (*L*, 166). Right at the beginning, McIlvanney plants this doubt about Jan's suitability. How can Laidlaw think he is accepted by someone who will not recognize his fundamental characteristic – his intellectual hunger? It is telling that in *Strange Loyalites* Jan leaves Laidlaw for a number of reasons which Laidlaw himself cannot gainsay, yet which emphasise her lack of any intellectual understanding of him. Jan's cruelty here is paralleled by Jeannie McPhater's action in 'End game' from *Walking Wounded*, where she deliberately puts Gus McPhater's copy of Schopenhauer in the bin under as much mess as possible – Gus is one of Graithnock's minor wonders, an autodidact. Previously, McIlvanney has taken some time to build up the justice of her case. Yet in the end she is found guilty, like Jan, of ignoring what makes a man most himself. Except in lust and acrimony, it seems almost impossible for men and women to communicate as partners in McIlvanney's work.

While McIlvanney accurately records many facets of working-class existence and the strength of character which many people show in living against the odds, working-class experience may in reality be less narrow than it appears in his novels. Nevertheless, in the essentials, it is a more optimistic vision than that of some of his contemporaries, as Douglas Gifford has pointed out:

> while McIlvanney and Spence certainly found more of epiphany and justification in their presentations of struggle and failure, Kelman remains true, like Alasdair Gray, to this tradition of enigmatic treatment of the nature/nurture controversy. That is to say Kelman and Gray, very different in so many ways, leave unanswered the questions as to whether their protagonists are victims of a Scottish, deprived post-war and grey environment and upbringing, or whether the faults lie essentially in themselves.[8]

Given that McIlvanney does provide a more engaging vision than Kelman and Gray, the question of where McIlvanney locates evil is not quite so straightforward as his work sometimes seems to suggest. This theme leads directly into the debate between socialism and existentialism which characterises McIlvanney's fiction.

On the face of it, *Docherty* is based on a socialist analysis of society which locates evil precisely among capitalist individuals and structures. Tam is a miner. His life is physically hard, and the money he earns is only just enough to live on. He upholds basic standards of decency as a bulwark against a dehumanising society. He supports Keir Hardie and believes that one day his policies will achieve a more just society. However, the difficulty of living humanely against such odds takes its toll on him, and he finds himself overreacting violently when he goes out to fight a peeping tom. But the coming of the First World War, and the physical and mental wounds which it inflicts on his son Mick, make him realise that 'His previous authority over his own existence was a joke'.[9] From then on, Tam fights a rearguard action against forces which he cannot control or influence. Despite his despair, he still castigates his son Angus when he discovers he has decided to contract to mine coal privately in order to earn more money. Rather than make a contract with his employers, Tam is waiting for a new order to be born when life will be different. Mick, who has become a communist because of his wartime experiences, asks him, disbelievingly, when such a time will come:

> 'When it comes. Ah don't ken when. When the yins that ken aboot these things can make it happen. An' they will. Me. Ah'm jist keepin' the accoonts clean. A kinna tallyman. Ah ken hoo much is owed. An' Ah'm no' settlin' fur less.'
>
> 'Ye canny believe that, feyther.'
>
> 'Son. Ah canny no' believe it.' (*D*, 258)

Tam dies in an accident, saving the life of a fellow miner.

'An awesome wee man' is how Tam is summed up by his friends, and *Docherty* has attracted some attention recently on this score. In his essay, '"Oor ain folk"?: National Types and Stereotypes in Arcadia' ('*OAF*'), Roderick Watson has argued that in the early modern period it was common for Scottish writers to describe national identity as 'static, pastoral and hence entirely contained within a closed system'.[10] He argues that this is true of both Kailyard and anti-Kailyard literature. Watson sees the same tendency in *Docherty*, with 'the wee man' and 'the hard man' being characters in a novel who can 'easily be trapped and crushed by larger social and economic forces' (p. 138). Watson contrasts the documentary tone of the descriptions in *Docherty* with the inner rage which the narrator feels about the way the people have been treated. However, Watson also argues that 'it is the "scientifically" determinist outlook behind such a voice which *guarantees* the characters' continuing status as "bodies", as elements contained in a closed and fictive pressure cooker' (p. 139).

Watson is not saying that, because of this counter-pastoral mode, *Docherty* is somehow bad fiction; rather he says that 'the book's style is directed to a fully-realised effect' (p. 140). He does note, however, the frequency with which Scottish writers employ these modes. While I agree with most of Watson's analysis, I am uncertain how it can be argued finally that, though Watson sees McIlvanney imposing a subhuman status on his characters, this is 'a fully-realised effect'. If McIlvanney, who is fully aware of the dehumanising effects of society on his characters, does not show the vitality they possess despite their circumstances, then he must have failed in one of his stated aims for *Docherty*, which was 'to give working-class life the vote in the literature of heroism' (*SS*, 231).

Rather, it seems that there are clear signs in *Docherty* that McIlvanney himself is antagonistic to the reduction of what should be fully-fleshed characters to anonymous phrases. Watson says that the characterisation of Tam briefly defies this view, but after his death the novel reverts to its usual view. This seems to be the crux of what McIlvanney is trying to achieve. Although the narrator's usual tone may be a determinist one, there are other times when he speaks existentially and generates a defiance of what seems a closed universe. When the narrator says at the end that Tam's gift to his friends was to enlarge their sense of themselves, his gift was *precisely* to expand that phrase or tag which life used to describe them and to make it into something recognisably human. The characterisation of Conn performs a similar function.

Conn, like many other 'young, imaginative boy' characters in the Scottish novel, resists, often with little success, the identities which the closed fictional world gives him. Of Conn, McIlvanney writes: 'The Bringan was where he could escape from the arbitrary and frequently harsh identity which High Street impressed on him' (*D*, 126). While it could be argued that this is merely a flight from the counter-pastoral to the pastoral, it is significant that in the rest of McIlvanney's work questions of identity are expressed through his existentialism, the main function of which is to call into question all given identities.

McIlvanney has written of his debt to the European existentialist writers Soren Kierkegaard, Albert Camus and Miguel de Unamuno. These three writers, a Danish Protestant theologian, a French novelist and a Spanish Catholic who lost his faith, are an eclectic choice. Generally they reject systems, like Marxism, which seem to impose on humanity burdens which it cannot bear. Instead they take as their starting point the absurdity and meaninglessness of existence and assert that, despite this, man must make choices which affirm his humanity in spite of absurdity. Camus writes that man must revolt:

> That revolt is the certainty of a crushing fate, without the resignation that ought to accompany it . . . That revolt gives life its value. Spread out over the whole length of a life, it restores its majesty to that life . . . It is essential to die unreconciled and not of one's own free will . . . The absurd man can only drain everything to the bitter end, and deplete himself . . . and in that day-to-day revolt he gives proof of his only truth which is defiance.[11]

There could be no clearer commentary on Tam Docherty's life and death than this, nor a clearer summary of the kind of existential ideas central to McIlvanney's fiction.

However, in *Docherty*, existentialism is subordinated to the conscious socialism which Tam espouses, and this is one of the reasons why the ending is unresolved. No matter how resolute and upstanding Tam was, his nobility did not change the social and economic terms in which he existed. As usual, Scottish history allows no escape even for the best of men. The confrontations of the 1930s were followed not by a period of justice for the working class but by the Second World War, though thereafter by a period of political consensus in which prosperity was more evenly shared. This seems to have caused McIlvanney some uncertainty. He notes in 'A Shield Against the Gorgon' that he actually wrote 30,000 words further than the present ending of the novel, presumably following the narrative of the sons. Importantly, however, in an interview with Ian Bell, McIlvanney claimed that a need to leave the past and concentrate on the present lay behind his move into the Laidlaw stories.[12] Not only was there a technical problem to be solved, there was also a thematic one. Though there was no continuing historical confrontation – rather the reverse – there *was* a continuing personal search for justice. This search is encapsulated in Laidlaw, a man perplexed by the meaninglessness of life. Laidlaw's watchword is to have 'the courage of your doubts', not to act according to someone else's second-hand analysis but to choose to act justly in an absurd environment. Thus, at the end of *Laidlaw*, instead of a chase (which is how *Tony Veitch* ends), Laidlaw gets to the murdered girl's father just as he is about to kill the murderer and rehearses the facts of his inadequate fatherhood to him, forcing him to doubt for a split second certainties about his own existence as a hard man which he had previously taken for granted. This uncertainty allows Laidlaw to arrest the murderer safely.

It was not until *The Big Man* that McIlvanney returned to the unresolved problem of *Docherty*. Like the 1930s, the 1980s too was a period of political confrontation. However, by shifting the central perspective from socialism to existentialism, McIlvanney addresses the difficulties of history in a different way. Instead of success being judged by how far conditions have changed, it is judged by how well a person can live in *whatever historical circumstances exist*.

The Big Man is one of these clichéd phrases which Roderick Watson identified as indicating a cast of Scottish types rather than characters. That is exactly how Dan Scoular feels about himself as the man whom Thornbank has chosen as its local hero:

> what they needed him to be they had partly accustomed him to pretend to be. He meant something in the life of Thornbank and he tried to live inside that meaning as best he could, like a somnambulist pacing out someone else's dream.[13]

Thornbank needs a hero because the economic dislocation of the 1980s has left it without employment or hope. Dan is redundant, coping with the challenge to identity that process brings; 'the slow, cumulative realisation that you didn't matter' (*TBM*, 101). Even the past is suspect. In this depressing atmosphere, Dan tries to hang on to the warmth of past life, the life summed up in *Docherty*, though sometimes he thinks he is making it up. Life has lost meaning, direction and authenticity.

Not surprisingly, Dan does not feel up to the task of unifying his local community. Whereas the choices which his parents made seemed black and white, it is more confusing for him to work out which actions he should take. The 'big man' has to find out who he is. Dan rejected education as a means of financial gain; now he is tempted to crime. He is asked to take part in a bare-knuckle fight for which he will be paid. Although the fight is illegal, it does not seem morally wrong, just as poaching did not seem iniquitous to Tam. However, when Dan discovers how his opponent Cutty Dawson has been forced into the fight at grave risk to his health, he begins to realise that agreeing to fight will lead him into a life of violence, where every penny he earns will be directly gained from someone else's misery. At the party after the fight, Dan is asked to inhabit a new image of himself just as false as the Thornbank image. It is false because it refuses to recognise the violence and deception of the fight:

> The identity they were trying to give him didn't relate to where he had been . . . They weren't celebrating him, they were celebrating the surrogate means he had given them of reaffirming their own lives without responsibility to what was past. (*TBM*, 192)

Matt Mason offers Dan a life of wealth and of meaning – but the meaning is based on the bastard sense of himself which the party offered. Matt offers to make Dan his son. Matt's real sons are being educated for a respectable middle-class life, but Matt wants Dan to inherit his criminal business. Matt speaks about how he made it out of the Gallowgate and how he will fight to protect himself. Matt's deprivation was real, but Dan cannot accept the interpretation of life – self-interest – which Matt has arrived at. He strikes Mason and takes some of his money to give to Cutty.

But Mason was not the only father whom Dan fought – he also fought his own father. When he was a teenager, Dan's father fought him in an attempt to instil in him the old working-class code. These old standards wrack Dan. He sees their honour but feels that they have become irrelevant:

> Cutty had lost. His father had lost. All those self-defeatingly brave men of his boyhood had lost. Like their champion, Cutty had tried to deny the truth of his own situation, had agreed to unfair odds, had tried to impose the strength of his will on impossible circumstances. (*TBM*, 202)

Dan also sees that his father had an intimation of this hopelessness in his fight against Dan. He was fighting against 'all the changes he felt coming, the loss of crucial principles' (*TBM*, 115).

At this stage in the novel, McIlvanney reflects on one of the major strands of the Scottish novel – conflicts between fathers and sons about history and the nature of the inheritance that the sons should have. In *Waverley* (1814), Edmund Waverley rejects the safe Hanoverian inheritance for the wild Jacobite dream. No matter how he schemes in *The Entail* (1823), Claud Walkinshaw cannot entail his property so that history will take the course he wants it to. In *Weir of Hermiston* (1896), Archie Hermiston refuses to support his father's authoritarian harshness. In *Sunset Song* (1932), Will Guthrie emigrates to Argentina rather than accept the poverty of his father's farm and his father's severe treatment. Scotland's history is one of its remaining unifying features: and because that history is characterised by conflict, Scots are often defined by their attitudes to conflict. Significantly, alert writers such as McIlvanney continue to repeat independently larger patterns of the national culture of which they disclaim direct knowledge.

Walking Wounded, a collection of short stories, shows the Scottish accent of McIlvanney's existentialism clearly.[14] Many of the characters here dream. Dreaming is another category close to the heart of the Scottish novel, where it is often seen ambivalently. Waverley's Jacobite dreams are beautiful, and satisfy his imagination, but would bring destruction and poverty if they came true. As analysed by turn-of-the-century writers like Neil Munro and J. M. Barrie, dreaming is a formidable barrier to engagement with Scottish life past and present. Gilian in *Gilian the Dreamer* (1899) almost succeeds in forgetting that the Clearances took place by feeding on powerful dreams, myths, of the Highlands. Peter Pan is the boy who does not want to grow up, perhaps because – like his forerunner in *Sentimental Tommy* (1896) – he would find life restricted, couthy and dull. These earlier dreams, which are directly related to the absence of any political nationhood into which local societies may mature, mask historic injustices and present powerlessness, though Barrie and Munro avoid the full implications in their work. McIlvanney is aware that his characters dream, and he knows they dream because of the lack of political or personal justice. Hurt and sadness come from both personal and institutional sources. In a society which does not want them, and in a universe which is hostile, people comfort themselves by dreaming, by escaping from vicious realities. If the possibility of action is denied, then dreaming is all that is left.

The culmination of all these themes can be seen in *Strange Loyalties*. The thematic expansion which occurred in *The Big Man* is still here and is indeed extended into other areas of life: Laidlaw's investigative journey takes him out of the west, south to the Borders and east to Edinburgh; the theatrical imagery which enhanced the scenes of domesticity in *The Big Man* returns; and McIlvanney uses paintings as a simple and effective source of symbolism. All these ingredients combined make *Strange Loyalties* more mellow than any previous novel. McIlvanney's growing confidence means that there are fewer over-written passages in the later novels, and the move to first-person narration in *Strange Loyalties* means that some of the verbal pyrotechnics now become a function of characterisation, to which they are more suited, rather than of narrative. This suits the tone of the book, which is often reflective. These changes in background, incidentals and narration make the cerebral journey easier than Dan Scoular's exhausting mental progress in *The Big Man*.

Thematically, *Strange Loyalties* takes up where *The Big Man* ended, with the extension from a socialist to an existential analysis. Laidlaw is still perplexed by guilt, universal in character:

> My ideal dock would accommodate the population of the world. We would all give our evidence, tell our sad stories and then there would be a mass acquittal and we would all go away and try again.[15]

Laidlaw fears that his guilt will make him unable to recognise the truth and stop him gaining access to understanding. His sense of guilt is accompanied by a respect for other people, an inheritance from his parents.

During his investigations, Laidlaw realises that some people's loyalty, their means of making life coherent, forces them into strange decisions. When these loyalties conflict with greater loyalties – 'loyalty to the truth and loyalty to the ideals our nature professes' – then it is time to force a choice of loyalties and see which one is the stronger (*SL*, 186). While it is this insight which reveals to Laidlaw the tactics he must use to trap Matt Mason, it is also, ironically, the reason for Scott's death. He too had strange loyalties.

Here, McIlvanney takes up a kind of incident which occurs in more than one of his novels: a difficult youthful experience of emotional [illegible] death. Instead of the somewhat fantastic fight at the centre of *The Big Man*, the episode at the centre of *Strange Loyalties* is of more immediate and enduring relevance: a fatal accident. Three men with whom Scott Laidlaw, Jack Laidlaw's brother, shared a flat as a student were involved in a fatal hit-and-run accident just before they were to graduate. Years later, not long before he died, when Scott's guilt was overpowering, he summed up to one of the others, Michael Preston, what he felt. All four had been setting out on life and were looking for success and approbation. However, by abandoning the man they killed, he became their judge. Michael Preston explained that the agreement

> denied Scott's nature. Which was to follow the honesty of his idealism to the bone. It was a death-sentence. We killed Scott as well as the other man . . . Scott took the pain most, for all of us. (*SL*, 276)

Scott left two paintings: symbols of McIlvanney's dual concerns. One is a painting of the industrial wasteland that Scotland has become; the other is of Scott's personal vision of guilt. The second painting, a pastiche of da Vinci's 'Last Supper', has a mixture of Christian and pagan imagery. McIlvanney's writing about guilt reflects the existentialist concern about the disorder of human existence and man's alienation from his deepest self. In his book *Existentialism*, John Macquarrie has written that the existentialist formulation of guilt is on this point not dissimilar to the Christian formulation of sin, in which guilt as a symptom of alienation from God plays an important role.[16] This perhaps explains the ease with which McIlvanney uses Christian imagery to make his own points. Christianity's formulation of guilt would also stress the universality of guilt, the corruption of the seeker, the misplaced loyalties which disfigure the lives of others, and the fact that the man we kill is our judge. However, there is so far no indication in McIlvanney's thought that guilt can be covered or removed. Rather, it must be borne: it is suggested in *Strange Loyalties* that 'This guilt was not absolvable. All I could do was take my share of it. I took the secret into myself' (*SL*, 279). Together with the bearing of guilt goes the determination to live a better life:

> I would have to try and learn to live with it as justly as I could . . . I would begin again to try to be a good father to [my children]. (*SL*, 280)

There is no redemption and no escape from the necessity of living up to standards which are humanly unreachable. Under this scheme, those who realise in however small a way that they are compromised, like Fast Frankie or Michael Preston, are tolerated. Those who deny their own brokenness, like Anna and Ernie Milligan, or those who think they are impregnable, like Dave Lyons, are beyond the pale.

From the outset of his writing career, William McIlvanney saw the need to map unfictionalised experience. From there he interacted with older patterns of Scottish society and identity, even though he has written that many of the most important direct influences on his writing were non-Scottish. This capacity to look out from Scotland and engage with cultural patterns from other places is a continuing feature of Scottish society. His socialism encouraged his exploration of working-class life, but it was his existentialism – which coexisted with his political beliefs – that became the force for unity and development within his work. The need to write in a language which is accessible led to the Laidlaw books and the character of Laidlaw. Technical innovations did not take the same form as those of other writers, but his work shows a functional technical progress born of his desire to communicate. The unjust treatment of workers, whether in the 1930s or in the 1980s has been explored in McIlvanney's work, and a coherent political position underlies it. That position requires social justice of a kind which respects the individual. McIlvanney takes risks in communication which do not always pay off. However, his commitment to the common man, a commitment which has an honourable history in Scottish culture, informs his writing at all levels. With compassion and honesty, he clearly reflects many things that many Scots feel about their own times. This is hardly the achievement of a lightweight author.

NOTES

1. William McIlvanney, 'Preface' in *Surviving the Shipwreck* (Edinburgh: Mainstream Publishing, 1991), pp. 11–14, p. 13.
2. William McIlvanney, 'Being Poor' in *Scotland: the Real Divide*, ed. Gordon Brown and Robin Cook (Edinburgh: Mainstream Publishing, 1983), pp. 23–6.
3. Douglas Gifford, *The Dear Green Place?: The Novel in the West of Scotland* (Glasgow: Third Eye Centre, 1985), p. 14.
4. Kelman has talked about this issue in an interview with Kirsty McNeill, 'Interview with James Kelman' in *Chapman* 57, 1989, pp. 1–9.
5. William McIlvanney, *Laidlaw* (London: Hodder and Stoughton, 1977; reprinted Coronet, 1990), p. 190. Subsequent references are to this edition.
6. Penelope Lively, *According to Mark* (London: Heinemann, 1984).
7. Isobel Murray and Bob Tait, 'William McIlvanney: *Docherty*' in *Ten Modern Scottish Novels* (Aberdeen: Aberdeen University Press, 1984), pp. 168–93, p. 169.
8. Douglas Gifford, 'Discovering Lost Voices' in *Books in Scotland* 38, 1991, pp. 1–6, p. 5.
9. William McIlvanney, *Docherty* (London: George Allen and Unwin, 1975; reprinted Coronet, 1985), p. 210. Subsequent references are to this edition.
10. Roderick Watson, '"Oor Ain Folk"?: National Types and Stereotypes in Arcadia' in *Nationalism in Literature: Third International Scottish Studies Symposium*, ed. Horst W. Drescher and Hermann Volkel, Scottish Studies 8 (Frankfurt: Peter Lang, 1989), pp. 131–42, p. 131. Subsequent references are to this edition.
11. Albert Camus, *The Myth of Sisyphus* (1942), trans. Justin O'Brien (1955; reprinted Harmondsworth: Penguin, 1975), pp. 54–5.
12. Ian Bell, 'Hunting for Morality in Scotland's Myths', *The Scotsman*, 16 April 1983, p. 4.
13. William McIlvanney, *The Big Man* (London: Hodder and Stoughton, 1985), p. 101. Subsequent references are to this edition.

14. William McIlvanney, *Walking Wounded* (London: Hodder and Stoughton, 1989).
15. William McIlvanney, *Strange Loyalties* (London: Hodder and Stoughton, 1991), pp. 255–6. Subsequent references are to this edition.
16. John Macquarrie, *Existentialism* (London: Penguin, 1976), p. 204.

FURTHER READING

Autobiography

'Growing Up in the West' in *Memoirs of a Modern Scotland*, ed. Karl Miller (London: Faber and Faber, 1970), pp. 168–78. This essay, together with the autobiographical writing in *Surviving the Shipwreck*, is an important source of working-class experience and aspiration in its own right.

Criticism

The two early novels are discussed in F. R. Hart, *The Scottish Novel: A Critical Survey* (London: John Murray, 1978). *Docherty* is briefly noted in Alan Bold, *Modern Scottish Literature* (London: Longman, 1983). There is a full discussion of *Walking Wounded* by Gavin Wallace, entitled 'Stubborn Resplendence', in *Cencrastus*, Spring 1990, pp. 32–3. The later novels were reviewed as they were published in Douglas Gifford's regular reviews of Scottish fiction in *Books in Scotland*.

Five

Myths and Marvels

John Burns

There is something of a critical orthodoxy in Scotland at the moment which maintains that for a novel to be acceptable it must deal only with contemporary urban life. In many ways, this is a necessary and healthy corrective to the widespread neglect of such subject matter in nineteenth-century Scottish fiction, but it seems just as limiting in its own way, denying a particularly vital strain in Scottish fiction: the strain of legend and myth. This now includes many literary elements, but in essence it goes back to that extraordinary rich oral tradition of storytelling, song and poetry which is such an important part of the Scottish imagination.

This tradition, as Douglas Gifford has shown,[1] has given a distinctive 'flavour' to the Scottish novel. It is central to Scott and Hogg and the best of Stevenson. It underpins much of the best work of the novelists of the Scottish Renaissance, Gunn, Gibbon, Linklater and Mitchison. For Gifford, these writers, for all their individual differences, share an awareness of the value of legend and myth and of the need to reassess the value of the 'primitive' which was such an important part of the development of 'modern' art in Europe earlier this century. Their access to the rich oral traditions of Scotland gives their work a unique and lasting resonance.

This chapter looks at three novels, all published in the last decade, which grow out of a shared awareness of that same tradition. Not all of them use Scottish material in a Scottish setting, but they do reveal a consciousness steeped in that archaic tradition, together with a delight in inhabiting the ambiguous landscape of legend and myth which is so congenial to the Scottish imagination. George Mackay Brown's *Time in a Red Coat* (1984), Sian Hayton's *Cells of Knowledge* (1989) and Harry Tait's *The Ballad of Sawney Bain* (1990) are remarkable feats of the imagination, their audacity of form and subject matter showing a tremendous confidence (two of them are first novels) on the part of contemporary Scottish novelists. This can only bode well for the future.

Time in a Red Coat is George Mackay Brown's third novel, and, like *Greenvoe* (1972) and *Magnus* (1973), it eschews conventional linear narrative in favour of a kaleidoscopic range of stories and images which ultimately coalesce to tell a story of strange and haunting beauty. The book tells the story of a young girl who wanders through the centuries, turning up whenever and wherever there is a war. While the girl herself does not seem to age until near the end of her journey, her white coat becomes progressively more stained and tattered through the effects of war. It is a story about both the survival and the cost of innocence in a violent and chaotic world.

It is clear from the outset that this is no conventional novel. The first chapter is set in the palace of a great Khan and describes a masque performed in front of the palace on a day on which the peasants and ordinary people are allowed inside the palace gates. This is an imaginary world very remote in time and space from the Orkney which is the normal backdrop for Mackay Brown's work. At first glance, it is nearer to the closed, highly ritualised worlds of Mervyn Peake's Gormenghast or Alasdair Gray's 'Five Letters from an Eastern Empire'. Many of the characters seem to have strayed in from one of Breughel's paintings, or from Mackay Brown's own Hamnavoe: the smith, the girl from the flax field, the butter girl.

The Masquer himself is an extraordinary character, 'wearing a coat of a hundred colours. His face was splashed white and purple and gold.'[2] Announcing that he is without musicians and assistants and that he will have to perform the Masque solo, he then appears to go into a trance. He performs a puppet show which creates different responses in his audience, as if to suggest that if you do not approach the Masquer's art with an open and responsive mind you will miss the significance of what he is doing. Like all good storytellers, too, the Masquer seems always to be changing, never allowing his listeners to pin him down in the way that audiences so love to do. And just as we, another audience, try to pin the Masquer down as an image of George Mackay Brown the storyteller, his Masque is itself seriously disrupted by the incursion of another storyteller, a boy who runs into the palace garden from the mountains, tearing his way through the crowd to tell another story whose 'message' is not immediately clear.

> 'My father says there's a sound of iron on stone . . .'
>
> 'Iron on stone!' cried the Masquer. 'What kind of message is that?'

> 'Barbarians,' said the boy trembling. 'There's a breach in the Wall.' (*TRC*, 91)

It is war that has disrupted the Masque of Peace. The order of life in the palace and throughout the Empire will be changed by the war. The great wall has been breached and the barbarians have broken through. Just as this happens, a girl is born in the palace and the princess's cries merge with the scream of a palace peacock. Two figures, one in black and one in white, silently make ready to offer their wisdom to the new-born child and offer sharply contrasting ways of looking at the world. For the White Guardian, life is light, love and delight; for the Black Guardian, the world is a place of torment, destruction and death. The rest of the book is taken up with the new-born child's journey through this strange and terrible world that can seem so different to each of us.

This first chapter sets the tone for the rest of the book. It is a rich text of shifting surfaces whose 'meaning' is fluid and relative to the perspective of the observer. Even in those places where the author seems to speak directly to the reader, or when the girl herself offers an interpretation, the reader is aware that the explanations are partial and incomplete. The language is, for the most part, the language of fairytale and legend, with no attempt to make characters or dialogue naturalistic. Mackay Brown presents us with a startling vision of a world at once wholly imaginary yet immediately recognisable. There is also a disturbing tension between the often luxuriant imagery and the short, terse sentences, similar in effect to the language of some of Iain Crichton Smith's more surreal short stories. Extraordinary things are depicted with no further comment, and peculiar juxtapositions occur with no explanation, like the scream of the peacock chiming with the cries of birth.

The girl herself is a disturbing character. When we first meet her, she is like an ivory doll or 'a corpse rigged out and bedizened for a funeral pyre' (*TRC*, 16). To Mistress Poppyseed, who had rescued her from the invading barbarians and who had brought her up, she is 'a dove in a cage'. She is silent all the time while Mistress Poppyseed explains to her that she is to be married to a rich man and her new life will begin. Realising that she is being promised one cage instead of another, she flees, walking out into the world she has never seen before and setting off on her long journey. On this journey, she turns up in different places and times, sometimes as herself, sometimes seen as a dove, always as a symbol of innocence. At first, her journey seems rather aimless: she crops up in various archetypal settings, none of which can be located precisely by the reader. Many of these settings are elemental (river, well, forest), but gradually they can be seen to have more to do with the eternal settings of war. Gradually, too, it becomes clear that the girl is linked to water, and that her story re-enacts an elemental conflict between fire (war) and water (peace).

The journey through an apocalyptic landscape of horror and destruction becomes all the more appalling when the reader recognises his or her own time.

> Fallen burnt stones – silent waiting women – children with gaunt cheeks and pot bellies – men struggling in honeycombs of mud, men hung like puppets upon spiked wire between honeycomb and quagmire, endless canals or trenches that one imagined must stretch from sea to mountains – men in dung-coloured clothes running on with bayonets, men buckling . . . (*TRC*, 214)

In some mysterious way, the girl is an antidote to all this, taking upon herself much of the pain and guilt of a world that is violent and uncaring.

Finally, she becomes an old woman sitting by the fire telling her own story to her grandson. It is more or less the story we have just read, except that she tells it in reverse order: the old woman travels through the world becoming younger and younger as she goes until 'the coat she wore was white as snow or salt. But it smelt like a white rose' (*TRC*, 249). In drawing everything together into this image of innocence, and in showing us the living innocence of the old woman's grandson, Mackay Brown is reaffirming his faith in humanity: despite the lethal potential of nuclear weapons, the destructive aspect of life will always be balanced – and can perhaps be overcome – by the creative. The sea, the mysterious force that draws the girl, is at once full of the bitter salt of human tears and 'a vast incalculable environing presence' (*TRC*, 235), giving life and hope to humanity, as if to suggest that, for all its violence, the void that surrounds us is ultimately creative and life-sustaining. There is a place in this world-view for darkness and for light. By not showing the mechanics of how this works, the novel suggests that faith is not capable of a mechanical explanation: it is of a different order of experience. The ending is thus fully in keeping with the novel's technique, with the reader encouraged to make a 'leap of faith', a faith that emerges from the deep, archetypal levels of the story.

Set in the seventeenth century, *The Ballad of Sawney Bain*, by Harry Tait, tells the story of the new minister of the ironically-named parish of Trig, in Galloway. This man had been present at the trial and death of the semi-legendary Sawney Bain, the Galloway Cannibal. The minister is so powerfully moved by the figure of Bain that he develops an obsession with finding out the truth behind the legend, because what he has seen does not square with the Church's official interpretation. In doing so, he becomes drawn into the strange life of Bain's common-law wife, Agnes Douglas (commonly regarded as a witch), and the 'atheist, warlock and political renegade' Steven or 'Steenie' Malecky. The novel chronicles the minister's attempt to comprehend their story and, by so doing, comprehend something of his country's recent bloody history.

The plot is extended and intricate, and can only be pieced together by juggling with several narratives at once: into the minister's narrative are set Black Agnes's story written in her own words; Steenie's story as told by an earlier minister, Mathius Pringle; the minister's own account of his journey late in the book to search for Malecky in the Highlands; and countless other interpolated narratives of varying length and of varying degrees of 'truth' and importance. In its characters, setting and language, the book carries echoes of many earlier Scottish books and writers. The reader has to be particularly agile to get a firm foothold on this text, and there is a great deal of enjoyment to be had in making the attempt. But for all Tait's delightfully dry sense of humour, the book is essentially serious in import and intention. If the reader sometimes finds it hard to grasp what is happening, the minister, too, is struggling.

The world of *Sawney Bain* is like the world of *Macbeth*, where everything, it seems, is 'smother'd in surmise, and nothing is but what is not'. The central enigma for the minister is what actually happened in the cannibal cave. He simply does not know. When Bain was alive, he would not tell him; now that he is dead, he cannot. In a big book covering a long period of time, characters are seen in younger and older guises, or are seen through the eyes of other characters differently at different times. Both Bain and Malecky are seen by the Church as evil, yet in the Black Book of Agnes Douglas, and in the eyes of the people among whom they live, they are regarded as men of great spirit who give generously of themselves to those around them. Bain, in particular, is a puzzle to the minister: how could a man who so strongly professes himself a Christian, and whose children could recite Scripture, carry out the abominations alleged to have been perpetrated in the cave?

The minister can make little or no sense of it all. Near the end of the book, he says in his journal: 'I feel as if I am in a wilderness of lies'.[3] Like the reader, he is uncertain about what can and cannot be believed. He feels that he is caught up in a 'demoniac jig', but continues to wrestle with his obsession until it all but destroys him. Conditioned by his Christian outlook, his imagination can only conjure up horrors – not only the horror of cannibalism, but also the horror of fornication, which is seen throughout the book as perhaps the greater sin in the eyes of the Church. This is demonstrated most clearly in Tait's marvellous character Walter Hyslop, the Kirk Elder who scours the woods and wild places of the parish by night in order to discover and expose young lovers. Much of Hyslop's zeal is of course driven by repressed jealousy, since he is himself unable to achieve such warm contact with others. The minister, too, is similarly tormented. Agnes Douglas looms large in his imagination because her sexual openness disturbs him; and in his interest in the girl Helen Melville there seems to be an element of sexual prurience.

When Elizabeth Adams and William Black are brought before the Reverend Marten Gilmarten for the sin of fornication, the minister at first feels Gilmarten's attack on them to be out of all proportion to the offence; but then, in imagining their coming together, he immediately links them with Agnes Douglas and her 'incestuous brood', so returning him to the image of the cave:

> On summer nights they had sat naked round their fire gnawing at their neighbours' flesh, staring out across the flames to a world of which they had inherited a grossly corrupted knowledge of God and of themselves, and of anything that could be called goodness. (*BSB*, 230)

Then, in one of those moments, scattered throughout the book, in which the minister's perceptions seem to fall in on themselves, he looks back at the Reverend Gilmarten and imagines that he is 'dismembering the bodies of Elizabeth Adams and William Black, rending limb from body, splitting flesh apart, grinding bones into powder'.

Such sudden reversals of meaning throw the minister into an anguished state of religious doubt. Late in the book,

> He was suddenly struck horribly and forcibly with the idea that the Scots were hardly a Christian people at all. To them religion was a spear, a sword, and a gun, blessed by their tribal deity, to be used against their enemies. (*BSB*, 323)

In other words, religion is *used* by various groups in the pursuit of their own ends. Tait attacks this at times with satire, and at other times with a bitter anger because of its cataclysmic effect on individuals and on the nation. 'Discipline and order' are the key words in the Reverend Gilmarten's view of religion (p. 215). The Kirk has, for him, a civilising mission which will help smooth the way for 'complete union between Scotland and England' (*BSB*, 193). The substitution of this for a true religious vision causes much anguish for the minister. He is intelligent enough to know that this is wrong, but he is also limited by his social conditioning and by the troubled knowledge that somehow Christianity is 'right' for him. He is unable to reconcile these insights and forge a new kind of belief.

In his confusion, the minister is seen as an outsider, alienated from the people of his parish. This is his characteristic stance, perhaps exaggerated by the Church's explicit aim of *controlling* the people; but it issues towards the end in a 'blasphemous hatred for all things human' (*BSB*, 423). The use of 'blasphemous' suggests a recognition on the minister's part that this is a perversion of the natural way of things, but the feeling emerges insistently from his unconscious and is perhaps the only response of which he is finally capable when faced with the horrors of 'the cave' – all those unknowns which lie beyond the Church's power to discipline and control.

In Black Agnes's story, the minister comes face to face with characters who live by a different set of values, although – in keeping with the novel's desire to refuse glib certainties – those characters too do not always prove to be fully in control of their own destinies. In particular, Sawney Bain's move from genuine religious awe into an increasingly inhuman fanaticism causes Agnes much pain thoughout. But in general, it seems that the unholy trinity of Agnes, Sawney and Steenie represents a much freer approach to living, in that they do not feel the need to bow down before the false idols of a rigid and repressive Church. (The Church, after all, had been instrumental in the degrading and sadistic torture of Agnes.) Throughout the Black Book, which the minister reads with horror, the modern reader feels drawn to these three outlaws, although Tait's own feelings for them perhaps encourage him to overromanticise their life 'on the run'. The world of the Black Book is a different world from the minister's carefully-worded text: it is rawer, more alive. There is joy (and humour) for instance in its sexual encounters; there is despair and horror at the brutality of war; there is anger at the way in which Kirk and State are ruining Scotland between them.

Much of the vigour of this text comes from the fact that Agnes – quick and vital in her responses to the world – writes in Scots. Tait's Scots is thin, a little repetitive and occasionally rather odd in idiom, but despite this it is a brave attempt to do something that no other Scottish writer has sustained at such length.[4] Perhaps Harry Tait's achievement in *The Ballad of Sawney Bain* will encourage more Scottish writers (and readers) to tackle longer narratives in Scots.

Though any statement about the meaning of another novel of widely varying perspectives, Sian Hayton's *Cells of Knowledge*, must necessarily be tentative, it seems that it is also concerned with exploration of religion and the roots of spiritual awareness. Where *Sawney Bain* uses the imaginary world of the ballads and the historical world of religious warfare as a backdrop, *Cells of Knowledge* goes back to the tenth century, to the conflict between pagan and early Christian ideas and beliefs. Like Gunn's *Sun Circle* (1933), it is set at a crucial moment in the history of the Church, under threat from without, through the raids of the Norsemen; and from within, through the ultimately schismatic debate between the Celtic and Roman forms of religious observance.

The novel recounts the attempt of a scholarly monk to interpret three letters written by an older monk, Selyf, telling of his own attempt to understand and come to terms with the nature of a mysterious woman named Marighal who had arrived at his monastery seeking baptism. Marighal claims to have left her father's castle against his wishes, and throws herself on the mercy of the monks, who are uncertain just how to deal with her. As a woman, she is thought to be unfit for baptism. In a time of Viking raids and tribal wars, the monks are afraid that she might be a spy. And because of the strangeness that attends her arrival – she comes out of the darkness on a night of great storm and terrifying portents – there are doubts about who or what this woman is, and even a fear that she may be a demon sent to destroy the monastery. As the novel progresses, it becomes clear that these doubts are partly justified. One of the stories that Selyf later learns shows that Marighal is indeed no ordinary mortal, but belongs to a much older race of giants.

Soon, however, she begins to take part in the life of the monastery, receiving instruction from Selyf and another monk, Cadui. She does not complain about the austerity of the monks' way of life, surprises them by being able to read, and is humble and courteous in her dealings with Selyf and Cadui – though also sure of her own worth. When Cadui implies that women are not really fit to live the religious life, she asks if God's loving kindness would be taken from a woman who was strong, clever and free. Cadui's answer is typical of the (male) Christian attitude of the order: 'most certainly, for then she would not be womanly, and God would turn his face from the creature'.[5] Selyf, however, knowing that Cadui's attitude is too severe, hastily adds that this would not be the case if she observed the other duty of women, which is love. This sharp contrast between male and female perspectives is a prominent theme in the novel, one obviously still relevant today. Hayton is also keenly aware of the spiritual strength ascribed to women in Celtic mythology, and on one level the novel suggests that this quality may still exist and might be reawakened.

Marighal's intelligence is also seen in her awareness of some of the internal differences which are capable of turning Christian against Christian, and in her ability to see beyond this to something that is lasting:

> Whatever the disagreements that might arise among His followers, the words of the Master were food for the souls of these hard-pressed people, and this was the source of their endless patience. (*CK*, 27)

Yet, in spite of this kind of sympathy, she is eventually driven from the monastery – mistrusted because she is a woman, and intelligent, and because her intelligence is a challenge to the faith of the monks. She is possessed of vision beyond the limited range of the monastery, and is always willing to extend her knowledge of the world.

Her principal characteristic is her ability to change: her nature is fluid and flexible, and this even extends to shape-changing. At one point, she takes on the shape of a dog and follows her husband to battle, and for much of the novel there are actually two Marighals in existence at the same time. It is little wonder that the monks are afraid of her. When she weeps tears of blood, even Selyf is shaken, but affirms his own humanity and courage by concluding that 'as long as the woman remained meek and received instruction with gratitude, it was not possible to treat her as other than human' (*CK*, 36). When he finds her showing an obviously superhuman strength, however, in fetching stones to mend the oratory, Selyf grows mortally afraid of her. Later, too, he learns of miracles and marvels, such as the time when Marighal told a lover that in order to perform a heroic task he must first kill her, strip her flesh from her bones and boil them, 'until they are so clean of flesh not even a mouse would find a scraping' (*CK*, 117) The novel describes this incident in the delightfully gruesome detail common to authentic fairytales and to the early Celtic hero-tales and legends. It is a mark of Sian Hayton's skill that she writes here with perfect control. At this and other points in *Cells of Knowledge*, this may be achieved by using early Celtic texts – rather than the modern novel – as models. Part of the success of Hayton's work is that she avoids any kind of Celtic Twilight in favour of something altogether more real and lasting: her language conveys a seemingly *authentic* picture of the Celtic imagination.

Another aspect of this picture appears at the visionary moment when Selyf overcomes fear of Marighal, realising that mankind will be enriched by gaining something of the giants' knowledge and wisdom. Marighal tells him of her feelings on the day she is expelled from the monastery. Her rejection by the Christians hurt her deeply, since she had thought that 'when I joined the family of Christians, I would find humans with the charity to accept me' (*CK*, 189). She wandered distraught along the shore until,

> As I sat among the rocks in misery weeping my forbidden tears, calmness came over me at last, like the silence that comes in the middle of a storm. Idly for a moment I watched a sea-urchin moving under the surface of the water and as I looked a tiny breath of wind blew across the surface and made it shimmer. The shimmering stopped and once again I was looking into the dim water. Again the light came, shivering with delight, and was gone. And all at once the sunlight was a blinding joy to me . . .
>
> That instant was like the instant after birth when all the past flooded into my heart and it seems that I had known this joy from the first day of my life. I know that God lives and loves me and that His generous love illuminates all creation, whether we can see it or not. (*CK*, 190)

Marighal's need to enter our own mortal world may be driven by her recognition that the love and compassion which she discovers are qualities missing from the giants' domain – although she knows, too, from bitter experience that such qualities are not always present in the human world either. Yet even the marginal gloss at this point rings true: 'to love, then, is the whole of the Law, and there is no hope beyond that' (*CK*, 196). Even the cold heart of the scholarly monk who comments on Selyf's text is dimly aware of the profound Christian message here. Even when Marighal's father appears from the world of the giants, in the scholarly monk's dream, he tells him that he sees a 'new truth' in his daughter's new life. But he also leaves a stern warning:

> Whenever mankind forget my daughters, the clever, the kind and the wise, I will come forth and walk the world again, and I will increase their sorrow a thousandfold. (*CK*, 197)

The daughters seem to represent a kind of wisdom that humanity ignores at its peril, and from various hints scattered throughout the text this seems to be the wisdom to remain intuitive, open and alive to the marvel that is life.

This is also exactly the state of mind that has to be developed in order to read *Cells of Knowledge* itself. With the scholarly monk's commentary appearing as notes in the margin of Selyf's letters, the novel is very much concerned with the clash between pagan values and ideas and the various forms of Christian ones. The notes themselves are not of much help to the modern reader trying to interpret the marvels described in the letters, but they do sharply highlight the difference between the cold, priggish monk who lives by the letter of the law and uses his theology as a fixed standard against which he can measure everything, and the genuinely confused and questioning mind of Selyf. The arrival of Marighal disturbs Selyf, and his later quest to find her again shakes his mind out of its complacency. As the book progresses, Selyf (= 'self'?) grows in stature for the reader as he opens his mind to possibilities which threaten to engulf everything in which he believes.

Like *Time in a Red Coat* and *The Ballad of Sawney Bain*, *Cells of Knowledge* is not a conventional narrative. As well as the marginal glosses of one monk on another, the book is a shifting pattern of many voices, many stories, all carrying part of an intricate, cunning narrative. Glimpses of early Celtic texts such as *The Mabinogion* appear within layer upon layer of stories within stories, some echoing well-known legends and folk-tales, some straight from the imagination of the author. In its mixture of fantasy and history, its evocation of a world that is no more, and above all in its power to reveal more and more levels of meaning at each reading, *Cells of Knowledge* is an extraordinary first novel.

All three of these novels, however, powerfully extend the folk-tradition of oral storytelling through their use of different voices to carry the narrative, and through their constant reaching after archetypal characters and situations. All three move in the landscape of legend, myth and folktale. This is something that Scottish novelists have always done: by allowing a wider perspective on the world, it continues to generate a strikingly imaginative fiction.

NOTES

1. Douglas Gifford, *Neil M. Gunn and Lewis Grassic Gibbon* (Edinburgh: Oliver & Boyd, 1983), Chapter 1.
2. George Mackay Brown, *Time In A Red Coat* (London: Chatto & Windus, 1984; reprinted Harmondsworth: Penguin Books, 1986), p. 3. Subsequent references are to the Penguin edition.
3. Harry Tait, *The Ballad of Sawney Bain* (Edinburgh: Polygon, 1990), p. 412. Subsequent references are to this edition.
4. Fionn MacColla is the possible exception here. A translation into Scots by Brian Holton of the first chapter of the ancient Chinese classic *The Water Margin* appeared in *Cencrastus* 7 and 8 (1981–2). Interestingly, the historical background to *The Water Margin* – set during the 'mixter-maxter o the Five Dynasties' sturt and stour' – is analogous to that of *Sawney Bain*.
5. Sian Hayton, *Cells of Knowledge* (Edinburgh: Polygon, 1989), p. 20. Subsequent references are to this edition.

Part II

INNOVATIONS

Six

Tradition and Experiment in the Glasgow Novel

Edwin Morgan

The flawed but significant novel by Edward Gaitens, *Dance of the Apprentices* (1948), contains scenes and ideas that often seem to reverberate through more recent fiction. It deals, often very vividly, with a working-class family growing up in Glasgow in the earlier part of the century. In one scene, set at the time of the First World War, the young hero Eddy Macdonnel is about to be called up but decides to become a conscientious objector, not because he is averse to killing but because he sees it as a capitalist war in which as a committed socialist he wishes to have no part: he wants to make his protest on behalf of 'the wage-slaves of the tenement warrens'. He thinks about the fine speech he will need for the recruiting office, and he knows that books and writers are going to help him.

> Eddy picked up a copy of Jack London's *The Iron Heel* from an oval table littered with magazines, newspapers, caps and socks. Standing in front of the window in his shirt he read again the chapter from which he had borrowed ideas and phrases for his intended speech. He waved the book in the air and his eyes blazed, 'Long Live the Revolution!' he cried, quoting from the book.
>
> A top storey window of the opposite tenement opened and a young woman leant out and looked full at him. He dodged aside, blushing with shame, and sitting down, pulled on his trousers. Then he stood before the window again and began doing deep breathing exercises. Yes, he would tramp along the banks of the Clyde and make his decision today. He would have to miss John MacLean's Sunday Men's Class.[1]

Then Eddy and his brother Francis talk about Karl Marx and whether individual or mass action is more likely to defeat capitalism, and suddenly the two brothers switch from politics and start reciting alternate verses of Lewis Carroll: 'You are old, Father William, and ''Twas brillig and the slithy toves'. 'My it's a rare book *Alice in Wonderlan*',' says Francis. 'D'ye mind Alice at the tea-party?'

Eddy goes out for a walk with a volume of Keats's poems, 'intoxicating himself with rhythm and words'. This is the young self-educated man choosing for himself what he wants to read, what he feels he needs to read. John MacLean and Marx are to be expected, but Keats? There are some political passages in Keats, but that is not why Eddy Macdonnel reads him; Keats, with his lush descriptions of the world of nature, feeds his hunger for a beauty he cannot find in his ordinary life in the Gorbals, in a house where both parents are often fighting drunk; Keats represents his idealism, and also makes the point that Marx and MacLean are not enough. Lewis Carroll humanises the two brothers, shows they have a sense of fun, adds a pleasing touch of the incongruous. And Jack London, an inspiration for all proletarian writers and young socialists at that time, brings the world of art and the world of politics together. *The Iron Heel* (1907) is a powerful and uncannily prescient futuristic novel about the emergence of a fascist dictatorship, an alliance of big business, the military and a few complaisant trade unions, which forces all democratic groups to go underground and become guerrillas, winning eventually but only after a very long struggle. To Eddy, it gives both warning and hope. To a reader in 1991, Eddy's encounter with the book is like a foretaste of the highly imaginative penetration of realistic material he knows from the fiction of the 1980s. Gaitens's theme of frustrated idealism, his warm and yet at the same time highly critical evocation of the environment of an underclass, hits a nerve which is exposed again and again in later novels. It is not merely what the main character feels about his or her own life and ambition and future, it is a social idealism, a social concern. But how far can straightforward storytelling and character-drawing deal with it?

In Archie Hind's novel *The Dear Green Place* (1966), the young working-class hero, Mat Craig, is trying, against various odds, to write a novel. He reads a lot, like his father and grandfather before him. His mother, who hates ideals, thinks it is a waste of time. However, young Mat reads widely, not just the statutory Marx and Hegel, but also Dostoevsky, Scott Fitzgerald, Joyce and Yeats. His father had also devoured Balzac and Rabelais and the *1001 Nights*. But why all these exotica? Mat is uneasy. In a strong passage, he tells us why:

> All the background against which a novelist might set his scene, the aberrant attempts of human beings and societies to respond to circumstances, all that was bizarre, grotesque and extravagant in

> human life, all that whole background of violence, activity, intellectual and imaginative ardour, political daring. All that was somehow missing from Scottish life . . . [where] there was only a null blot, a cessation of life, a dull absence, a blankness and the diminution and weakening of all the fibres of being, of buildings not blown up but crumbling and rotten . . . [W]hat a writer should do is wrench his whole world up and put the mark of his thumb on it. Shove it into the violent torrent of events.[2]

This is a point of view which would be rejected by a more recent novelist like Kelman, who argues that it is precisely in dealing with the everyday texture of apparently *non*-dramatic details of life that the writer's main task lies. He too would read foreign novelists, but not out of what Hind's hero calls the 'sense of deprivation' of major events in Glasgow or Scotland. The function of the quoted passage is to raise these wider issues in the reader's mind and make him or her think about them in other parts of the book, particularly in the section where the hero takes a job in a slaughterhouse because he needs the relatively good money it pays. The work is described in detail, and vegetarian readers would be the better of a strong stomach. In a sense, the slaughterhouse scenes are meeting the demand that Mat had made for what he saw in Europe, something 'bizarre, grotesque and extravagant in human life', a background of violent activity. Yet, what the hero learns, as he gets used to the work, is that this work can be seen not as bizarre but as ordinary, a job which in our society has to be done, a job which in a city like Glasgow employs many men, who form a little society with its own habits and rules, its own bantering humour, its own heroes and bad hats. Because it leaves him so healthily tired at the end of the day, he has no energy left to write his novel; but of course the author, Archie Hind, writing about it, *has* the energy, and writes *his* novel, which is a good one. Does this therefore disprove Mat Craig's bitter complaint about the 'blankness' of Scottish life as a background for a novelist? Not necessarily, if one takes the broader view. The fact that Scotland has nationhood without statehood must leave its cultural life with a sense of the unfinished, the provisional, the potential, a situation that the novelist like every writer inherits willy-nilly and has to think about, often very creatively, as in Frederic Lindsay (*Brond*, 1983) and Alasdair Gray.

In the 1970s, one novel which took a hard look at the Glasgow environment and found it usefully inimical rather than 'blank' or 'null' was George Friel's *Mr Alfred M.A.* (1972). Mr Alfred is a seedy, heavy-smoking, virtually alcoholic, middle-aged, unmarried teacher of English in a fairly grim comprehensive; but despite his various shortcomings, he is well-read and well-intentioned – 'He wanted to love his fellowmen'. He does – only just – manage to hold down his job, but he has never really learned how to deal with people, and makes disastrous mistakes, like falling in love with one of his girl pupils and hitting one of the more insolent boys – in fact, he seems marked out for destruction. It is a farily black and bitter book, but also at times highly humorous. It moves relentlessly towards its conclusion in Part II, which is called 'The Writing on the Wall'. Mr Alfred has been told by fellow teachers that it is high time he wrenched himself out of the rut of the past, gave Shakespeare and Shelley a rest, and got himself into some Youth Culture. He lives in an area where gang fights are frequent, where there are fatal stabbings and where graffiti cover every inviting space. One night when he is in the street, drunk, after closing-time, he is mugged by four of his ex-pupils and left unconscious in a tenement back-close. This is where the book takes another dimension. The unconscious Alfred imagines that he is engaged in a long conversation with a young man called Tod who, as his name suggests, is really that old Scottish character the Devil. Tod asks him:

> 'What have you with all your education ever wrote to compare with Ya Bass?'
>
> 'Your Ya Bass?' said Mr Alfred. 'You mean you wrote Ya Bass?'
>
> 'It was me thought it up,' said Tod. 'Me and nobody else. All my own work. Alone I done it.'
>
> 'Did,' said Mr Alfred. 'Coriolanus.'[3]

Tod proceeds to give him a little lecture on the 'vulgar eloquence' from which 'a great vernacular poetry arises', alarming Mr Alfred as he warms to his theme of how graffiti are only the beginning of his anarchic assault on society. He has 'three principles': 'Deride, deface, destroy'. He wants not an empire, but chaos. 'From Omsk and Tomsk to Kirkintilloch, you're all on your way out. All you literary bastards. It's the end of the printed word. Everything's a scribble now. The writing's on the wall.' Alfred's last despairing remark is: 'When I look at what you've done to this city!' – but Tod's ominous reply before he disappears is: 'Go thou and do likewise'. Alfred, groggily coming to, follows Tod's advice, and is apprehended by the police after he has felt-penned on the nearest wall MENE MENE TEKEL UPHARSIN. GLASGOW YA BASS. He knows his Bible, and, as Belshazzar foretold the destruction of Babylon, Alfred foretells the destruction of Glasgow – except that it seems defiant to the last! Mr Alfred ends up in a mental hospital, saying in a mild voice: 'Turned out nice again today. No sign of children.'

Friel's novel no doubt reflects something of the public worry about gangs and graffiti in Glasgow in the early 1970s, though we are told that it is also in part autobiographical and that the author's disillusioned career as a teacher has injected an extra bitterness into the book. Be that as it may, it contrasts with Archie Hind's novel (which has a curiously static, even old-fashioned look) in at least acknowledging a hard thrust of change in the city. Glasgow, a place of change for the last thirty years, has sometimes seemed to be burdened, as far as its novelists are concerned, with certain stereotypes of approach, where image does not necessarily take over from reality but instead distorts reality through crude overcolouring and selective melodrama. It is a strange phenomenon that Alexander McArthur's *No Mean City* (written in collaboration with the London journalist H. Kingsley Long), first published in 1935, should still be in print and readily available in paperback on station bookstalls half a century later, each paperback edition as it comes out showing a slightly updated cover design, as if there were complete continuity, amounting almost to identity, between people in Glasgow today and people in 1935. Although it was the violence-packed action of the story which made its fame, it was in fact presented almost as a sociological document, with a preface (not reprinted in later paperbacks) stating:

> Unemployment and overcrowding are primarily responsible for conditions which may be paralleled in all great cities, but which are, perhaps, more conspicuous in Glasgow than in any other. It is only fair to add that no other city is makng a more determined effort to re-house and help its poorer citizens.[4]

There is no doubt that some chapters, notably 'The Sherricking of the King', have real historical interest. But it was the crude excitement of the whole story that made this novel the mainspring of a long-standing opportunism among publishers. McArthur's own posthumous novel, knocked into shape by Peter Watts and published in 1969, was called *No Bad Money* with an obviously son-of-no-mean-city title. Bill McGhee's *Cut and Run* (1962) was advertised on the Corgi paperback as 'A novel of the Glasgow street-gangs – in the tradition of *No Mean City*'. Authors are not responsible for their publishers' blurbs, but it has to be noted that John Burrowes's *Jamesie's People* (1984) became a Fontana paperback advertised on *its* front cover as 'A novel of the Glasgow slums in the tradition of *Cut and Run* and *No Mean City*'. Even when Alan Spence's collection of short stories, *Its Colours They Are Fine* (1977), was republished in paperback by Corgi, the lurid cover, showing a razor attack in a Glasgow street, was based on a photograph already used on the cover of *Such Bad Company: The Story of Glasgow Criminality* by George Forbes and Paddy Meehan (1982); and although there is a moment of such violence in Spence's book, it is quite untypical of these affectionate, humourous, sensitive stories. However, the publisher could not resist the image.

It is almost as if the Glasgow writer, like the Glasgow man, should not be seen to be soft, should not be seen to be not macho. Something which has lasted so long, and which has sold so many books, obviously cannot be simply written off, even if it is deplored. But it must surely be encouraging that it does not have the field to itself. Stereotypes have been shaken in various ways in recent years, and I am thinking not only of the widely recognised Gray and Kelman, but also of a number of new approaches by a variety of writers who do not form a 'Glasgow school' as such but who seem to share a general feeling that the city ought to be presented, or used, from unexpected as well as familiar angles, and in experimental as well as straightforward styles. Women writers have helped to extend this range, straightforwardly with Agnes Owens, experimentally with Janice Galloway. Owens's *Gentlemen of the West* (1984) is a short, lightweight, episodic, well-observed, very readable book, unusual in that she, a middle-aged woman, presents the story in the persona of a young bricklayer, in or out of work on the periphery of Glasgow, with most of the action centring on a local pub. The episodic nature of the book is reminiscent of Gaitens's *Dance of the Apprentices*, but Owens's hero, unlike Eddy in the earlier book, is very uncertain about what he wants, except that it is not what he has in peripheral housing-scheme Glasgow: he has no burning socialist convictions and he is not a reader; on the other hand, he is not an anarchic graffiti-merchant like the characters in *Mr Alfred M.A.* At one point, he is wandering through an old, abandoned, big house and, beside it, the burnt-out bothy where an older drinking crony of his, Paddy McDonald, now dead, had once lived. He thinks about ghosts, and almost wishes he could see one. 'Anything,' he says, 'just anything to give me a hint of something beyond.' Then, in a burst of macabre mischievousness, he puts up his only graffito: PADDY WILL RETURN. At the end, he goes off to the north-east of Scotland where he thinks work and money are to be found. Like the young hero of Kelman's *A Chancer* (1985), who leaves for London at the end of that book, he cannot articulate what he needs – 'anything to give me a hint of something beyond' – and this restless dissatisfaction and uncertainty, understandable in the 1980s, would have seemed strange to the novelists of the 1930s and 1940s.

Janice Galloway's *The Trick is to Keep Breathing* (1989) is about a woman as well as by a woman. Indeed, it is a virtual monologue by a young drama teacher who is living in a bleak housing scheme, feeling isolated, struggling to come to terms with the tragic death of a lover, tugged between anorexia and overeating, entering the world of health visitors, doctors, a mental hospital, finally coming through to self-forgiveness and sanity (we hope, though the end is ambiguous). It sounds grim, but is not, largely because of the wit and intelligence of the narrator and the break-up of the narrative with memories, letters, phone-calls, lists, snatches of conversation and little fragmentary messages that bleed off typographically into the margins. It is not specifically a book about Glasgow, but the Glasgow background which it uses, a postwar estate on the outskirts, with a poor bus service and few car-owners, graffiti everywhere, slaters slithering in the porch, seems perfectly designed to be of least help to someone trying not to go mad. As with learning to swim, 'the trick is to keep breathing . . . They say it comes with practice.'

With the emergence of women writers like Owens, Galloway and A. L. Kennedy (*Night Geometry and the Garscadden Trains*, 1990; short stories, downbeat but telling and often subtle), what of the macho? It is alive and kicking in Alex Cathcart's *The Comeback* (1986), which opens with a joiner being part-crucified with his own nails on the floor of a pub and ends with another sensational scene of tragic vengeance in the same pub as it apocalyptically crumbles about the characters. If being nailed by hands or feet to the deck is widespread big-city legend (which is not to say that it has not happened), Glasgow in 1991 has seen such an incidence of criminal violence as must remind us that there is still no mean number of very hard men in the city. Alan Spence, on the other hand, in the highly evocative, four-stranded narrative of *The Magic Flute* (1990), tracing the early lives of four boys growing up in Glasgow in the 1960s and 1970s, works towards something of the harmony suggested by the title, though only by the device of having the 'bad' boy of the four go to Belfast to be killed, while the 'best' boy, into music, peace and psychedelia, flies back to Scotland from America at the end with the rising sun streaming hope and a new life through the plane window. The Old Orange Flute, the flute of James Galway and the flute of Mozart all come together, and are indeed 'magic'; but what if the hard boy had stayed in his home town?

William McIlvanney's *Laidlaw* (1977) may have been underestimated because it is a detective thriller, a murder mystery, and that category may make it seem less serious than his mainstream novels like *Docherty*. *Laidlaw*, however, set in Glasgow, has much interest. The city of the 1970s is clearly identified, with places mentioned by name, from Kelvingrove Park to the old Muscular Arms pub, and the action covering different parts of the city from the centre to Drumchapel, Cathcart and Bearsden. But within this realism, and the accompanying excitement of a crime story, tracking down a girl's killer, McIlvanney sets as his central character the complex and unusual Detective-Inspector Laidlaw, who keeps in his locked desk drawer 'Kierkegaard, Camus and Unamuno, like caches of alcohol', who answers the tantrums of his wife (complaining that she and the children do not see enough of him) with 'Yes, I know. I also know the difference between *Hedda Gabler* and *East Lynne*. And you are *East Lynne*, missus', and whose work is distinguished by a tough humaneness and sympathetic understanding, a refusal to accept the police ethos of Them and Us. McIlvanney has sometimes been criticised for lending his pen too readily to the West of Scotland macho stance. If there is any truth in the criticism (the *East Lynne* factor?), this book must surely qualify it. Laidlaw is a hard man, but he does not share the standard prejudices expressed by his fellow-officers. The murderer turns out to be a sexually confused young man: after being involved in a homosexual affair which did not satisfy him, he has tried, with desperate and tragic results, to love the girl he eventually killed. When he is caught by the police, his homosexual friend, who had been genuinely in love with him, commits suicide. Laidlaw is the only one in the book who can understand and feel for this whole tangle of wasted lives. At the end, he takes a cup of tea to the boy in his cell. The boy is in a state of total misery and is bewildered by the action.

> Laidlaw saw the countless flecks that swam in the boy's eyes, a galaxy of undiscovered stars. 'You've got a mouth, haven't you?' Laidlaw asked.[5]

McIlvanney, like Lewis Grassic Gibbon, can get away with things that seem excessive. These last two sentences of the book do work (even though you can see how openly they are devised to work), on the basic level of human sympathy, a Glasgow hardness and a Glasgow empathy brought together.

Taking up McIlvanney's phrase about the 'galaxy of undiscovered stars' in the perhaps bisexual boy's eyes leads into another novel, *Towards the End* by Joseph Mills (1989), the first openly gay novel set in Glasgow with Glasgow characters. It mentions gay pubs and other places by name, presenting a range of relationships, and various degrees of 'outness', in an ordinary, unsensational way, as a part of the life of the city, linked to family and workplace and straight friends, exposed to occasional danger and violence but not really ghettoised. Interestingly enough, Mills uses an image not unlike the image of eyes and light found in *Laidlaw*. Paul, the young hero of the book, who is gradually discovering the complexity of relationships, looks up at a faulty display of Christmas lights in a shop, with the colours flickering, dimming and brightening again, and is reminded of the flashing strobe-lights of a disco he has been to, and the faces flickering there.

> I realised now that all the simple emotions burning in those coloured faces were far more complicated, made up, like the display, of a myriad of mirror, malleable components.[6]

Both Mills and McIlvanney are suggesting, in their very different ways, that much of Glasgow and its people is waiting to be discovered; and that this, if anything, is the keynote of most recent fiction. The jagged, compressed, episodic style of Thomas Healy's *It Might Have Been Jerusalem* (1991) drives the most frustrated, impoverished and sexually sinister of those inhabitants into scenes of Grand Guignol without losing the reader's attention. To other writers, the things that wait to be uncovered will only yield to a cool, measured, distanced approach.

Frank Kuppner's *A Very Quiet Street* (1989) is subtitled 'a novel, of sorts'. This remarkable book is a mixture of criminal investigation, autobiography and what one may call the fiction of speculation. It reinvestigates the case of Oscar Slater, a German Jewish immigrant who was jailed for almost twenty years for the murder of an old woman in West Princes Street in 1908 – a murder which it can now be agreed he did not commit. As the real murderer is still not known, though there are suspects, it remains an interesting and tantalising case – particularly as both the police and the law come out of it very badly. Kuppner himself was born and brought up in the house next to the one where the murder took place, and his memories and half-memories of boyhood in West Princes Street in the 1950s, his knowledge of and revisiting of the street and the area round about it – Glasgow's Square Mile of Murder as it has been called, because of a number of famous cases there a century or so ago – are intricately woven together with his reconstruction of the possible or probable past of 1908 in a way which recalls Proust, as does also the obsessional detail of street and close and door and window and architectural mass. There are loose ends, unfinished stories, unrelated incidents, as in life. Yet the book, turning its magnifying-glass on a single small patch of the city around Charing Cross, does in its maddening manner pull the reader forward. Borges, as well as Proust, would have found much interest in its mingling of fact and fiction.

In that book, Kuppner was trying to discover truths about the past. James Kelman, in his three novels (*The Busconductor Hines*, 1984; *A Chancer*, 1985; *A Disaffection*, 1989), is trying to discover truths about the present. He has underlined in an interview his belief that the most important part of this truth will come not from recounting highly dramatic events like murders and bank robberies but from following ordinary people about their business throughout a whole day. 'I think the most ordinary person's life is fairly dramatic . . . The whole idea of the big dramatic event, of what constitutes "plot", only assumes that economic security exists.'[7] This desire to convey the actual texture of life, with minimal authorial interference (what he calls the novelist 'colonising' the reader like a verbal imperialist), is familiar to us from James Joyce, one of the authors whom Kelman admires. But in the Glasgow context, where the fondness for strong drama, even melodrama, for violence of various kinds, has fuelled a fair part of the tradition, the absence of violence in Kelman (apart from one or two brief moments) is immediately striking and attractive and seems to signal a new spirit, as it does also in Alan Spence. There may be violence in the language, and in some of the anti-Establishment tirades; but in the main characters, for all their inadequacies and frustrations, there is an underlying decent tenderness which shows in Hines's obvious love for his young son and more spectacularly in the splendid scene where Pat Doyle, in *A Disaffection*, tells a story to his brother's two children and holds them spellbound. But the desire not to colonise the reader means that the Glasgow setting and characters can seem strangely disembodied. Although plenty of places are mentioned by name, and although people go about their business – football match, dog-racing, drinking in pubs, a wedding, a rolling mill – Kelman's determination not to overdescribe means that we hardly ever learn what the characters look like, or what they wear (except in the most general terms). This is perhaps commented on in *A Disaffection* when the disaffected teacher, Pat Doyle, disillusioned with teaching but also for inner psychological reasons on the verge of a breakdown, thinks in one of his interior monologues that he may be about to metamorphose like the character in Kafka's story 'Metamorphosis' who woke up one morning to find that he had become a large beetle.

> He seemed to be. It was highly likely. This sort of escapade happened all the time. Take Gregor Samsa as a for instance. He was a poor unfortunate bastard though having said that of course it would take a Giant to squash him. A Giant. A veritable Mammothian. And there were none of these lurking in this man's Glasgow, all of whose entities were so palpably impalpable.[8]

Both Hines and Doyle seem to be fighting impalpable powers, powers of darkness. Both can find nothing that really satisfies them in their work, in the state of the country, in their imagined future. Doyle, who has no wife or girlfriend, solaces himself by blowing long, melancholy sounds on two electrician's pipes he picks up in a backalley, a bizarre find, yet somehow very Glaswegian in its incongruity;

and they become magic pipes, as magic as Spence's flutes, when he enthrals his nephew and niece by talking about them. They are 'palpably impalpable'. Hines the bus conductor lives partly in the real world of the buses and partly in the world of his racy imagination; in his remarkable monologues, you can still see the real Glasgow, for which his favourite, repeated phrase is 'this grey but gold city', but it is transformed into a sort of collage of hopes and fears and angers which he is mentally unrolling for the benefit of his young son.

> How d'you fancy a potted history of this grey but gold city, a once mighty bastion of the Imperial Mejisteh son and centre of Worldly Enterprise. The auld man can tell you all about it. Into the libraries you shall go. And he'll dig out the stuff, the real mccoy but son the real mccoy, then the art galleries and museums son the palaces of the people, the subways and the graveyards and the fucking necropolises . . .[9]

Perhaps Kelman's characters do not have to be described: they reveal themselves, entertainingly and often very movingly, through voice, through speech, through punctuation and syntax. And the grey but gold city seems to shimmer and shade over like some great but partly tarnished and partly still-unrealised object, like the clouds which Hines's father used to sit looking at through his window in the evening in Drumchapel.

> He must have reckoned the view capable of curious tricks, tossing off rays of solace during the long hot summer evenings as the sun went down, that much needed glimpse of the indefinite for those who dwelled up the hill.[10]

Like Doyle's mysterious pair of pipes, rescued from the back of a building, Hines's father's 'much needed glimpse of the indefinite' comes from the window of a commonplace housing scheme. Doyle reads many books; Hines wants his son to read books; and this is reminiscent of Eddy Macdonnel in *Dance of the Apprentices*, the self-educated man who realises that ignorant people will not change society for the better. But in Kelman the social idealism is more problematic, and also much more interesting, in that there is so much power in the undefined, the indefinite, the grey but gold, the runner in the rain at the end of *A Disaffection* who does not know whether he is running from or to.

Alasdair Gray in his many books, but especially in *Lanark* (1981) and *1982, Janine* (1984), has the crucial importance of having seen that everything you want to bring to bear on a novel which you are projecting to yourself can and should be brought to bear. If you are an artist as well as a writer, you will not hesitate to make the whole book-design serve your needs, including layout, illustrations, varying typefaces and type sizes, unorthodox typography (somewhat as in concrete poetry) for special effects, blank pages for sleep and silence, and farewells to the reader like newspaper headlines. If you are aware of how far science fiction has come in the last hundred years, joining itself confidently with the aims of mainstream fiction as well as with the demands of sociopolitical fable or allegory where required, you will make use of the imaginative high-energy it can supply and has supplied, from *The Iron Heel* and *Metropolis* to *Brave New World* and *Solaris*. If you have an epic intent (as Gray had), you will rejoice in the fact that modernist dislocations of narrative order may chime very productively with the ancient epic command to thrust *in medias res*, and only later tell how things got that way; in addition, many traditional features of epic, such as the descent to an underworld, are used in *Lanark* to deepen the perspective in startling ways. And if you want to make use of autobiography (as both novels do, even though Jock McLeish in *1982, Janine* is made deliberately unlike Gray), you make no bones about getting down to the bones and basics of human life, the miseries and traps, the loves and hopes, the scrabblings and soarings, scorning to drown in the ludic sargassos of postmodernism into which you may certainly insert a toe.

All this is to say that Gray's work, however interesting it may be to critics and aestheticians, remains a large and strong and moving communicative act. Just as Kelman's bad language is undoubtedly a barrier to some readers otherwise well disposed, and there is nothing one can do about this unless and until *fuck* and its derivaties become more widely acceptable (as in fact seems to be happening), so Gray gives hostages to fortune in his lists of sources, influences and plagiarisms, the whole 'critic-fuel' as he himself calls it in *Something Leather* (1990), which has ample precedent if one thinks of Joyce, Urquhart and Rabelais, but which the very reader Gray wants to reach and does reach will find offputting and self-regarding. It would be very wrong, however, to allow impatience with these intellectual additions to spread into other non-realistic parts of the novels, to praise the central straightforward narrative of Thaw's life in Books 1 and 2 of *Lanark* as one clear note in the surrounding science-fiction static, or to admire the explanatory and redemptive retrospect of McLeish's earlier life in the second half of *1982, Janine* ('the moment when I start telling my story in the difficult oldfashioned way, placing events in the order they befell') at the expense of the typographical bonanza of his attempted suicide in the pages before. Dragonhide and salamander, mohome and intercalendrical zone and apocalyptic war, are all essential and thrilling components of the dimensionality of the book of Lanark's lives and times. And the most humanly moving moment of McLeish's long night's journey into day, when he at last finds he can shed tears in a flood of self-forgiveness, is presented not in a paragraph of narrative prose but in what is almost a concrete poem of page-centred *Ach*s. The unadventurous reader may strain and complain, but really has no escape. He is being opened up, like one of Janine's blouses, button by button, and a light is being shone on him. How uncomfortable! But it is all human, he discovers, and about Scotland, and Glasgow, and the state of the soul and senses, and the pilgrimages thereof.

Gray's books may be Glasgow-based, but they have much to say about the government of these islands, about capitalist society, about imperialism and small nations, about politics in general. In *1982, Janine*, he goes out of his way, in the Epilogue, to dissociate himself from the views of his hero, who says that Scotland is and always will be 'a poor little country'. Not so, says Gray.

> In fact Scotland's natural resources are as variedly rich as those of any other land. Her ground area is greater than that of Denmark, Holland, Belgium or Switzerland, her population higher than that of Denmark, Norway or Finland. Our present ignorance and bad social organisation make most Scots poorer than most other northern Europeans, but even bad human states are not everlasting.[11]

Yet if the sociopolitical concern so typical of the Glasgow novelist is still strong in Gray, so also are the less tangible idealisms. Like Hines's father staring from his window in Drumchapel, Lanark is much given to searching the sky, if not for signs and wonders, at least for light. When he first arrives in the gloomy, near-sunless deutero-Glasgow of Unthank, he cannot get Rima to understand his excitement as he sees a pearly light behind the tenements and tries to remember the word 'dawn'; he even tries to chase it down the street as it quickly fades. On his arrival at the Institute, he asks to see out of the window and is rewarded with a visionarily distant, intensely beautiful cloudscape from which he can hardly tear himself away. Later, Dr Munro asks him: 'Tell me, Dr Lanark, is there a connection between your love of vast panorama and your distaste for human problems?' This rebuke would hardly apply to the Lanark at the end of the novel, much chastened, and thoroughly acquainted with human problems. But as he sits waiting for the close of his life, an elderly man in Glasgow, his eyes devour the moving clouds and he is 'glad to see the light in the sky'. These gleams and portents, like the magic flutes and the magic electrician's pipes, add their necessary, indefinable, other-than-social dimension to the maturity of the Glasgow novel.

NOTES

This chapter is a reworking of material contained in the Alexander Stone lecture, delivered at the University of Glasgow in 1990.

1. Edward Gaitens, *Dance of the Apprentices* (Glasgow: MacLellan, 1948; reprinted Edinburgh: Canongate Classics, 1990), p. 128.
2. Archie Hind, *The Dear Green Place* (London: Hutchinson/New Author, 1966; reprinted London: Corgi, 1985), pp. 87–8.
3. George Friel, *Mr Alfred M.A.* (London: Calder & Boyars, 1972; reprinted Edinburgh: Canongate Classics, 1987), pp. 155–6.
4. Alexander McArthur and H. Kingsley Long: *No Mean City: A Story of the Glasgow Slums* (London: Longmans, Green, 1935), p. vi.
5. William McIlvanney, *Laidlaw* (London: Hodder & Stoughton, 1977; reprinted London: Coronet/Hodder & Stoughton, 1979), p. 224.
6. Joseph Mills, *Towards the End* (Edinburgh: Polygon, 1989), p. 168.
7. *Chapman* 57, Summer 1989, p. 9.
8. James Kelman, *A Disaffection* (London: Secker & Warburg, 1989; reprinted London: Picador/Pan, 1990), p. 164.
9. James Kelman, *The Busconductor Hines* (Edinburgh: Polygon, 1984; reprinted London: Dent, 1985), p. 90.
10. Ibid., p. 130.
11. Alasdair Gray, *1982, Janine* (London: Cape, 1984), p. 345.

FURTHER READING

Burgess, Moira, *The Glasgow Novel: A Survey and Bibliography* (Motherwell and Glasgow: Scottish Libraries Association and Glasgow District Libraries, 2nd ed., 1986).

Gifford, Douglas, *The Dear Green Place?: The Novel in the West of Scotland* (Glasgow: Third Eye Centre, 1985).

Murray, Isobel and Tait, Bob, *Ten Modern Scottish Novels* (Aberdeen: Aberdeen University Press, 1984).

Seven

Resisting Arrest: James Kelman

Cairns Craig

REALISM AND RESISTANCE

Since the publication of his first collection of short stories, *Not Not While the Giro* (1983), and his first novel, *The Busconductor Hines* (1984), James Kelman's fiction (*A Chancer* (1985), *Greyhound for Breakfast* (1987); *A Disaffection* (1989); *The Burn* (1991)) has had an enormous impact on the nature of writing in Scotland in three crucial areas: the representation of working-class life, the treatment of 'voice' and the construction of narrative. Central to all three is Kelman's refusal to accept the definitions of what counts as 'literature' in contemporary society, his defiant rejection of the categorisations within which modern writing is created and consumed. At one end is his determination to make writing connect directly with the 'lives of ordinary people':

> In our society we aren't used to thinking of literature as a form of art that might concern the day to day existence of ordinary women and men, whether these ordinary women and men are the subjects of the poetry and stories, or the actual writers themselves. It is something we do not expect. And why should we? There is such a barrage of élitist nonsense spoken and written about literature that anything else would be surprising.[1]

At the other is his denigration of the modes by which fiction is constructed to avoid the 'real' world in which those 'ordinary men and women' have to survive:

> Ninety per cent of the literature in Great Britain concerns people who never have to worry about money at all. We always seem to be watching or reading about emotional crises among folk who live in a world of great fortune both in matters of money and luck . . . Or else we are given straight genre fiction . . . The unifying feature of

> all genre fiction is the way it denies reality. This is structural – in other words, if reality had a part to play in genre fiction then it would stop being genre fiction.[2]

For Kelman, the bulk of fiction – and even of 'literature' – is an evasion of reality, in content or in form – and 'literature' itself is a way of preventing writing from becoming engaged with that reality, since it is the product of an educational system whose business is to ensure that people 'discover how not to appreciate the potential of literature as a living art form, as a dynamic activity that might involve their friends, family and neighbours'.[3]

With that central thrust to his conception of writing, Kelman's fiction sets out to resist becoming 'literature' by a fundamental commitment to realism in content and style; it is from that commitment to 'realism' that the three factors listed above derive.

Presentation of working-class life

Kelman's novels are located quite differently from traditional narratives of working-class life. Working-class fiction, in the sense of fiction written by working-class writers rather than writings about the working classes, has focused primarily either on the skilled working class, whose ambitions towards a better and more comfortable life are frustrated by the capitalist environment in which they work (*The Ragged Trousered Philanthropists*, *Saturday Night and Sunday Morning*), or on the tragic impossibility of escape from the working class for those with special gifts, either physical or mental (*This Sporting Life*, *From Scenes like These*, *Kes*). Underlying both narrative structures is the drive to confront both characters and readers with a realisation of the fundamentally destructive nature of the industrial process and the enormous sacrifice in energy and creativity required to resist its dehumanising pressure. Such a narrative strategy can only work where there is a perceived value in the protagonist and/or the community under threat, and that value is essentially directed towards the possibility of a future in which the value of the individual or community will be redeemed from the destructiveness of the present. Working-class fiction is dominated, therefore, by the implication of a lost potential, whether individual or social, and has to take its focus from characters whose experience is viewed as being, in some sense, central to the whole of working-class life in that loss. It is for this reason that the protagonists of working-class fiction are often members of the skilled and politically aware 'labour aristocracy', or have a special talent that focuses some aspect of working-class interest outside of the life of the factory, some aspect which enforces the sense of community and solidarity which capitalism attempts to destroy.

Kelman's novelty in this context is that it is not the skilled, the potentially politically active working class, who are the location of his fiction; it is those who are marginalised from traditional working-class values, who do not believe in the possibility of communal political action, who do not believe in the viability of a personal escape from their conditions. Kelman's depiction is not of a working-class *community* so much as of a working-class world which has become atomised, fragmented, and in which individuals are isolated from one another – a world in which political hope has been severed and only economic deprivation remains. It is a working class, in other words, without a possible salvation through the political or economic transformation of history.

The difference between Kelman's presentation of working-class life and the traditional version can be seen clearly if we compare his work with the major contribution to working-class fiction of the 1970s, William McIlvanney's *Docherty* (1975). *Docherty*'s focus is on the heroism of the working-class survivor, a heroism based on a belief in a fundamental set of communal values: by the end of the novel, those values have not yet been translated from the individual to the society of which he is a part, but such a translation is held out as the possibility on which redemption of working-class lives will be based. If the defeated hero's nobility can be emulated and made politically active, redemption is still possible. Kelman's central characters, on the other hand, are always those who see the illusoriness of such traditional modes of solidarity, and who have no faith in traditional modes of working-class self-improvement: however much they may look back nostalgically upon a world of communal solidarity and directed struggle, they know it to be redundant. Like bus drivers on one man buses, it is every man for himself; like schoolteachers who try to liberate, they are part of the prison they are trying to help their wards escape from; like the gambler, they know that everything has a chance but that there is little in their lives that they can actually control.

Kelman's novels, then, take place not in the traditional sites of the working-class struggle for power (the trades unions, the educational system as liberator), nor in the traditional sites of working-class escape from work and exploitation (sport, domestic solidarity), but along the margins of that traditional working-class life. And they do so because that traditional life has been decimated: founded as it was on heavy industry, on the idea of a mass society whose masses could be brought into solidarity, it has been wiped out by the destruction of the traditional Scottish industries. Kelman's central characters are symbols of the collapse of working-class life into a dispirited and isolated endurance: there is no hope of transformation; there is no sustenance in community. In Kelman's fiction, there is a brutal awareness that the Scottish working class, who saw themselves as the carrier of historical change in the days of McIlvanney's Docherty, are now the leftovers of a world which has no need of them; their choices are limited to acceptance of the atomisation of social improvement, or submission to becoming fodder for the only industry they have left – the poverty industry. There is no way out that is not a denial of a possible solidarity; there is no solidarity that can be activated to change the world. There is only anger and nostalgia.

The treatment of 'voice'

Kelman's realism requires an authenticity to the presentation of his characters' voices that refuses to compromise with traditional conceptions of 'Scots' and the orthography that writers have adopted for Scots speech. Kelman transliterates into a phonetic orthography that seeks neither to patronise nor to dignify the actuality of Scottish speech:

> I'm no prejudiced at all, you just stick up for them.
>
> I don't. I just tell the bloody truth, as I see it.
>
> I'm no saying ye dont, but let's face it as well Pat, ye do like to be different.
>
> Naw I dont.
>
> Your maw's right, said Mr Doyle. The same with bringing back the belt, you've got to be different there too.
>
> Tch da.
>
> Nay tch da about it – you've aye been against the belt. But at least the weans'll show some damn respect. And you canni deny it.[4]

'Ye' and 'you' are mixed in this speech, traditional Scottish words – 'weans' – with vernacular pronunciation – 'canni'. It is not rendered in terms of an ideal of the Scottish working-class as maintainers of a distinctive Scots language, but in terms of a specific geographic pronunciation. More importantly, however, what Kelman has done is to allow that language to fuse together with his own narrative voice so that the distinction between the language of narration and the language of dialogue is dissolved. The lack of grammatical markers for speech means that the text moves indiscernibly from spoken, to thought, to narrated language:

> Mrs Doyle sniffed slightly: Yous'll end up arguing.
>
> Patrick nodded. After a pause he swallowed a mouthful of tea and resumed eating. He took another slice of bread and wiped up the sauce at the rim of his plate. His da was looking at him. Pat

glanced at him. They both looked away. It was quite sad because it was hitting old nerves or something and shouldni have been causing such a big kerfuffle. He looked at his da again but there was nothing he could give him. He couldnt. He couldnt give him anything. He didnt deserve to be given anything. So how come he should be given it? People get what they deserve in this life. Even parents. Maws and das. They don't have a special dispensation. Except maybe from the queen or the pope or any other of these multibillionaire capitalist bastards. But no from their equals, they don't get any dispensation from them. So fuck off. (*D*, 113)

The third-person narrative voice that relates facts in the world – 'he swallowed . . . Pat glanced . . . They both looked' – merges into the reflective third-person voice that interprets characters' states of mind – 'He was quite sad' – which then fuses with the characters' own thoughts and the language in which they speak to themselves – 'He couldnt give him anything. He didnt deserve to be given anything. So how come he should be given it?' – which in turn becomes true interior monologue – 'So fuck off'. Kelman's particular use of free indirect discourse not only allows modulation between different perspectives (third-person narrator, first-person thought) but also allows modulation across different linguistic registers. In particular, what is characteristic of Kelman's style is the fusion of the spoken with the written, so that the narrative voice itself can take on the characteristics of a speaking voice. By this method, Kelman has found his own very specific means of overcoming the distinction between English (as the medium of narration) and Scots (as the medium of dialogue) which has proved a constant dilemma to Scottish writers. The liberation of the narrative voice from the constraints of written English is an act of linguistic solidarity, since it thrusts that narrative into the same world which its characters inhabit.

The interweaving of spoken and written forms of speech is made more emphatic by Kelman's refusal to use inverted commas as speech markers. The text is designed visually to resist that moment of arrest in which the reader switches between the narrative voice of the text and the represented speech of a character, and what this does is to create a linguistic equality between speech and narration which allows the narrator to adopt the speech idioms of his characters or the characters to think or speak in 'standard English' with no sense of disruption. The text, therefore, constructs a linguistic unity which resists the fragmentation and isolation that the novels chart as the experience of their characters. Unity of voice replaces unity of political or social purpose as the foundation of solidarity: the text *enacts* at a linguistic level what it points to as absent in the world, a communality that transcends the absolute isolation of the individual human being. The fulfilment of working-class values that can no longer be completed in politics or in history is completed *textually* – resisting the arrest of solidarity and of political action by a linguistic substitution that insists on unity even as it presents disunity.

Narrative

In Kelman's narratives, context massively dominates over event: the plots are extremely limited, the 'happenings' undramatic, the context and characters' reflections upon them everything. In fact, Kelman might be said to be fulfilling Virginia Woolf's assertion that the novel ought to examine 'an ordinary mind on an ordinary day', exploring the 'myriad impressions', the 'incessant shower of innumerable atoms' that 'shape themselves into the life of Monday or Tuesday'.[5] The detailing of the minimal events and acts of a day – the making of coffee and the rolling of cigarettes are endlessly repeated actions of Kelman's protagonists – resists the power of plot to falsify the real. The crises which Kelman's protagonists face – and they are all in one way or another on the edge of mental breakdown – are not resolvable by action and event; they are conditions of suffering which are permanent, reflecting the stasis, both political and social, of the worlds which they inhabit. There is no way out: the condition continues. It cannot be arrested and there is no respite from it. All of Kelman's protagonists are condemned to go on, restlessly and relentlessly bearing their unbearable alienation, precisely because the ultimate falsehood would be to cease to be aware of suffering. They must resist any rest from the torment that they suffer as strongly as the world which they suffer resists any transformation:

> There are parties whose attention to a variety of aspects of existence renders life uneasy. It cannot be said to be the fault of Hines that he is such a party. A little leeway might be allowed him. A fortnight's leave of absence could well work wonders. A reassembling of the head that the continued participation in the land of the greater brits
>
> Fuck off.[6]

The voice of sensible social and behavioural accommodation – 'A little leeway might be allowed him' – is recognised as falsifying the Busconductor Hines's need to refuse 'a fortnight's leave of absence' as any kind of solution to his crisis. The crisis is the condition, and it has no social solution: social palliatives have to be resisted because they simply provide a rest which allows people to be returned to the very world that has made them sick.

Kelman's narratives are not concerned with progressions along a temporal trajectory of events; they are concerned with an unchangeable context into which human beings are thrown and from which there is no escape. They are concerned fundamentally, therefore, not with the progress implied by a narrative sequence but with repetition – repetition as the systematisation and dehumanisation to which working-class people, above all others, are subjected, a subjection which is the denial of their existence as human subjects and the affirmation of their status as subjects of the Great British realm:

> it has never been acutely necessary to think. Hines can board the bus and all will transpire. Nor does he have to explain to the driver how the bus is to be manoeuvred. Nor need he dash out into the street to pressgang pedestrians. Of its own accord comes everything. (*BH*, 154)

The alienation which previous generations of working-class writers had envisaged as being an event that had occurred at some earlier point in history, and which could therefore be overcome by another historical event, has become an unchallengeable context. Hines's identity is in being a Busconductor: his role has taken him over and he cannot evade it; the reification of his identity is such that he cannot simply drop being a Busconductor as he might take off a uniform. Busconducting for Hines is life – a terminal condition. In such a world, there can be neither tragedy nor redemption, because both imply the power of event, and therefore of narrative, to change the self or the world. For Kelman's characters, there is only endless repetition, repetition which becomes a structural principle of Kelman's art in a formal mimesis of the real world in which his characters are trapped.

It is by this re-envisaging of the nature of working-class life and the realism which is required to represent it that Kelman's fiction has transcended all the paradigms of previous writing about the working classes. Kelman's working-class realism is tactical rather than essential, for what is essential is that the working-class characters, and especially the marginalised working-class characters who are his protagonists, are the sites not of a social – a class – conflict, but of an existential awareness from which most human beings are insulated by their society. The alienation of the working class becomes the context not for the exploration of social issues and possible political improvement, but for the exploration of humanity's existential condition. Kelman's tormented characters become heroic because of their continuous and restless need to confront the fact of being absurdly and gratuitously thrown into an existence which makes no sense and has no place for them. It is this that justifies the connection of Kelman's fiction not with the work of the British working-class realist writers of the 1950s and 1960s, but with the continental traditions of Kafka, Camus and Beckett. Kelman's protagonists are Sisyphus figures, rolling a cigarette rather than a rock, as they wait for Godot. They may inhabit a real Glasgow, but it is Glasgow which exists to put them on trial, and in that trial it is transformed into a Kafkaesque distortion by which Drumchapel becomes 'the District of D'.

ALLEGORIES OF BEING

According to the existential tradition, we are 'thrown' into being, and there is no foundation which connects our individual 'being' with any ultimate and meaningful Being. We are the products of the random and the accidental: within such an existentialist framework, no necessity underpins and validates the human condition.

It is this 'thrownness' and randomness of existence that Kelman confronts in *A Chancer*, where Tammas's obsessive betting is the medium through which the randomness of existence is allegorised:

> Dog 2 paid 2/1 on the tote a place, giving £1.50 in return for the 50 pence. And if he had backed the dog as a straight win on the tote he would have received more than four quid but so what, it was irrelevant, it had nothing to do with it – a mistake to even think it. He had £1.50 in his pocket and it had come from nothing, and that was the only point.[7]

In gambling, the human being confronts the source of his own being, or the lack of it: money created from nothing; life staked on the accident of the future:

> Ach . . . John had opened the *Adviser* and was reading the tipster's comments on the race. This guy fancies Real Smooth, he said to Tammas, what d'you think man?
>
> It's got a chance.
>
> Tch, according to you everything's got a fucking chance!
>
> John! that's the whole fucking point! (*C*, 166)

The Chancer is he who knows what everyone else seeks to conceal: the equality of all options in a world that has no reality except the present.

That is why Tammas is presented to us as an 'accidental' character: he lives with his sister and her husband, but shares nothing of his life with them. His origins are unstated: when he hitches a lift at the end, he disappears into a future defined by the chance of where the lorry is going. The accidental nature of all existence is what his gambling gives definition to:

> He knew the betting forecast on the race, the favourite being reckoned an even money chance. There was nothing else he needed

> to know. Not now. He had backed it and that was that, either the horse would win or it would lose. There was not anything in between. (*C*, 253)

'Not anything in between' establishes the space of an unrealisable and indefinable nothingness against which being defines itself, a nothing which is not just the absence of something, but a fundamental negation of all existence. Between the short scenes which make up the novel, it is as though Tammas appears out of and returns to that nothingness. The white spaces and line of points which divide the sections are not simply conventional symbols of time passing: it is not that we feel that unnarrated events have occurred and time has passed, but rather that existence has been suspended, as though Tammas's being has been suspended, until the next scene begins. The process of narration brings things into existence; when narration stops, existence ceases:

> Tammas stared at the dogs breaking and racing to the 1st bend. He was nodding, and he continued nodding as they rounded it and headed up the back straight. He dropped his programme to the ground; he turned and muttered, See yous in the bar.
>
> . . .
>
> He wakened early on Christmas morning; ben the front room he switched on the electric fire and the television. (*C*, 168)

No bets, no existence, because no awareness of the existential as opposed to the contingent reality of the world around him.

This effect is emphasised by a deliberate opposition within the novel's narrative method: the events of the novel are presented from Tammas's consciousness, and yet the narrative insistently refuses us access to his thoughts. We are seeing the world from Tammas's point of view, but seeing him as though he were only available to us from a third-person perspective. Thus, the above passage continues:

> There was a packet of cigars lying on the mantelpiece, a present from Robert and Margaret. He unwrapped the outer covering and extracted one, smelled it quite closely from end to end before inserting it in the corner of his mouth. And he gazed at himself in the mirror. When he struck the match for it he inhaled and coughed on it, and began to sneeze. In the kitchen he blew his nose, made a cup of instant coffee. He doused the cigar in the water gathered at the drain in the sink. (*C*, 168–9)

The narrative is closely focused on Tammas's immediate perceptions, and yet we are told nothing about he contents of his consciousness, only about his actions. It is the reverse of an interior monologue: rather than the whole world being present in a character's thoughts, the character's *actions* are his whole world. Immediate action and event are the only realities because the inner world of thought is nothing. In Tammas, Kelman has constructed his own version of Camus's Meursault: he is the outsider, whose consciousness of the existential condition means that he must live in entire dislocation with the ordinary human world and its emotions; he is the negater of all the values which chain us to our social world as though it were the ultimate reality.

The one moment when Tammas is tempted into that social world is when he spends time with a woman – Vi – and her daughter Kirsty. Vi describes her problems with her daughter as arising from the fact that 'it's just the two of us. I mean because it's only the two of us' (*C*, 186). With Tammas there, they become a threesome, but a threesome that is not a proper family unit, just as Tammas, his sister and her husband ('The three of them ate in silence' (*C*, 136)) are also a failed threesome. The transformation of the isolated one into the communal three, a three which is also a one, is an echo of that defiance of mathematical logic by which Being itself, in the Christian tradition, is both unitary and a trinity; such a transformation may be impossible for Tammas in a world where 3/1 and 1/3 are simply odds and where all the chances are equal, but it is a transformation which obsesses Kelman's other protagonists.

> Here you've got a family comprising husband wife and wean whose astounding circumstances are oddly normal. This trio are as 1. But the husband is to be no doubt leaving his job of work to take to another. And the reason is clear: he has failed to make a go of things at this the third time of asking. It is his considered opinion that the door must soon be shown him for being a bad busconductor. And in the long run it'll probably prove possible that just being an actual conductor will be reason enough because 1-man-buses are the vehicular items of the not too distant future. (*BH*, 80)

Hines, the soon-to-be-redundant second on the soon-to-become-1-man-buses is obsessed by the impossibility of realising the unity in multiplicity that would allow him to escape the isolation of one and become part of some larger unit. He can neither leave the buses nor remain; he can neither suffer in isolation nor merge into the identity of the family unit; there is no redemption of the three into one or the one into three:

> the 3 of them, the trio of persons sir, the through thick and thin yins you see sir him and Sandra and the Paul fellow – that's the wee man – the 3 of them, the trio of persons sir the 1, the unit, that impetus for continued survival viz the bastarn grub in the pot,

> howsomever it be better known as the loaves and the fishes sir . . . (*BH*, 93)

The transcendental, logic-defying unity of the trinity is impossible: Hines lives only the world of time, a modern Charon whose passengers do not cross to the other side, but simply cross and recross the empty and meaningless spaces of the city. The Busconductor is the time-keeper of the world's journeys, but he himself journeys nowhere, travelling out only to come back, travelling forwards only to reach a terminus which is no conclusion. The Buscondutor is an emblem of modernity: a world structured by endless, restless travel, an existence dominated by time; indeed, the Busconductor's existence is dominated by the need for *over*time. Kelman's presentation of the Busconductor is conducted in a realism so intense that it becomes its own opposite, an allegory of the modern condition where all conception of Being has disappeared:

> inasmuch as Hines could eventually, could have become
>
> He was wanting that becoming.
>
> This is what it's about. Now then: . . . (*BH*, 98)

Where Tammas in *A Chancer* has annihilated the past and knows only the moment when future chances realise themselves in the singularity of the present, Hines knows only a present that is always turning to past (even though 'the present should not be said to be yesterday' (*BH*, 86)) and 'the immediate past is not only today but also tomorrow' (*BH*, 81). Thus, when Hines confronts the garage Inspectors over his failure to turn up for work, he takes his son with him and thinks: 'This is one of these wee moments in life which you're earmarked to remember once I'm dead and buried (*BH*, 183). The moment of crisis has to be seen as already over and done with, its becoming concluded. Hines cannot ever *become* anything – fulfil his 'lad o' pairts' potential, for instance – because he sees all becoming as already over: he cannot *make* a future because he sees it as already completed and past, structured with the same finality as a bus timetable. He is metaphysically incapacitated because no future has any reality that is not identical with the past. He wants to give up being a bus-conductor but cannot because no future is envisageable in which he does not remain the same identical bus-conductor. He can only imagine giving up if he can turn it into an already completed past action: 'I need to jack it; I want to have jacked it' (*BH*, 65).

The Busconductor lives in a world of necessity, but a necessity which is severed from the foundations of Being: he is part of a self-contained system which is its own justification, but has no connection with any underlying reality that can give the system a meaning. The only eternity is the eternity of repetition – 'I'm sick of this eternal busconducting sir' (*BH*, 39) – and the repetitious world is a self-contained and self-perpetuating system from which the mind recoils into the construction of its own alternative realities.

What connects the Busconductor Hines to Patrick Doyle, the disaffected schoolteacher, is that both suffer from a mind that is an endless generator of hypotheses, hypotheses which have a local logic and rationality but which cannot overcome the sheer brute stuff of the real. The dynamic of their deepening despair is an exponential intensification of hypothesis-creation, a vast excess of intellectual energy over which they have no control and which continually realises the impossibility of its hypotheses having any grip on the actuality of immediate existence:

> he proceeded to traverse the flagstones up the stairs and into the closemouth. Is this fucking Mars! Traversed the fucking bastarn flagstone onto the planet fucking Vulcan for Christ sake
>
> except that it no longer exists. That poor old nonentity Vulcan, being once thought to exist, and then being discovered not to exist! That's even worse than being declared fucking redundant, irrelevant, which was the fate of ether upon the advent of Einstein. Whether it existed or not had become irrelevant to the issue. Fuck sake. Ether. After all these centuries . . . (*D*, 252)

Far from being figures of Glasgow realism, Hines and Doyle are paradigms of a culture which has discovered the emptiness, the groundlessness of its own systems of knowledge: those systems float free, valid or invalid; are all redundant or will be redundant and give no succour against the immediate brute reality of the present. Each is a closed system (a 'closed mouth'), over which the mind walks as though it is a solid reality ('bastarn flagstones') until it is discovered not to exist, not to *have* existed because 'irrelevant to the issue' – to the way out. That is why Doyle is 'the bloke who can show Gödel's Theorem to the average first-year class in a sentence' (*D*, 14). Gödel's theorem demonstrates that all systems of knowledge are founded upon some principle which they cannot themselves justify and which have to be validated from some other system: there is no absolute and self-contained – i.e. necessary – truth; all truths are dependent, and potentially redundant. That is their 'sentence': those who set out to teach truths are sentenced by Gödel to an endless and self-defeating task. The system of their knowledge is 'true' only as long as its unjustifiable and dependent first principle is not questioned from without, but, since all systems are of that kind, their inevitable redundancy is already assured. Knowledge as power turns into the purely aesthetic value of system-building:

> I'm so much bigger than you, he said, these are my terms. My terms are the ones that enclose yous. Yous are all enclosed. But

> yous know that already! I can tell that just by looking at your faces, your faces, telling these things to me. It's quite straightforward when you come to think about it. Here you have me. Here you have you. Two sentences. One sentence is needed for you and one sentence is needed for me and you can wrap them all up together if you want to so that what you have in this one sentence is both you and me, us being in it the gether.
>
> Please sir!
>
> Yes sir?
>
> Do you think we shouldn't be here?
>
> Aye and naw. Sometimes I do and sometimes I dont. I think your question's fine. I think for example in Pythagoras you'll find ways of looking at things, at flitting from one thing to another. And oddly enough it really does have to do with transmigration and maybe even with certain taboos. It makes things fucking really interesting. (*D*, 26)

The effort to come at the reality of being ('us being in it the gether') dissolves into making 'things fucking really interesting': but things do not fuck, and neither does Doyle, locked out from participation in the process of being, enclosed within systems which he cannot accept, generating new systems which he knows to be illusory.

That is why Hegel and Hölderlin are the ghosts who haunt his imagination: the lucid and ludic system-builder and the poet descending into madness and obsession. They are the two poles of the romantic imagination – one dominating reality (briefly) and revealing the order of Being, the other subjected to a world that cannot make more than fragmentary sense. Between them stands Goethe's Werther, whose obsessive love for a married woman Doyle's relationship with Alison repeats, but whose suicide Doyle cannot emulate, because even love is only a cultural hypothesis, an enclosed system, a way of making 'fucking really interesting':

> I'm an authority on Goya who was three years older than Johann Wolfgang von Goethe whose love affair with the beautiful Kathchen Schonkpf
>
> fuck off. That includes Werther. (*D*, 258)

Kelman's protagonists are questers after Being: each is an uncomfortable and discomfiting character because, like Hines, 'when all's said and done he is a negation. Being a negation is peculiar' (*BH*, 202). They come at Being by negating the systems of thought through which we enclose and tame existence: their life is one of continual refusal, and their refusal makes others uncomfortable by making them aware, however briefly, of the problem of Being itself:

> It was the word of course, arse, she didnt like it and hadni been able to cope when he had said it. It was an odd word right enough. Arse. There arent many odder words. Arse. I have an arse. I kicked you on the arse. This is a load of arse. Are-s. It was an odd word. (*D*, 146)

The purpose of Kelman's protagonists is to kick us into awareness of our Ares, our Areness.

EVADING THE POLIS

> Funny how come so many officers-of-the-law crop up these days. Patrick appears to be surrounded by them. Everywhere he looks. (*D*, 209)

Kelman's protagonists are always running up against the police: Tammas encounters them as early as page 20 of *A Chancer*, Hines is always on the lookout for inspectors who will book him, and in *A Disaffection* two 'polis' stand guard at the gates of school, symbolising the school's real function, the policing of the lower orders on behalf of a dictatorial society: Doyle 'went to uni and became a member of the polis' (*D*, 139). Like Tom Leonard's poems in Glasgow vernacular, Kelman exploits his transcription of local speech to make a point: the 'polis' are the representatives of the 'polity' ('we're responsible for it, the present polity' (*D*, 149)): the police dominate the *polis* as envisaged in ancient Greece and replace the ethic of free citizens in a shared community with repression and the continual threat of violence. The ideal city community has dissolved into isolated and terrorised individuals, who in turn are dissolving into fragmentary and multiple identities, an inner disharmony to match the outer chaos.

The problem for Kelman's protagonists is that the ideal of community which they seek is unenvisageable ahead of them: it is already lost and defeated in the past. That is why, for Doyle, the year 1770 accumulates significance: it is the year of Hegel and Hölderlin's birth, of Beethoven's, of Wordsworth's, of the birth of revolution in the Americas. It is the year in which germinates the great harmonies of romantic music and the vision of a harmonious citizenry; but it is also the year from which will spring Hegel's master-slave conception of history and the American imperialism against which Doyle rages so impotently throughout the book. The harmonies of that romantic assault upon the traditional order of reality turn into madness and echo only faintly in Doyle's front room as he plays on his electrician's pipes, just as the assertion of economic and political independence echoes only faintly through the strike which Hines engenders in the bus depot. The vision of revolt against the existing order and the creation of a harmonious polis is what is mocked by the conclusion of *A Disaffection*, when Doyle, wandering the city, is considering throwing a brick through the windows of the big institutions:

> There was a pair of polis across the street who needless to say were observing him openly and frankly and not giving a fuck about him noticing . . . They half-turned from him. They had appeared at the very thought of insurrection, the very thought and they were there. (*D*, 336)

Running away, he is chased and brought down, resisting arrest: 'And there they were is that them there, the polis, the flying rugby-tackle to bring him down, in mid-flight . . .' (*D*, 337). The romantic flight towards a higher and more harmonious world is undone in the dialectic of master and slave.

In this inner disharmony, the individual fragments into a multiplicity of conflicting voices, each as limited and insecure as the hypotheses which float across the real.

> Was it to be taken seriously. Of course, shouted a voice. Whose fucking voice was it. Funny how voices come along and shout, just as if they were something or other, knowledgeable fucking parties perhaps, that knew what was going on. (*BH*, 164)

It is the energy of this inner dialogue which Kelman has exploited in *The Busconductor Hines* and *A Disaffection*, the fragmentation and chaos of their inner lives pitched against the enforced social order of the external world. But the more chaotic those inner worlds become, the more desperately they desire order, harmony; the more they seek harmony, the more they encounter the false and policed orders of the external world and recoil from them. There is no escape from his dialectic: Hines wills to give up being a bus-conductor but will not; Doyle will give up being a teacher, but cannot stop sounding like one. They shuffle back and forth, desperate for a rest, but unable not to go on refusing to become part of the polis, continually resisting arrest – and a rest.

NOTES

1. 'The East End Writers' Anthology, 1988', *Channels of Communication: Papers from the Higher Education Teachers of English Conference held at Glasgow University* (Glasgow: HETE 88, 1992), p. 21.
2. Ibid., p. 25.
3. Ibid., p. 24.
4. James Kelman, *A Disaffection* (London: Secker and Warburg, 1989), pp. 112–13.
5. Virginia Woolf, 'Modern Fiction', 1919; reprinted in *Collected Essays* (London: The Hogarth Press, 1966), vol. II, p. 106.

6. James Kelman, *The Busconductor Hines* (Edinburgh: Polygon, 1984; reprinted London: J. M. Dent and Sons, 1984), pp. 181–2. Subsequent references are to the Dent edition.
7. James Kelman, *A Chancer* (Edinburgh: Polygon, 1985; reprinted London: Picador, 1987), p. 62. Subsequent references are to the Picador edition.

Eight

Innovation and Reaction in the Fiction of Alasdair Gray

Alison Lumsden

Typical recent criticisms of the work of Alasdair Gray have described it as an exploration of, and an imaginative escape from, the systems which serve to entrap and enclose the individual.[1] Such readings of his fiction suggest that it is both innovative – a term which implies a pushing against the limits of accepted boundaries – and radical.

It is certainly the case that what concerns Gray thematically is the ways in which his protagonists are entrapped within systems and structures – be they political, economic or emotional – which serve to limit their capacity for love and freedom, and bring about their personal and societal dissolution. In *Lanark* (1981), Nastler claims that his novel is about just such a process of disintegration:

> The Thaw narrative shows a man dying because he is bad at loving. It is enclosed by your narrative which shows civilization collapsing for the same reason.[2]

It appears that what renders both Thaw and society 'bad at loving' are precisely these systems which close off (like dragonhide) their means of escape and the emergency exits which might provide a route back to their humanity, leaving them encased within structures which ensure their self-destruction.

In *Lanark*, such systems are explored at both a personal level – most specifically in the Thaw narrative – and at a social one, as the Lanark sections of the novel expand Thaw's personal nightmare into an image of a corporate hell where man is both metaphorically and literally 'a pie which bakes and eats itself'. Here, the systems which support such a structure are vast, anonymous entities, the 'creature' which – as Lanark discovers – the individual cannot finally challenge in any real way. Rima points out:

> You dragged us here from a perfectly comfortable place because you disliked the food, and what good did it do? We still eat the same food. (*L*, 430)

Any compensation or 'emergency exit' which is to be found in the novel lies, then, not in the public realm but in the way in which individuals, in their own lives, may attempt to challenge the structures which seek to enclose them. This is what Thaw/Lanark must ultimately learn. 'Yet I did no good, Sandy', Lanark tells his son, 'I changed nothing':

> Of course you changed nothing. The world is only improved by people who do ordinary jobs and refuse to be bullied. Nobody can persuade owners to share with makers when makers won't shift for themselves. (*L*, 554)

And it is his realisation which provides some compensation within the engulfing systems which the novel describes, as Lanark – certainly less brutal and more responsible than his earlier Thaw incarnation – meets his death both 'glad' and 'saddened', aware that he can do little to challenge the vast corporate systems which circumscribe his life, but also that, as an individual, he may still choose to live his life as honestly and freely as possible within this arena.

This mixture of the personal and the social is one which persists throughout Gray's fiction with varying degrees of sophistication. In *The Fall of Kelvin Walker* (1985), this thematic trope emerges in the novel's exploration both of Kelvin's attempt to break free from personal restrictions into a form of existentialist freedom, and of the more social Calvinist system which serves to enclose him within a repressive and destructive framework.[3] For Kelvin, social and religious pressure prove more powerful than a personal desire to assert his own will, and as a result he moulds his new-found freedom in the form of the structures which have shaped his childhood. At the end of the novel, consequently, it is no surprise that he should return to his father, his father's religion, and the town of Glaik which shaped this ethos.

Calvinism, however, proves to be more of a straw man for Jock McLeish in *1982, Janine* (1984), for what this novel explores is a man eventually freed – at least partially – from an image of God as repressive as Mad Hislop, but replacing it with a 'still small voice' which offers compassion and capacity for redemption which Jock had thought impossible.[4] The bondage in which Jock's image of God holds him is paralleled in the novel, as Robert Crawford points out, with the bondage imposed upon him by his emotional fears, with the state of Scotland, and with the bondage of Janine by Jock himself within his sexual fantasies:

> For Gray's imagination the theme of a contest against physical and intellectual entrapment has remained central. In *1982, Janine* Jock McLeish is at the same time a supervisor of security installations and a man constantly compelled to escape from reality through his own fantasies which not only involve bondage but also become for him a form of entrapment. Again, with horrible ease, escape seems to become another kind of imprisonment. Paralleling Jock's sexual fantasies are his musings on Scottish politics: Scotland too seems in bondage, but no escape is envisaged which would not be another form of enthralment.[5]

Yet, while as Crawford says, there may be no means of escape offered for Scotland in the novel, it does suggest that there may be some kind of freedom for Jock himself within that system. Certainly, the night in which the novel takes place seems to teach him – in the wonderful form of the Ministry of Voices, a polyphonic, multiplistic catharsis which challenges the entrapping forces of an authoritarian system – a way of preventing one's past from becoming a form of enslavement. 'Listen look back the past is that fountain where all springs stream' (*J*, 182), says the voice of God, suggesting that the only way to escape the trap of the past is to confront it. It is by this means that Jock is released into temporality – allowing his past to become a past-tense narrative rather than an ongoing nightmare – and thus finds a way to proceed. While the end of the novel may question how long this new commitment might last, it is clear that Jock has found some kind of freedom within the context of the novel – a freedom which at least allows him to envisage (if not put into practice) an alternative life for himself and thus similarly liberate Janine, allowing her to take control of her own narrative.

In *1982, Janine*, sexual fantasy is clearly used as a form of bondage for both Janine and Jock himself, but in Gray's recent novel *Something Leather* (1990), sexual fantasy is itself used as the route to a kind of personal freedom for its protagonists.[6] Here, Gray explores personal restrictions and the need for the characters in the novel to break out of these restrictions which they themselves, their pasts or their social positions have imposed upon them. Again, while social freedoms may be difficult to achieve (the working-class characters find it difficult to escape the traps which restrict their lives), freedom may be achieved at a personal and emotional level, as June, head shaven and tatooed, casts off her inhibitions to find greater fulfilment and happiness:

> In the leather shop she buys a black belted coat with big lapels and a military-looking hat with glossy skip. She contrives to be served by the assistant who introduced her to the Hideout, and at one

point removes her glasses and says, 'Do you remember me?' After a wondering stare the assistant says, 'Yes! . . . Did you find that place you were looking for?' 'Oh yes.'

'So you're happy now?' says the assistant, smiling.

'Yes', says June, smiling. (*SL*, 231)

Thematically, then, Gray's work seems to suggest that, while the vast economic and political structures which form systems of entrapment – Lyotard's overarching grand-narratives of our age and society – may be difficult, if not impossible, to challenge, the individual may nevertheless find some kind of freedom *within* these frameworks.[7] While Gray does not suggest that such freedom comes easily (for Jock and June it is, on the contrary, a compensation won only after much pain), his fiction implies that it may provide some antidote to the larger societal forces which serve to restrict freedom.

Interesting and well-handled as this thematic exploration is, however, it may hardly be described as innovative in any real sense, for the conclusions which Gray's work implies are in fact fairly traditional, classically bourgeois ones. Not surprisingly, then, it is not for these thematic explorations that Gray's fiction has been hailed as innovative, but rather for its stylistic experimentation and dexterity. Such dexterity is used to explore the far more postmodern, reflexive question of the ways in which the traps created by the process of writing and imagination – those traps which destroy Thaw in *Lanark* – may themselves be challenged within the work of fiction which is itself of course an imaginative construction.

It is here, then, in Gray's reflexive handling of this paradoxical situation that, it is argued, his work may be recognised as innovative and experimental, and, since such questions place his work in the context of other international fictional developments in the recent past, as postmodernist.

And yet it is possible that Gray's treatment of this reflexive paradox *is itself* a form of containment, for there are ways in which his work does not *challenge* the sources of its own creativity but rather *accepts* that reflexivity may provide a creative impasse which renders, as Crawford suggests, each form of escape simply another form of enthralment. It is necessary to explore whether this acceptance of the postmodern predicament in Gray's fiction may finally constitute not real innovation, but *reaction*.

Certainly, a reactionary position seems to be implicit in Gray's handling of postmodern techniques and strategies. While Gray himself rejects the application of this term to his own work, it seems clear that not only the strategies used in his novels, but also the issues which are raised within them, can be seen to be broadly in tune with those fictional developments which have appeared in the past twenty years and which have been described as postmodernity. Randall Stevenson, for instance, has traced convincing stylistic parallels between Gray's work and that of 'postmodern' innovators from Flann O'Brien to Peter Ackroyd.[8]

Strategies and techniques alone, of course, do not constitute postmodernism – such features have been found in various forms since the advent of the novel. Postmodernism is, rather, an attitude and a response to precisely the awareness of linguistic reflexive entrapment which we have seen explored in Gray's work, precisely the predicament which Nastler raises in his conversation with Lanark, for instance:

> 'I will start,' said the conjurer, 'by explaining the physics of the world you live in. Everything you have experienced and are experiencing, from your first glimpse of the Elite cafe to the metal of that spoon in your fingers, the taste of the soup in your mouth, is made of one thing.' 'Atoms', said Lanark. 'No. Print. Some worlds are made of atoms but yours is made of tiny marks marching in neat lines, like armies of insects, across pages and pages and pages of white paper.' (*L*, 485).

However, what is arguably most interesting about his statement is that as a postmodernist 'comment' it is embarrassingly *passé*, for, as Stevenson's essay, along with Gray's own Index of Plagiarisms suggests, such notions were, by the time *Lanark* was published, very familiar ones, and hardly in need of statement in this bald fashion within Gray's fiction.

Randall Stevenson suggests, somewhat tentatively, that what may be happening here is a form of 'post postmodernism', as if Gray, aware that there is no radical path left for the writer (even a postmodern one), is opting to offer only a pastiche of postmodernism itself which necessarily pre-empts – and therefore short-circuits and to some extent escapes – its own inevitable containment.[9]

To read Gray's work in this way is certainly critically dextrous, but it also seems problematic. In the first instance, it raises the problem of how we as readers are to recognise such pastiche, for, after all, there is only a fine line between pastiche and bad writing, and greater evidence seems necessary before Gray's novel can be admonished. Certainly, although these words belong to Nastler rather than Gray, such pedantry is not lacking from Gray's fiction in general, and it is possible that what is presented here in Gray's Index of Plagiarisms and Epilogue is not a *pastiche* of postmodernity, but, quite simply, rather clumsily-handled metafictional strategies.[10]

More significantly, if, to give Gray the benefit of the doubt, what *is* explored in *Lanark* is the more sophisticated question of how there may be no radical path available to the writer, no imaginative escape route from inevitable entrapment, Gray's response to this position still seems to owe more to reaction than innovation. For if Gray's response is, as the term 'post-postmodernism' implies, simply to accept inevitable entrapment and to write it into his fiction as an inevitable part of the imaginative process, such a position is in danger of providing its own rather comfortable 'escape route' from innovation and one which is in the end clearly reactionary.

'The sun also rises', states Nastler in Gray's Epilogue, suggesting that there is nothing new under the sun and that, indeed, the attempt to escape the inevitable conclusion to his novel is not even worthy of his time. In the face of this, Lanark is right to protest, and indeed he does win a victory – however insignificant – against Nastler's quietism. *Lanark* as a thematic and artistic whole, then, does somewhat paradoxically continue to resist inevitable entrapment. Yet, while this may be the case, it appears as if the author of it is less willing to admit that there may be some ground to be gained against containment within his own structural strategies. Significantly, while the words of the Epilogue must in the end be attributed to Nastler, the Epigraph of the novel can be more directly attributed to Gray:

> I started making maps when I was small
> Showing place, resources, where the enemy
> And where love lay. I did not know
> Time adds to land. Events drift continually down,
> Effacing landmarks, raising the level, like snow.
> I have grown up. My maps are out of date.
> The land lies over me now.
> I cannot move. It is time to go.
>
> (*L*, 560)

Moving though this familiar postmodern trope may be, the speaker's decision that it is 'time to go' now that his 'maps' – his familiar and secure yet entrapping structures – are out of date seems, after all, a type of quietism, a refusal to attempt to draw *new* maps which may, in the end, prove to be reactionary.

Certainly, while the *thematic* impulses in Gray's work remain uneasy with any position which settles with an inevitable and inescapable notion of entrapment, it seems as if Gray himself repeatedly reinforces this containment within the tropic architectures of his work, thus reinforcing a position which may, finally, be less of a *critique* of entrapment than a form of containment itself. Thus, a position which seems to conclude only that there may be no way of escaping the large-scale economic and social structures which serve to entrap the individual becomes too easily one which, in its *own* structurally reflexive fatalism, also denies the individual the local or lesser successes which Lanark, Jock or June at least in part achieve on a thematic level.

Again, a very similar problem results from Gray's handling of Scottish material in his fiction. Thematically, Gray often uses Scottish themes and aspects of experience to great advantage, using particularly Scottish tropes of entrapment to explore more widespread issues. In *1982, Janine*, for example, Calvinism is used as a trope wherein Gray examines the ways in which Jock creates a rigid social code (a God as authoritarian as Mad Hislop) with which to limit his own freedom. In such instances, Scottish themes are used to their full advantage and, as they have been in the best of Scottish fiction, with a tropic impulse with resists parochialism.

However, there is also an element in Gray's work which serves to limit this expansiveness, pulling it *back* towards a particularly Scottish and depressingly parochial field of reference. At such points in Gray's fiction, Scottish themes are no longer used as critiques of entrapment, but are, on the contrary, means of containing Gray's fiction *within* a particularly disenchanting sphere. Outlining Kelvin's failure at the close of *Kelvin Walker*, for example, Gray suggests, albeit parodically, that it is his Scottishness which is the source of his misery:

> At the age of forty he became 293rd Moderator of the General Assembly of the United Seceders Free Presbyterian Church of Scotland and married a girl less than half his age who bore him six children, none of whom are very happy. (*FKW*, 141)

For Jake and Jill, however, things are somewhat easier:

> In their late thirties she and Jake had a child almost (but not quite) by accident, then got another by adopting the wholly accidental child of a friend.
>
> These children are often happy.
>
> It is easier for them.
>
> They are English. (*FKW*, 141)

Such a conclusion at the end of the novel suggests that, in the face of social structures which entrap individuals (here, the fact of being Scottish), there is no escape possible. Yet the thematic impulse of *The Fall of Kelvin Walker* seems far more complex: Kelvin's failure is more of an *individual* one than a *Scottish* one. The conclusion of the novel then seems to work against its own thematic impulses and those within Gray's fiction in general, pulling it back, despite the humour, into a kind of parochial containment which can only be seen as an unnecessary limitation.

While Gray has claimed that it is the business of the novelist to avoid the role of moralist, this impulse in his fiction seems an undeniably didactic reflex; a reluctance to leave his fictions *free* in some more ambiguous area where the reader may or may not read some direct social issues (most frequently the state of Scotland, or even more parochially Glasgow) into them.[11]

This type of containment can be very clearly seen in operation in *1982, Janine*, where in the course of the novel itself Jock's personal entrapments are allowed to exist as a metaphorical parallel for the state of Scotland. Through his *tropic* use of Scottish material, consequently, Gray presents a critique of the Scottish statement within the fictional form of Jock's narrative. This device is for the most part handled skilfully, with Scottish material being explored as an organic and natural part of the novel, alongside parallel themes of a more universal nature. In the Epilogue of the novel, however, the speaker (Gray? A. G.? the Author?) comments:

> And now a personal remark which purely literary minds will ignore. Though John McLeish is an invention of mine I disagree with him. In chapter 4, for example, he says of Scotland, 'We are a poor little country, always have been, always will be'. In fact Scotland's natural resources are as variedly rich as those of any other land. Her ground area is greater than that of Denmark, Holland, Belgium or Switzerland, her population higher than that of Denmark, Norway or Finland. Our present ignorance and bad social organisation make most Scots poorer than most other north Europeans, but even bad human states are not everlasting. (*J*, 345)

Again, metaphoric expansiveness is narrowed down to the specific, as the author ensures that his own opinions on the state of Scotland will form part of the structure of the work of fiction. These opinions surely serve only to *contain* the fictional whole, limiting its field of reference and the wider thematic impulses which it has achieved.

A similar kind of containment also occurs in *Something Leather*. In this, the latest of Gray's fictions, the setting is not overtly Scottish, is not contained within a specific topography, and the suffering and social injustice portrayed within it seem 'universal' issues. However, at the end of the novel, Gray again pulls his material back towards a specifically Scottish, even Glaswegian, issue, cutting his critique to the size of a parochial polemic:

> It was now clear that June was a new woman, and to describe how she used her newness would limit it. There was a clear hint that having been liberated by the work of Senga and Donalda, June (the professional person) and Harry (the inherited wealth person) would cut themselves off from the poorer folk and have fun together. You need not believe that ending, but it is how we normally arrange things in Great Britain. It is certainly how things were arranged in Glasgow in 1990, when that city
> was the official capital of Europe –
> culturally speaking. (*SL*, 251)

While one could argue that this material is not intended to be read entirely seriously, it does serve to operate as a form of containment within Gray's fiction, pulling the tropic impulses in his own work back towards a specific and limited field of hectoring reference.

More significantly, if these particularly Scottish forms of entrapment (forms which, we should note, Gray himself places within his fiction) are being used as the basis of a critique of containment within Gray's work, they seem, ultimately, to point towards a dangerous complacency – a position wherein the fact of Scottishness (a fact which, after all, is fairly unchallengeable for many of Gray's readers) itself forms an inevitable form of entrapment, thus rendering us, like Kelvin, inescapably doomed to a parochial misery and quietistically forced to return to the Glaik that bred us. Such an argument seems perilously close to an excuse for mediocrity (or at least misery).

Finally, containment also emerges in Gray's work in its relationship with criticism – a relationship which again, while seemingly presenting a *critique* of containment, ultimately *dictates* an inevitable containment of and for itself. A familair feature of Gray's work from *Lanark* onwards has been its epilogues and 'critic fodder'. As with Gray's other reflexive strategies, it is possible to read such material in terms of critique, seeing it as an attempt to short-circuit the inevitable containment of the radicalism of fictional writing by critical commentary. However, again it seems important at least to suggest that by this strategy Gray may only be timidly seeking to contain responses to his fiction, 'drawing the poison' of potential critical debate so that it can only take place within the reflexively pre-emptive terms that Gray has prescribed for it, thus again stifling rather than supporting any real radicalism in his fiction.

Certainly, such 'critic fodder' serves not just to pre-empt but even to 'define' the reader of Gray's work. In *Lanark*, Lanark comments: 'I thought epilogues came after the end', and Nastler responds:

> Usually, but mine is too important to go there. Though not essential to the plot it provides some comic distraction at a

> moment when the narrative sorely needs it. And it lets me utter some fine sentiments which I could hardly trust to a mere character. And it contains critical notes which will save research scholars years of toil. (*L*, 483)

Such a statement, however comic, serves to circumscribe Gray's reader, presupposing that he or she will inevitably be a 'research scholar' or critic. And while again these words belong to Nastler, they express a position which does not seem that far removed from Gray's own. While the Epilogues of *1982, Janine* and *Something Leather* may come more conventionally at the end of the novel – and thereby in part at least outside the fictional construct proper – they show a similar impulse to that found in Nastler's own, namely a desire to control (and thus limit) the terms of the debate, and a consonant unwillingness to allow the text to stand alone from what might be seen as the entrapping and stifling practice of the sort of 'research-scholar' criticism which Gray/Nastler welcomes.

Such material in Gray's work, then, initiates a safe (because invited) dialogue between critic and author, a dialogue which inevitably circumscribes the arena of criticial response, and, more importantly in the context of this study, inevitably contains the scope for *real* radicalism, *real* innovation within the work of art. Such acceptance of the inevitable encroachment of entrapping systems (be they our Scottishness, the inevitable process of criticism, or, as for Jock, the acceptance of our own personal role as failures) is in the end only a form of retreat, a form of *collaboration* with these systems themselves. For to insist on such trapping systems is, as Jock paradoxically demonstrates, a way of avoiding what freedom might be gained, what responsibility we might have to make the world around us (or the fictional process) more tolerable.

It is, then, hardly surprising that the first major work of criticism to appear on the work of Alasdair Gray should be one which bears his own designs and which places him foremost in the list of acknowledgements.[12] Such a position was, perhaps, inevitable, for to offer a 'critique' of entrapment in the way in which Alasdair Gray does in his fiction is ultimately to cooperate with that process of 'entrapment' itself.

Whatever may be the successes of Gray's fiction, then (and they are considerable), it is at least arguable that within this context – a context which is becoming all too familiar in Scottish writing – his much-heralded 'critique' of the inevitability of entrapment is not one of them. Such a critique, surely, can only be convincingly offered by one who has explored every means of escape. While Gray's protagonists June, Jock and Lanark gain dignity from their restlessness in the face of their own containment and the limited victories which they do in the end and against all odds win, Gray on the contrary seems all too willing to accept the inevitable fact of his own 'structural' reflexive defeat, and, indeed, to dictate the terms of it. While, then, his protagonists may find some form of radicalism with which to confront the systems which serve to contain their freedom, Gray, in his handling of postmodernism, in his use of Scottish material and in the genial, almost masonic dialogue which he initiates with academic criticism, is content with other prizes. Perhaps, after all, his fiction provides us not with *critiques* of containment, but rather a series of containing strategies; not with means of *escape*, but comfortable terms of surrender.

NOTES

1. See, for example, Cairns Craig's essay 'Going Down to Hell is Easy: *Lanark*, Realism and the Limits of the Imagination' in *The Arts of Alasdair Gray*, ed. Robert Crawford and Thom Nairn (Edinburgh: Edinburgh University Press, 1991), pp. 90–107.
2. Alasdair Gray, *Lanark: A Life in Four Books* (Edinburgh: Canongate Publishing, 1981; reprinted London: Grafton Books, 1982). All subsequent references are to the Grafton edition.
3. Alasdair Gray, *The Fall of Kelvin Walker* (Edinburgh: Canongate Publishing, 1985, reprinted Harmondsworth: Penguin, 1986). All subsequent references are to the Penguin edition.
4. Alasdair Gray, *1982, Janine* (London: Jonathan Cape, 1984; reprinted Harmondsworth: Penguin, 1985). All subsequent references are to the Penguin edition.
5. Robert Crawford, 'Introduction', *The Arts of Alasdair Gray* (pp. 1–9), p. 5.
6. Alasdair Gray, *Something Leather* (London: Jonathan Cape, 1990; reprinted London: Picador/Pan, 1991). All subsequent references are to the Picador edition, to which Gray added a new concluding sentence (p. 251).
7. See Jean-Francois Lyotard, *The Post-Modern Condition: A Report on Knowledge*, translated by Geoff Bennington and Brian Massumi (Manchester: Manchester University Press, 1984), p. 15.
8. Randall Stevenson, 'Alasdair Gray and the Postmodern', in *The Arts of Alasdair Gray* (pp. 48–63).
9. Stevenson, p. 56.
10. Gray, of course, is at times well aware of his own pedantry, commenting (in his Nastler guise) in *Lanark*, for example: 'The critics will accuse me of self-indulgence' (481). At other times, however, it appears in a less playful form, such as when Jock gives lengthy accounts of the state of Scotland in *1982, Janine*; accounts which seem to owe more to polemic than artistry.
11. 'It's a pity that storytellers can't be moralists', writes Gray in 'Postscript' to Agnes Owens, *Gentlemen of the West* (Edinburgh:

Polygon, 1984; reprinted Harmondsworth: Penguin, 1986), p. 137.

12. I refer to *The Arts of Alasdair Gray*, which, while containing much useful information and critique, clearly stands in a rather peculiar relationship to the author himself.

FURTHER READING

Gray, Alasdair, *Unlikely Stories, Mostly* (Edinburgh: Canongate Publishing, 1983).

Gray, Alasdair, *McGrotty and Ludmilla, or The Harbinger Report* (Glasgow: Dog and Bone, 1990).

Imhof, Rudiger, 'Chinese Box: Flann O'Brien in the Metafiction of Alasdair Gray, John Fowles and Robert Coover', *Eire-Ireland* (Spring, 1990), pp. 64–79.

Murray, Isobel and Tait, Bob, 'Alasdair Gray: *Lanark*' in *Ten Modern Scottish Novels* (Aberdeen: Aberdeen University Press, 1984).

Whyte, Christopher, 'Alasdair Gray: Not a Mirror but a Portrait', *Books in Scotland* (Summer, 1988), pp. 1–2.

Witschi, Beat, 'Defining a Scottish Identity', *Books in Scotland*, no 34, pp. 5–6.

Nine

Iain Banks and the Fiction Factory

Thom Nairn

When asked what his new novel *The Crow Road* (1992) was about, Iain Banks replied: 'Well it's about 147,000 words at the last count, but seriously, it's about Death, Sex, Faith, cars, Scotland and drink'.[1] His remarks may come closer to the truth than his book jackets and reviewers. Regardless of their likenesses and differences, his novels are rarely about what they appear to be about.

It is almost a decade since the appearance of Banks's first, mysteriously much-maligned novel, *The Wasp Factory* (1984). In the intervening years, he seems to have committed himself to convincing us that 'Iain Banks' is actually the trading name of some kind of writers' collective. His mainstream novels are in themselves eclectic enough in terms of genre. The black, absurdist *The Wasp Factory* is often, dubiously designated 'horror'; *Walking on Glass* (1985) is a hybrid of science fiction and realism; *The Bridge* (1986) is an equally dense interweaving of genres; *Espedair Street* (1987) is a 'rock 'n' roll' novel; and, more recently, *Canal Dreams* (1989) seems a bizarre collision of Robert Ludlum and J. G. Ballard. *Canal Dreams* also shows especially clearly Bank's affinities with the kind of contemporary thriller-writing practised, for example, by Household in *Rogue Male* (1939) or John Le Carré in *The Perfect Spy* (1986).

This diverse body of work is further complicated by the existence of Iain M. Banks, the name under which the author publishes his science fiction – or space operas, as he prefers to call them – *Consider Phlebas* (1987), *The Player of Games* (1988), *Use of Weapons* (1990) and the short stories in *The State of the Art* (1991). Due to limited space, the focus here will be on his mainstream writing: his work outside the science-fiction field (though it is rarely far from its edges) is his most interesting, and

Banks himself regards *The Bridge* as his best novel to date.[2] This, however, is not to demean the science fiction: *Consider Phlebas* is often flabby and unrealised, but *Use of Weapons* is exceptional, and there is some wonderfully malicious material in *The State of the Art*.

As his first published novel, *The Wasp Factory* offers a logical point of entry to Banks's work, though he has pointed out on many occasions that it was the seventh he had written but the first he had revised. Set in the North of Scotland, it focuses intensely on growing up in a society where machismo is paramount. Much of the novel's black humour lies in our belief that the central character, Frank, has had his genitals eaten by a bulldog as an infant. As a result, he is the meanest of the mean, typifying Banks's pervasive interest in quasi-feral anti-heroes. *The Wasp Factory* quickly became notorious for depicting the burning of dogs; there are also bombed and disembowelled rabbits, more than a little necromancy, wasps fried in 'the factory', and the occasional surreal murder – such as the dispatch of cousin Esmeralda, caught in the entrails of Frank's giant kite and unleashed over the North Sea. Frank is philosophical about this murderous approach to adulthood:

> That's my score to date. Three. I haven't killed anybody for years, and I don't intend to ever again. It was just a stage I was going through.[3]

That so many English reviewers failed to note any humour in *The Wasp Factory* says a good deal about intrinsic differences of outlook between Scottish and English society, suggesting the presence in the former of a darker, more complex, perhaps not altogether creditable sense of humour.

The novel as a whole is a rich, intriguing tapestry of shrouded sexual symbolism (disrupted watercourses, ruptured dams); totemic ritual; hints and omens; bizarre, quirky dialogue and behaviour; inbuilt socio-political commentary; and an often reality-defying use of language: Banks manages to make a battle between Frank and a seriously disgruntled rabbit fraught with tension, gore – and credibility. The novel's dense texture is gripping from the outset, invites investigation, and needs several re-readings to unravel: the mysteries of 'the factory' are dark, malignant and impenetrable. We know something complicated is wrong with Frank, but need to find out more. His macabre lifestyle, beliefs and history unfold in a meticulous catalogue of atrocities: collision, minor apocalypse and revelation are consistently imminent. On whatever level the novel is approached, it holds the reader. Only the squeamish and humourless need beware.

Like Lennox in *The Bridge*, Frank is an ideal exemplar of, in one of Hugh MacDiarmid's favourite phrases, the 'absolute propriety of a gargoyle's grinning at the elbow of a saint'.[4] Quirky, complex, pointed humour, a diverse parade of atrocities, and much else in Banks's work likewise recalls the Caledonian antisyzygy, the dichotomy so beloved by MacDiarmid. Potential schisms in the individual (schisms are piled on schisms of all kinds) are constantly present in Banks's fiction, making it comparable to R. L. Stevenson's *Dr Jekyll and Mr Hyde* and James Hogg's *Confessions* or *The House with the Green Shutters*, or Alasdair Gray's *Lanark*. Yet Banks has expressed doubts about the place he may or may not occupy in a specifically Scottish literary tradition, as well as some dubiety about Scottish literature itself. The antisyzygy, after all, is far from exclusively Caledonian: the same holds true of the most distinctive feature of *Walking on Glass* and *The Bridge*, which is their fusion of diverse styles of hard realism and quasi-science fiction, hardening the realist base while delving into some fairly strange subjective zones.

The real nature of this fusion is clarified by Randall Stevenson's observations, quoting the postmodern theorist Brian McHale to help explain the work of Alasdair Gray:

> As Brian McHale suggests, postmodernism and science fiction can '. . . be seen as siblings, sharing a common descent in the twentieth century: the two ontological sister genres, science fiction and postmodernist fiction, have been pursuing analogous but independent courses of development . . . along parallel but independent tracks'.[5]

As Stevenson goes on to explain, Gray's *Lanark* (1981), like the work of Brian Aldiss or J. G. Ballard, significantly diminishes the independence of these 'tracks', fusing postmodern stylistic pyrotechnics with blunt realism or largely fantastic, science-fiction scenarios. It is very much this sort of fusion which is apparent in *Walking on Glass* and *The Bridge*, Banks himself remarking: 'I don't think *The Bridge* would be the way it is at all if it wasn't for *Lanark*'.[6] Such tactics do bear some oblique comparison with the Ballads, with 'Tam o' Shanter', with R. L. Stevenson, with *A Voyage to Arcturus* (1920), with MacDiarmid's later, stranger excursions, or with some of the work of Muriel Spark and Edwin Morgan, as well as Alasdair Gray. But there are also related developments in the writing of Umberto Eco, Thomas Pynchon, Keri Hulme, or Günter Grass – Banks himself has cited Grass's *The Tin Drum* as a formative influence. Recognition of some of these affinities with a wider, international context of writing, as well as the Scottish one, helps make Banks seem a less odd or isolated figure.

At any rate, *Walking on Glass* is one of Banks's strangest novels: if it is flawed, as the author believes, it is also much underrated, exemplifying some of the complexities which associate Banks with the context of writing outlined above, as well as preparing the ground for subtler work in *The Bridge*. *Walking on Glass* consists of three apparently unrelated narratives, each of which is sustained through five subsections, while a sixth offers some sort of illumination. Each narrative has a central character: the lovelorn art student Graham Park, moving through an apparently realistic setting in contemporary London; the rampantly paranoid Stephen Grout, believing himself to be some kind of interdimensional warrior, trapped in exile; and Quiss, who *knows* that he *is* an exiled interdimensional warrior. Each of these narratives develops systematically as the subsections unfold. Playing games, however, is Banks's stock in trade, and he plays them with characters and readers alike. As the narrative moves through Park/Grout/Quiss/Park/Grout/Quiss etc, the distinctions grow befuddled and the diversity of the scenarios begins to break down. Loading his text with symbols, images, cross-references and tangled coincidences, Banks allows settings, events and characters to filter from one narrative to another, undermining our assumptions until we begin to lose track of which of these narratives can be accepted as the real one. Banks makes us play detective as we try to pin down links in a chain which, as well-trained readers, we are convinced must exist.

The role of the author is also foregrounded, and increasingly questionable. Given the subtextual questions of authorial position and the nature of storytelling – like a good postmodernist, Banks makes us doubt everything – it is not surprising to find books themselves assuming a central role. 'The Castle of Bequest', for example, where Quiss is confined, is described as 'built very largely of books . . . filled full of hidden, indecipherable lettering'.[7] This seems all the more suspicious if we move back eight pages into Grout's bedsit in London:

> His room was full of books; thick, dog-eared, broken-spined gaudy-covered paperbacks. They lay on the floor, stacked on their sides because he didn't have any proper shelves. The floor of his room was like a maze, with tower-blocks of books, whole walls of them set out on the thin carpet and holed linoleum so that only small corridors for him to walk in remained between them . . . Coming back to the place drunk, especially when he couldn't find the light switch, was horrendous; he would wake to a sight like Manhattan after a severe earthquake. In paperback. (*WG*, 30)

This setting is eerily anticipatory of the structure of the Castle of Bequest, just as Grout's drunken devastation – or his looking in his books for things 'locked away in his brain somewhere' – prefigures Quiss tearing the castle to pieces in search of clues and meanings.

What is happening here? Are Grout and Quiss somehow the same Being? Is Quiss some manifestation of Grout, a subjective projection or part of his unconscious mind? These are only a sample of questions raised by myriads of calculated parallels, mirrorings, echoings riddling the novel. *Walking on Glass* begins to seem a palimpsest of never fully-decipherable possibilities, as, in turn, the castle comes to seem a palimpsest within a palimpsest, while we, like Grout, read the novel awaiting the click of revelation. At the end of the Quiss narrative, in a cheekily self-reflexive gesture, we are left with a character reading, in a book with no cover and no title page: 'He walked through the white corridors' (*WG*, 233). These, of course, are the opening words of *Walking on Glass* itself. Several commentators have recently remarked that we may already be in the midst of a post-postmodernist age, where the postmodern itself becomes the butt of elaborate jokes. Banks's work as a whole can easily accommodate such a concept.

Or many others. Banks allows space for the possibility that the Quiss-world functions as a science-fiction allegory supplementing the real-world scenarios occupied by Grout and Graham, all of which may be employed to explore the social and political breakdown of *our* world. In the sixth section of the novel, we are left with an embittered Graham wandering in the debris of the Grout scenario, just as we leave Grout amid the symbolic trappings of Quiss's. On one level, this is a conclusion on the side of the acceptably real, though, simultaneously, it is an allegorical exploration of the unconscious mind. As the apparent controller of Bequest, the seneschal, observes, 'we can be sure of nothing' (*WG*, 228). Art *is* a funny business and a dubious one. This novel is about that as well.

At one stage of *The Bridge*, it is remarked that:

> Dr Joyce looks profoundly unconvinced (I don't blame him really, this is all a pack of lies), and shakes his head in what may well be a gesture of exasperation.[8]

Godot is invoked in *Walking on Glass*: mention of 'Dr Joyce' indicates another of Banks's antecedents. If anything, *The Bridge* is quite literally 'a stream of unconsciousness'. The suggestion that it is 'all a pack of lies' could also be construed as another postmodern anti-flourish, reminding us of the instabilities of fiction, mocking postmodernism in its sheer blatancy. At any rate, the entire narrative is compounded of instabilities of one kind or another, Banks twisting off on divergent tangents and subjecting his readers' and characters' sense of reality to disruptive disjunctions. We are back to palimpsests here; wheels within wheels; veneer beneath veneer; and to the question of what *The Bridge* might be about.

In one way, the bridge in question is the Forth Railway Bridge, at least for some of the time: for the rest, it is something else a bit bigger. Throughout, it is imbued with a multiplex symbolism which defies compact analysis. The structure of the novel itself is at least as complex and tangled as the engineering reality on which it is based. Its many deviant strands, however, do depend – like Alasdair Gray's *Lanark*, which it often parallels – on two intimately-related primary narratives. One is fantastic, though nevertheless probably closer to reality. The other is realist. The scenario of the first narrative is the Bridge-World, the domain of Orr, a fantastic world where the railway bridge is expanded to gigantic proportions. Dr Joyce asks Orr – a stranded, memoryless refugee on the bridge – what he sees as he peers from the windows of the doctor's surgery. Orr, whom he is trying to cure, replies: 'I see a fucking great bridge', and BIG it is:

> Its sloping sides rise, russet-red and ribbed, from the granite-plinthed feet set in the sea nearly a thousand feet below. Those latticed flanks are slabbed and crammed with clusters of secondary and tertiary architecture; walkways and lift-shafts, chimneys and gantries, cableways and pipes, ariels and banners and flags of all shapes, sizes and colours. There are small buildings and large ones; offices, wards, workshops, dwellings and shops, all stuck like angular limpets of metal and glass and wood to the massive tubes and interweaving girders of the bridge itself. (*B*, 22)

Just as *The Wasp Factory* hinges on magnifications or intensifications of one kind or another, so too Orr's Bridge-World is a massive expansion of the Forth Railway Bridge, its bizarre, endless, tubular interiors housing a multitude of caricatures, deviants, walking symbols and expanded banalities. Through this, Orr wanders in search of he's not quite sure what: identity, meaning, knowledge, love, the secrets of an apparently documented but extinguished library. Yet, as in *Walking on Glass*, there is nothing stable to be counted on: corridors, tunnels and lifts are moved or cease to exist with ease, while televisions and telephones do whatever they want, plugged in or not. The place is multiplex, and Banks maximises its potential: it is a subjective hinterland constructed of phallic tubing, a complex latticework corresponding to diverse social strata, to disruptions and apparent meaninglessness, with direction an implausible concept.

Yet, paradoxically, the bridge is also pattern, structure and calculation personified, power and cohesion – a curiously, disturbingly re-emergent shape, echoed in fishing nets and net stockings, always in the corner of the eye. In the midst of clustered chaos, Orr does not have sufficient perspective to appreciate this. It is only on the second narrative level, with Lennox, that these hints of realities and achievements begin to coalesce, making it possible to join some of Orr's dots.

This second narrative follows Lennox from roughly 1965 to 1985, when he is in his thirties. It traces his path to affluence, his tangled love life and his systematic descent into a confusion and disorientation which he numbs – or accelerates – with an escalating intake of alcohol and hallucinogens. As his uncertainty and instability grow increasingly visible, some kind of impending crash is clearly signalled, and duly takes place within sight of the bridge. It is a collision with self as well as the bridge, surrealistic scenarios of collision pervading the novel in nefarious permutations. When Lennox wrecks his car, the last recorded image from the road bridge being the railway bridge, it becomes easy to identify the Bridge-World of Orr as Lennox in coma, his life mirrored, echoed and laid increasingly bare as we are drawn through the macabre tapestry of the Bridge-World, gradually putting two and two together.

Banks grew up in Queensferry with the bridge an omnipresent background, and the realist segments of *The Bridge* – given the precedent of *Lanark* – are intriguingly suggestive of the incorporation of biographical material, or perhaps the exploration of another self who might easily have been. Like *Lanark*, *The Bridge* may be partly autobiographical: like *Lanark*, it also features acute, satirical perspectives as well as surreal characters and scenes. 'The Barbarian', for example, is a send-up of male sexuality, also providing through the dense Scots of his monologue (here describing the monkey which rides on his back) a good deal of the black humour which lurks in the novel:

> It wiz this majishin that geez this thing, cald it a familyar soay did an it sits on ma showder and gose jibber fukin jibber oll bludy day it gose. I cany stand the dam thing but am stuk with it I suppose and it wi me too, cumty think ov it. (*B*, 61)

That the two are shackled, and the Barbarian's Scots verges on the illiterate while the 'familyar' is a master of RP, has as much to do with the state of 'the Union' as it does with the inside of Lennox's head.

Banks successfully achieves his own union in *The Bridge*. As the Bridge-World crumbles, its superior surreality begins to concede to the real scenario of contemporary Edinburgh. Tangents converge eerily but convincingly, worlds come closer, overlaps grow more distinct. Banks never loses control, guiding us unerringly through the elaborate web of his novel. In this work and elsewhere, his success is first and foremost as a storyteller, rather than a prime innovator. In fact, Banks's success as a storyteller is largely based on a readiness and a capacity to assimilate such a diverse menu of already-existing literary techniques: modernism and postmodernism, dirty realism and surrealism, fantasy and science fiction, William Burroughs and Edgar Burroughs, all seem equally integrated in the various burrowings and borrowings of his imagination. Integral to all this is his openness to language at all levels. The Scots of the Barbarian, for example, is loaded with paradox and ambiguity, as is the military terminology tactically deployed in *The Wasp Factory*. A further asset is Banks's fascination with the nature of stories themselves, and how and why they are told. Equally, his repeated focus on time and the tricks it can play occupies an important role in establishing narrative structures and facilitating the range of forms they take in his work.

Such factors are also prominent in his science fiction. Mad machines and deviant drones and phones show an awareness of diverse areas of contemporary literature – and trash – which helps Banks open up new shapes and potentialities for the science-fiction genre while also remaining in touch with classics such as Doc Smith or Robert A. Heinlein. Banks performs the same kind of surgery with the thriller in *Canal Dreams*, cross-fertilising a politically-volatile situation with a near-future scenario.

Banks has thus shown no signs, so far, of settling down into a cosy corner. He is always trying for something new, and even if – as in *Consider Phlebas* – he does not wholly succeed, this at least leaves a ragged edge in his work which sits paradoxically and interestingly with his concern for the state of the art. Likewise, if his tales do not always gel or communicate, this can produce – for an increasingly tentative perception of reality in the 1990s – a paradigm more convincing, if frustrating, than anything that could be offered by a neatly-finished package. It will be interesting to see what Iain Banks's fiction factory has produced by the year 2000; but, like the man said, that's another story.

NOTES

1. Interview with Iain Banks in *Festival Times*, 17–23 August 1991, p. 57.
2. 'A far better book – it's the best of the bunch in terms of the actual craft of the novel.' Iain Banks, interviewed in *Radical Scotland*, no. 42, December/January 1990, p. 27.
3. Iain Banks, *The Wasp Factory* (London: Macmillan, 1984; reprinted London: Abacus, 1992), p. 42.
4. Often borrowed by MacDiarmid, the phrase is taken from C. Gregory Smith, *Scottish Literature: Character and Influence* (London: Macmillan and Co., 1919), p. 35.

5. Randall Stevenson, 'Alasdair Gray and the Postmodern' in Robert Crawford and Thom Nairn, eds, *The Arts of Alasdair Gray* (Edinburgh: Edinburgh University Press, 1991), p. 57.
6. Interview in *Radical Scotland* (see note 2).
7. Iain Banks, *Walking on Glass* (London: Macmillan, 1985; reprinted London: Abacus, 1991), pp. 38–9. Subsequent references are to the Abacus edition.
8. Iain Banks, *The Bridge* (London: Macmillan, 1986), p. 13. Subsequent references are to this edition.

Ten

Of Myths and Men: Aspects of Gender in the Fiction of Janice Galloway

Margery Metzstein

There is a danger, when discussing Scottish fiction, of creating a misleading homogeneity; of seamlessly combining and making indistinguishable diverse ingredients such as Scottishness, the history of Scottish literature – and gender. This produces a passable malt, labelled 'wha's like us? Damn few, and they're a' deid.' But this writer is sceptical, and wishes to avoid that vat of self-congratulatory delusion. This writer is Scottish – and also female.

As a Scot who chose to study English literature, I was slightly bemused to discover that this was, indeed, *all* I was to study, give or take the occasional American or Irish writer. This may have been naive. In any case, I soon turned to Scottish literature, but discovered that my reactions to this were multiple: shame at my ignorance, delight at discovering 'new' writers, anger at the omission of these writers from school timetables, and finally more bemusement, for two reasons. On the one hand, I could not identify with the idea of Scottishness which I was being asked to don like a tartan shawl. On the other, all the writers on the course were male. The absence of books by Scottish women writers seemed to suggest a lack of talent, or that they did not exist. There were very few women writers on the English literature course either. When I questioned their absence from both courses, I was told that if they had to be unearthed then they couldn't be any good anyway.

It is worth quoting in this context a writer who – until restored by recent feminist scholarship – suffered as much as any from this kind of erasure of women writers from our history. Dorothy Richardson remarked in 1924 that there is

> no illusion more wasteful than beginning all over again; nothing more misleading than the idea of being divorced from the past. It

> is, nevertheless, quite probable that a feminist insistence on exhuming hatchets is not altogether a single-hearted desire to avoid waste and error.[1]

Richardson insists on the harmful effects on women of the continuously recycled fiction which cancels their past. This fiction gives the false impression that each generation of women is a new type, leaving them adrift, cut off from their forebears. Maybe her remarks could also be read as suggesting that women might rebury a few hatchets in the skulls of their male contemporaries for the sheer hell of it.

What has any of this to do with Janice Galloway? Another case of personal axe-grinding? Another humourless feminist, nagging on about some unimportant matters from her past? These questions are not merely rhetorical, nor the issues raised only subjective; rather, they are central to a discussion which challenges generalising terms like 'Scottish writer' for its erasure of the problematics and specificities of both nationality and gender. As will emerge here, there are significant similarities between Dorothy Richardson and Janice Galloway. Although 'nurtured' in Scotland, Galloway's writing is important in the context of a wider history of women's writing, one which resists definition by malestream culture, and which has been edited out of the histories or canons of writing much as Richardson suggests. If included at all, it has been subsumed into the language of 'universalism' or 'nationalism'. By focusing on gender issues, I hope to present a reading which recognises Galloway's 'tenacious talent',[2] elucidates the importance in her writing of a feminist consciousness, and opens up the notion of Scottishness by questioning the concept of identity which it inevitably constructs and the applicability of this to women writers.

AN EXPERIMENTAL NOVEL

Janice Galloway's novel *The Trick is to Keep Breathing* (1989) has been praised for its experimental approach to form and typography. To verify this, it is necessary only to let the book fall open at any page. Divisions in the text are emphasised by two main scripts. Encountered at the very beginning, the italicised script tells the story of the death of Joy Stone's lover, Michael. The other story, recorded in standard script, is set in the present, in which the reader is given access to the inner and outer lives of the main character. Galloway also uses a number of other devices (lists, playscripts, marginalia, signs, speech bubbles) to break up the writing and fragment the text. However, the two main scripts, juxtaposed together on the opening pages, read as follows:

I can't remember last week with any clarity.

> I watch myself from the corner of the room sitting in the armchair, at the foot of the stairwell.[3]

Not being able to remember and watching herself are interrelated aspects of Joy's present tense, which is marked by an inability to function on an everyday level and a surreal sense of disconnection from her body and the objects and events in her world. It might simplify matters to call Joy's condition 'a nervous breakdown', but I want to resist this term. It too readily normalises and contains the condition and inadequately describes the strong sense of alienation which accompanies this character's disintegration of self. The problem is a loss of identity, which has been addressed by many women writers but perhaps most arrestingly by Emily Dickinson:

> After great pain, a formal feeling comes –
> The Nerves sit ceremonious, like Tombs –
> The stiff Heart questions was it He, that bore,
> And Yesterday, or Centuries before?
>
> The Feet, mechanical, go round –
> Of Ground, or Air, or Ought –
> A Wooden Way
> Regardless grown,
> A Quartz contentment, like a stone –
>
> This is the Hour of Lead –
> Remembered, if outlived,
> As Freezing persons, recollect the Snow –
> First – Chill – then Stupor – then the letting go –
> ('After Great Pain')

This poem could in many ways stand as a powerful synopsis of Galloway's novel and as a dissection of the different stages of grief and its emotional impact. As the last line of the poem indicates, it is the stage of 'the letting go' that Joy Stone needs to reach, and in fact does, by the end of the novel. Before reaching this stage, Galloway uses the process of moving through grief as a means of foregrounding certain conditions of daily life which can be the norm for women who, although not suffering from a nervous breakdown, can be said to be in grief.

This indicates that the book works at several levels. If forced into a linear plot, then the novel can be summarised as one woman's experience of death and the devastating effect which this has on her personality. However, as already stated, this narrative is fractured and the effect is that incidents and objects are examined in a detail which both threatens to overwhelm the main protagonist and becomes a thing-in-itself for the reader.

Pat Kane refers to this aspect of the novel and calls the conjunction of form and content 'a textual materialism which comes across not as arid experiment but as a necessary emotional device'[4] – and, perhaps predictably, links this aspect of her writing to 'the wounds inflicted by the damage of late-capitalist life in Scotland'. While I have some reservations concerning this last statement, it does usefully suggest the condition of *anomie* where objects and the material threaten to engulf Joy Stone in her effort to move through endless days. On the other hand, objects and their base material use also act as an anchor for her sense of displacement and provide a gloss of normality.

At the beginning of the novel, when the health visitor calls, Joy uses the ritual of tea and biscuits to convey her ability to cope – to indicate that she is a sane, 'normal' woman, capable of fulfilling the role of organised, welcoming housewife:

> I burst the wrap soundlessly and make a tasteful arrangement. I polish her teaspoon on my cardigan band. No tea pot. I make it in the cup using the same bag twice, and take it through as though I've really made it in a pot and just poured it out. (p. 20)

It could be argued that Galloway demonstrates here that the norm – being acted out by a character who is so alienated from it is possible in a 'late-capitalist' society because the housewife, and her accepted role, are indeed products of that society – part of the hidden costs of a severely estranged group whose labour and personhood are cancelled out, are disguised by their familiarity. It is in this sense that Joy's breakdown can stand as an exemplar for women and all those others who are pushed to the margins of capitalist society and can, by virtue of their position, be described as grieving.

In part, the reason for the disembodiment of Joy is that she has no place to grieve. Her lover, Michael, had a wife, although separated from him, and this leaves Joy only one possible role, that of mistress. Therefore, when Michael dies, the smooth machinery of legitimised institutions judders into action and operates to negate and label Joy Stone. Her presence must be denied. If she is not mother-wife-daughter-sister, who is she? There is no legitimate name for her in relation to Michael, which means she *must* not exist. The assigned name, *mistress*, finds its closest synonym in the word *prostitute*, and these terms confer on a woman a role limited to a degraded sexuality. They also simultaneously convey a horror of the sexually active woman.

Adorno and Horkheimer discuss this issue in the *Dialectic of Enlightenment*:

> Prostitute and wife are the complements of female self-alienation in the patriarchal world: the wife denotes pleasure in the fixed order of life and property, whereas the prostitute takes what the wife's right of possession leaves free, and as the wife's secret collaborator – subjects it again to the order of possession: she sells pleasure.[5]

Although it is clear that Joy does not 'sell pleasure', her position would certainly be easier to accommodate within this system if she did. While Michael's wife is 'given her place' at his funeral, and Joy is an embarrassing presence, both roles are potentially interchangeable. The problem is being a woman who cannot be, or refuses to be, defined:

> 1. The Rev Dogsbody had chosen this service to perform a miracle.
> 2. He'd run time backwards, cleansed, absolved and got rid of the ground-in stain.
> 3. And the stain was me.
>
> I didn't exist. The miracle had wiped me out. (p. 79)

When Joy reacts with anger to this sermon by sending the Rev. Dogsbody a letter, she is taken to task by the headmaster at the school where she teaches:

> Boss: I thought you were a realist but you haven't been very realistic about this.
>
> Employee: I don't think that what happened at that service had anything to do with realism. Quite the reverse. I think it was in terrible taste.
>
> Boss: I don't see what you mean. I don't see that at all . . . I explained to you at the time. I thought you understood. (p. 75)

The trouble with Joy is that she always does the wrong thing; that she does not fully understand what is expected of her. Paradoxically, although she is 'losing the place' in terms of her prescribed role in society, and does not in a sense exist, she does have enough of a sense of self to be a thorn in the flabby flesh of those authorities with whom she comes into contact.

At various points in the novel, Galloway reproduces dialogues which read like short scenes from a play script. These often occur with men who have, or think they have, power over Joy, and range from interviews with her doctor or psychiatrist to conversations with her ex-boyfriend or betting-shop boss, Tony. The game they want Joy to play is that of the obedient, pliant other who will be the good patient, the distant ex-lover or the gratefully seduced. Part of Joy's 'illness' is her unpredictability. She cannot *behave* any more, and the powers of constraint which used to operate through an internalised model of the 'good girl' no longer function successfully. Joy reflects on how far she has deviated from this model:

> I used to be so *good* all the time.
> [where good = productive/hardworking/wouldn't say boo]
> . . .
> [where good = value for money]
> . . .
> [where good = neat, acting in a credit-worthy manner]
> If I was a good [i.e. patient, thoughtful, uncomplaining] girl long enough I would reap the reward. (pp. 81–2)

Joy finds out that there is no reward, and the immutable material fact of Michael's death becomes the catalyst which leads to her breaking down the good girl that she had become and beginning to imagine new possibilities for herself. Hélène Cixous discusses this kind of process in 'The Laugh of the Medusa' in relation to women and the inner censoring of their desires, using herself as an example:

> And I, too, said nothing, showed nothing; I didn't open my mouth, I didn't repaint my half of the world. I was ashamed. I was afraid and I swallowed my shame and my fear. I said to myself: you are mad! . . . Who, feeling a funny desire stirring inside her (to sing, to write, to dare to speak, in short to bring out something new), hasn't thought she was sick? Well, her shameful sickness is that she resists death, that she makes trouble.[6]

Joy finally 'resists death' by imaging herself as a swimmer, 'not a natural swimmer' but confident that she can learn – 'the trick is to keep breathing' (p. 235). The image of a swimmer is a particularly significant one since Joy's mother died after attempting to drown herself, while Michael died, accidentally, by drowning. It is only at the point when Joy is able to see herself as a swimmer that she can forgive herself, that she can find her own voice. The voice at the end of the novel is also the self-reflexive voice of the author, of the woman writer who has, to recall Cixous, opened her mouth, who has taken hold of the pen and refused to accept that the pen is organically the prerogative of the male.

In this respect, Galloway can be read as a link in the chain of women writers who have forged their female protagonists from the unpromising material of a recognisably male stereotype. Thus Charlotte Brontë's Lucy Snowe, in *Villette*; Dorothy Richardson's Miriam Henderson, in

Pilgrimage; or Catherine Carswell's Ellen Carstairs, in *The Camomile*, are all close relatives of Joy Stone, in that they risk cliché in their construction, yet are transmuted into figures who break the mould of masculinist discourse. All of the aforementioned characters start out as teachers: Snowe and Henderson are governesses, while Carstairs and Stone are music and drama teachers respectively. Each author, to a greater or lesser extent, uses this conventional figure and prises open the gap between the defined role and the woman who inhabits it. The tension within each character, and their fascination, lies in the extent to which what Cixous calls 'the funny desire stirring inside' is allowed to overflow and disrupt the confines of their already-defined 'femininity' ('The Laugh of the Medusa', p. 317). This desire is not primarily sexual, although it is sexually-charged; it is rather the desire, as Cixous puts it, 'to bring out something new', to recreate, whether a work of art or themselves. The authors and their characters, their creations, can be said to intersect in that both are, in a certain sense, engaged in writing texts of '*jouissance*', which is to be understood in the Barthesian sense of paradox – against the doxa of received views of women and of texts which have inscribed these views. Barthes's concept of *jouissance* incorporates the idea of a 'radically violent pleasure which shatters, dissipates, loses'.[7] This concept provides an enabling framework within which to read Galloway and the other novelists mentioned, as it does not underestimate the pleasure and the pain involved in rewriting and reconceptualising crystallised identities.

BLOOD: 'HIDEOUS PROCESSES'

I have subtitled Galloway's collection of short stories 'hideous processes' because I wish to continue the association with Dorothy Richardson and because it ironically relates to a view of women which has been with us for some time and which is targeted in some of Galloway's stories. The phrase is quoted from *Pilgrimage*, and occurs at a moment of crisis for Miriam Henderson. Under the word 'Woman', in the index of a set of encyclopaedias, Miriam finds the definition:

> *inferior*; mentally, morally, intellectually, and physically . . . her development arrested in the interest of her special functions.[8]

Miriam realises, with rage, that she is being defined here, that she is one of the 'women [who] stopped being people and went off into hideous processes'. What Richardson presents is a version of woman, written by eminent Victorian men.

A modern version of this 'old story' can be read in 'Blood', the title story in Galloway's collection. The words, written not in an index under 'Woman' but on a cubicle door of the girls' toilets are:

> GIRLS ARE A BUNCH OF CUNTS.[9]

Although starker than Richardson's phrase, both sets of words lock into a single ideology which continues to delimit women in terms of their biological difference from men, and to use this difference as a form of insult. Richardson's processes – menstruation and the menopause – are seen as 'hideous' from a male point of view in her novel, which is exactly the point about Galloway's 'BUNCH OF CUNTS' in her short story. The intersection of both phrases exists in the simple fact that cunts bleed. The inverse of this, bleeding cunts, foregrounds the hostility and fear which transforms a statement of fact into one of abuse. Janice Galloway has remarked that women need to reclaim language and, as an example of this, that some women use the word 'cunt' as an affectionate term for the labia. While feminists may disagree about the possibilities of reclaiming language and this much-maligned word, it is nevertheless clear that a reclamation is at work in 'Blood'.

The story opens in a dentist's surgery, where an unnamed schoolgirl has a tooth removed. The blood which results is described in some detail:

> Blood made a pool under her tongue, lapping at the back of her throat and she had to keep the head back instead. Her lips were too numb to trust: it would have run down the front of her blazer. (p. 2)

Presented ironically and humorously, the dentist is typified by the song he sings, a kitsch country-and-western number, 'Ruby'. The title of this song and its lyrics have a chain of associations in the story: the colour of blood/woman/uncontrollable sexuality/lips (both sets)/menstruation – in other words 'hideous processes', which arouse fear.

The dentist tells his female assistant to give the schoolgirl a white pad to stop the blood spilling from her mouth. He provides sanitary towels instead of cotton wool. This crass offering is pivotal to the coda at work in the story. The association of blood and sanitary towel comes together after the girl has passed the aforementioned slogan on the toilet door and discovered that she is menstruating. In an effort to escape from her embarrassing messiness – as defined by the dentist and the slogan – the girl goes to the music room: 'It would be good to get out of here, get to something fresh and clean, Mozart and the white room upstairs' (p. 6). The music room proves to be only a temporary haven. Although practising Mozart on the piano becomes a way to forget her female viscosity – her bleeding which spills over and is a constant reminder of her female status – this does not last. A male student, who teaches cello, interrupts her playing. This student, previously described as 'being afraid of girls' (p. 7), confuses the Mozart with Haydn, the girl opens her mouth to correct him and the blood runs free, 'spilling over the white keys and dripping onto the clean tile floor' (p. 8). The boy, who has been moved by the music to forget himself and his fear, flees at the sight of the blood. Blood then becomes a powerful symbol in this story for those aspects of the female which cannot be contained and which cause fear, whether evinced as a patronising jocularity or a more marked revulsion, but most importantly force the female into a guilty paradox, on the one hand complicit with the ideology which equates woman with guilt, on the other resistant, yet unable to escape from its tentacles.

Two other stories, 'Frostbite' and 'Fearless', deal with more overt forms of masculine fear of women. The eponymous character in the latter, and the drunk in the former, direct their aggression, held against specific women, randomly at women in general. Both the abuse and the fear which this arouses in women are foregrounded in each story and are clarified by Galloway at the end of 'Fearless':

> The chink and drag from the close-mouth in the dark, coming across open, derelict spaces at night, blustering at bus stops where I have to wait alone. (p. 115)

The 'I' in those lines is again unnamed, but usefully open so that any woman can interpolate herself into the subject position and identify with it.

There are many more aspects of this collection which deserve to be singled out, but I will end by mentioning 'David'. This story takes the most positive aspects of female sexuality and unites them with those of the male. It is a celebration of love and lust, both touching and erotic, which simultaneously challenges and breaks several taboos – the still-prevalent taboo surrounding older women in relationships with younger men; of the female schoolteacher and male pupil. We have met David before. Described here as 'sullen behind the blonde fringe needing cut', with 'unnatural blue' eyes (p. 36), he also appears in Galloway's novel, in which he is introduced as an ex-pupil:

> David was someone in Sam's class. I thought he was moody and unpredictable. Our paths crossed at school though I never taught him. (*The Trick*, p. 131)

This account of David is interchangeable with the description of him in the short story.

'David' builds up to a climax in which teacher and pupil express an almost tangible attraction. Galloway pares away extraneous words to create a rhythm and flow which carries readers into the core of the story. This is particularly difficult when writing about the sexual act, since the wrong choice of words can lead to bathos or absurdity and a shattering of the erotic moment. Galloway glances off the mechanics of sex, and instead suggests the intensity of the participants' response by foregrounding the texture and overwhelming presence of their bodies:

> Our teeth touched, mouths open. I felt him swallow, the skin on my lip stretch till it split, a sudden give from the tightness and I was sliding my hands, tugging on the thin shirt: ridges of warm rib beneath my fingers rubbing my palms on the warm sides of his jeans, the length of seam. (*Blood*, p. 38)

From a feminist perspective, this writing can be seen as a successful attempt to reclaim the language of sexuality from an arid, sterile, male-driven perspective which has often objectified and reduced both characters and readers. In the words of Hélène Cixous:

> It is impossible to define a feminine practice of writing, and this is an impossibility that will remain, for this practice can never be theorized, enclosed, coded – which doesn't mean that it doesn't exist. But it will always surpass the discourse that regulates the phallocentric system . . . It will be conceived of only by subjects who are breakers of automatisms, by peripheral figures that no authority can ever subjugate. ('The Laugh of the Medusa', p. 323)

In my introduction, I suggested that the term 'Scottish writer' constructs an identity which is not applicable to women writers who are Scottish. In this discussion, I have attempted to link Galloway's writing with other women writers and feminist issues because it seems to me that there is a very real danger of once again burying the past and present of women's specific concerns underneath the universal heading of 'Scottish writer'. This is not to deny that Galloway's writing produces a recognisably Scottish cultural milieu and uses the language and rhythms of speech specific to the West of Scotland. However, I have been engaged in problematising the idea, which still appears to be current in critical writing and elsewhere, that women writers can be easily assimilated and appropriated as 'Scottish writers' when the identity constructed by critics has relied on a masculinist perspective, based on the works of largely male writers. This is especially important when Galloway herself analyses and questions the often negative effects of Scottish male culture on the female. From this point of view, it seems more important to resist male constructions of national characteristics which pose as gender-neutral, at least until they have shown themselves capable of listening to the voices of women, writers or otherwise, who have opened their mouths against the doxa of what it is to be Scottish, or a Scottish writer.

NOTES

1. Dorothy Richardson, 'Women and the Future: a Trembling of the Veil before the Eternal Mystery of "La Giaconda"', *Vanity Fair*, April 1924, p. 39.
2. John Linklater, 'Novelist in the Shop Window', *Glasgow Herald*, 19 May 1990, p. 27.
3. Janice Galloway, *The Trick is to Keep Breathing* (Edinburgh: Polygon, 1989), p. 7. Subsequent references are to this edition.
4. Pat Kane, 'Authors who come up with the Goods', *The Scotsman*, 28 April 1990, p. 4.
5. Theodore Adorno and Max Horkheimer, *Dialectic of Enlightenment* (London: Verso, 1979), p. 79.
6. Hélène Cixous, 'The Laugh of the Medusa' in Dennis Walder, ed., *Literature in the Modern World* (Oxford: OUP, 1990), p. 317. Subsequent references are to this edition.
7. Roland Barthes, *Image Music Text*, trans. Stephen Heath (London: Fontana, 1984), p. 9.
8. Dorothy Richardson, *The Tunnel* (1919); reprinted in *Pilgrimage* (London: Virago, 1979), II, p. 220.
9. Janice Galloway, *Blood* (London: Secker and Warburg, 1991), p. 5. Subsequent references are to this edition.

Part III

NEW READINGS

Eleven

Divergent Scottishness: William Boyd, Allan Massie, Ronald Frame

Douglas Dunn

As is well known, Scotland is susceptible to self-inflicted disfigurement. In fiction (as in much else), the primary source of distortion and simplification stems from a contest between nationalist impulses, often vernacular, and Unionist motives. Inevitable as this tension is, in starkest outline it can be said to originate in how the name 'Scotland' has ceased to accord with a nation-state in political culture, except in the amorphousness of active controversy and inert sentiment. Much, if not all, fiction and poetry, however, suggests that a coincidence between literature and nationality is far more assured, even if still prone to dispute.

Against a contemporary background in which fiction will often be read politically, novels and stories which appear to devalue their nationality will tend to seem mischievous, ungainly, irresponsible or willing to avoid the historical moment. It can be slippery ground for a critic. Nor should it be gainsaid that its tackiness is a matter of social class and education. Easy movement between social classes might be a Scottish Myth (or it might not), but in fiction at least it certainly seems less nonchalant and disinterested than in Scott's time. Demotic Scots and English dialogue, together with English prose narrative, assert a phenomenon very close to a complete social representation in Scott's novels. Vernacular Scots dialogue and English literary prose on the same page suggest two fairly obvious and different levels of self-awareness of a kind with which contemporary novelists are either impatient or incapable. For it to exist, a writer has to be in a position to acquire a genuine familiarity with spoken Scots idioms as well as an appropriate prose capacity in the common language. Glancing mimicry in either language is insufficient for a novelist to whom a Scottish social vision is important. In recent years, James Kelman has complicated the diagnosis by breaking down the traditional split between English narrative and dialectal speech, its cadences, intonations and syntactical habits. He has done this by insisting on the expressive unit of his characters with their author's obligations to them and their locale. Kelman's achievement can be admired, but it is hard to see how it can be exemplary for Scottish fiction as a whole. Even if it is admitted to be a perennial dimension of Scottish writing that its innovative, self-renewing desires and tussles often take the form of vernacular upsurges, it can be a source of anxiety that their consequence can be to exclude other writers (and readers) from the contemporary picture. There is an atmosphere of 'political correctness' which encourages social narrowing in favour of a working-class, left-wing, vernacular authorship. More than a hint of perverse cultural censorship can be detected in the critical favouritism of the day; and as it is one which denies the full identity of the country, it can be considered serious. Here too, though, overstated leftist, radical, conservative and nationalist tactics can be understood. They are resistant and self-protective as well as lashing out at political opponents. Instinctively or by design, they counter further inroads on local or Scottish phenomena of one kind or another, while, in the case of recent Glasgow fiction, an identity and a dignity have largely been created as if for the first time.

What has to be avoided is gruff small-mindedness, with its grimly regressive fury. Whether emanating from the Left or the Right – and we will see this – all that is achieved is an evasion of the actual demography of the country. Obstinately holding to a primarily vernacular definition of Scottish writing, for example, fails to include fiction (and poetry) whose momentum is loyal to other priorities, some of them imaginative or expansive. Muriel Spark's appraisal of herself and others as of 'Scottish formation' seems, for many, too humane and broad. A critical mentality exists which applauds R. L. Stevenson for 'Thrawn Janet', but which ignores Henry James's estimate of Stevenson as the finest English prose stylist of his time. All that is served by such a belittling notion of the art of fiction is the disfigurement which pride can encourage.

> Our school was in Scotland, was in almost every respect a Scottish public school, and yet a strong Scottish accent was a real stigma. Indeed, any regional accent was parodied mercilessly. When people spoke with a strong Scottish accent we would make harsh retching sounds in the base of our throats or emit loose-jawed idiot burblings . . . To us the locals were 'yobs', 'oiks', 'plebs', 'proles', 'peasants', and 'yokels'. It now seems to me astonishing to recall

the patrician venom we would express, like aristocrats faced with imminent revolution – a curious mixture of contempt, fear, guilt and jealousy. They lived, after all, in the real world beyond the school grounds, and however superior we congratulated ourselves on being, there was no escaping the fact that they were freer than we were – and that grated. I am sure that we in our turn were looked on as revolting, arrogant, nasty snobs. By no means a harsh judgement.[1]

An education like William Boyd's – Gordonstoun, then the universities of Nice, Glasgow and Oxford – would seem to set him apart decisively from James Kelman, Alasdair Gray and William McIlvanney. Or does it? As well as socially mixed, nationality can be a scattered phenomenon. Born in Accra in 1952, Boyd's 'Scottish formation' is of the kind that could be called diasporic. None of his novels, however, is set in Scotland in such a way as to make it 'about' a Scottish theme, although *The New Confessions* (1987) could be an exception. More than one Scottish reader will have asked: '*Is* Boyd a Scottish writer?' Keeping racial prissiness to one side, there is sense to the question; and the answer could be: 'Yes; but being a Scottish writer doesn't mean the same for him as it does for Kelman, Gray or McIlvanney'. It is a fine distinction, however, and far from a disqualification. In another sense, the distinction is starker. Boyd's fiction depends on concerns other than his presence in Scotland or a relationship to recent political crises and their literary significance. So, for that matter, does Muriel Spark's. Mrs Spark lives in Italy, which seems to be a 'better' address for a Scottish writer than London. She is often referred to as the finest living Scottish novelist, which seems to imply either that *The Prime of Miss Jean Brodie* (1961) outweighs almost everything else she has written, or that a cosmopolitan fictitiousness is acceptable – and that last admission is not always predictable in Scottish taste.

Those 'loose-jawed idiot burblings' and 'harsh retching sounds' are worrying in Boyd's candidly self-critical description of his Gordonstoun years. There is something obsessive about them, too. In *An Ice Cream War* (1982), Felix, the central character, finds himself, in the middle of the 1914–18 war in East Africa, attached to a Scottish sergeant, Gilzean.

'Aye, sir. I'm Sergeant Gilzean.'

He then said something Felix didn't understand.

'I beg your pardon?' Felix said.

'I said "Fegs it's a bauch day", sir, Gilzean repeated patiently, as if this was an activity he was accustomed to. 'I'll just make siccar they beanswaup porters look swippert with your gear.'

'Oh. Yes. Fine.'[2]

Such an encounter is angling its comedy at – shall we say – a non-Scottish readership, or that section of Scottish readers which finds dialect a joke and whose own way of speaking is already differentiated from it. Is it funny? Is it reprehensible? Is it Scottish? It could be possible to opt for all three, while trimming the third. English novelists, however, have hardly shirked from poking fun at other English men and women of all social classes. It might suggest too nervous a sensitivity on the part of Scottish readers to find Boyd's humour irritatingly condescending. What seems likely is that his heart is in the right place but that he is let down by sheer inexperience. There seems to be a desire to get a Scottish character, or *something* Scottish, in there. A little later, Felix and Gilzean find themselves disposing of dead bodies by pushing them into a river.

> 'They're for the kelpies,' Gilzean said. He seemed unusually depressed, Felix thought, far more so than normal.
>
> 'What a way to go,' Felix said, wondering if he should ask what kelpies were. Fish? Crocodiles? (*ICW*, 301)

Boyd knows what a kelpie is. Not to tell the reader is an act of Scottish possessiveness, or anglified Scottish archness. It has the status of an unexplained joke within the novel's 'British' register. 'He only understood one word in three,' the narrator says of Felix's listening to Gilzean, 'but this time he thought he knew how the little man felt.' Simultaneously a gesture of sympathy and of condescension, it is a statement which expresses Boyd's limitations as a Scottish novelist. On the relatively few occasions when Scottish dialogue is necessary to him, he can't help himself – he caricatures it.

Boyd's cosmopolitan reach is one largely of a comic restlessness, round pegs in square holes, unlikely people in unlikely places. Imperial echoes are sounded in *An Ice-Cream War*; its story recalls *Four Feathers*, even if Boyd makes little of what seems an opportunity for a more penetrating or thoughtful discursion on British and German colonialism than his comic tendencies permit. As with Waugh, Linklater or Kingsley Amis, even a critical comic vision is one which Boyd finds it difficult to use without curbing seriousness in favour of the entertainments of misadventures and consecutive bungling, especially to the fore in *Stars and Bars* (1984). A penchant for the rendering of near-catastrophic amusement looks like a peculiarly English state of affairs. It is the tradition in which Boyd habitually works, although, in Smollett and Linklater, there are sound Scottish precedents.

Morgan Leafy, in *A Good Man in Africa* (1981), for example, shares several propensities with Amis's Jim Dixon. One of them is an ability to find himself in embarrassing situations. Boyd locates Leafy's social class precisely:

> Checking up [Dalmire's] A-level and degree results in his personal file, Morgan had been amazed to discover how much worse Dalmire had done than he. And yet, and yet *he* had gone to Oxford, while Morgan went to some concrete and plate-glass building site in the Midlands. He *already* owned a house – in Brighton, legacy of some distant aunt – while Morgan's UK base was his mother's cramped semi-detached. And yet Dalmire had been posted abroad as soon as his training was over while Morgan had sweated three years in an overheated office off Kingsway. Dalmire's parents lived in Gloucestershire, his father was a Lieutenant-Colonel. Morgan's lived in Feltham, his father had been a catering manager at Heathrow . . .[3]

Even in the minor ranks of post-Imperial British diplomacy, posted to the provincial capital of Kinjanja, the accident-prone Leafy is riotously out of place. A dose of clap leads to some easily-anticipated comedy of the Lucky Jim variety.

> 'Right,' he said briskly. 'Let's have a look.'
>
> 'You mean?' Morgan cleared his throat. 'Off?'
>
> 'Aye. Breeks down. The lot.'
>
> Morgan thought there was a good chance he might faint. With trembling fingers he undid his trousers and let them drop to his ankles. Too late he remembered his baggy, perished underpants. He felt his face blaze with miserable embarrassment as he unfastened the safety pin holding up his useless Y-fronts. (*GMA*, 149)

The doctor, Murray, is of course a Scot. For the most part, he is presented through Leafy's ratty, fidgety point of view: 'Actually I can't stand the man. Sanctimonious, Calvinistic so-and-so . . . hectoring, bullying – sort of moral storm-trooper'. There is even Murray's 'dry Scottish accent'. Leafy wonders, too, if in these 'stern features' he discerns 'the moral rectitude of a latter-day John Knox'. No reader will be taken aback either when Murray is seen declaring his principled stand over Adekunle's corrupt land-dealing, and giving the bum's rush to Leafy's offer of a substantial bribe on the African politician's behalf. Murray is the 'good man' of the title (with, perhaps, some ambivalent tilting in the direction of the harried Morgan Leafy). His competence and conscientiousness throw into relief the high English botchery of Her Britannic Majesty's representatives in Nkongsamba and the worldly calculations of the local political set. Boyd, however, concentrates most on Leafy. As a result, the story of an expatriate Scottish doctor – the comic potential of which was never very promising – becomes a sideline while remaining essential and perhaps closer to the book than Boyd was prepared to allow in the actual writing of it. Predominantly *English* comic expectations could have got in the way of a more complete realisation of Murray as a character. It is as if Boyd *likes* a Scottish element to be present in his books, but feels it aesthetically and perhaps commercially hazardous to give it its head.

The closest he comes to taking that risk is *The New Confessions* (1987). Early pages in the book set up some basic myth-making. John James Todd, the narrator whose life is the novel's subject, is born in Edinburgh in 1899. His mother, the daughter of an Argyllshire laird, dies at his birth, and Todd grows up torn between dislike and suspicion of his father, a professor of clinical anatomy. He has a fat, disagreeable elder brother, later to become wealthy. Oonagh, the family's housekeeper-nanny, hails from Lewis. Edwardian Edinburgh is convincingly evoked, as is life in an eccentric Borders school, Minto Academy, for adepts of maths and music, and each plays its contributory part in Boyd's portrayal of Todd's childhood and adolescence. In turn, *their* function is to justify the hero's subsequent wandering and self-dependence. When he runs away from school, supposing himself in love with his mother's recently-bereaved sister, he realises 'the first indication of a dangerous tendency in my character: the long view, the long term, rarely attracts me. It is the here-and-now I find alluring', a pattern which recurs to provide 'swift satisfaction followed by disastrous remorse'. Prudence, caution, the sensible weighing-up of possible outcomes, are habits of mind associated with stay-at-homes; and it is noticeable how much of Boyd's fiction is drawn to anywhere except here. That capricious visit to Todd's Aunt Faye dramatises a preliminary sexual embarrassment; it also disabuses Todd of his suspicion that his real father is an Englishman. The curve of the first two chapters is one in which a young man is obliged to recognise his father and nationality. 'I couldn't be sure of anything and so chose to rely entirely on myself', Todd writes in the 1972 of the book's present tense, by which time he is on the beach at the Villa Luxe, by the Mediterranean, at a remove from his life's events, rather like Hope Clearwater in *Brazzaville Beach* (1990). 'Discontinuity', says Todd, 'sudden random change', is 'the real currency of our lives', a theme prominent in *An Ice-Cream War*, and exploited comically in *A Good Man in Africa* and *Stars and Bars*. In both *The New Confessions* and *Brazzaville Beach*, uncertainty, and the unpredictable, are supported by business about mathematics. What can happen in life with 'strict brutal force' is acknowledged in the theorising intellect as capable of grace and elegance.

Discontinuity, sudden change, a predilection for short views and constant movement, figure strongly in John James Todd's life and mind. Even well into his seventies, his Scottish accent long gone, and rootless, Todd still hangs on to his nationality. At least, he corrects those who think he is English. Boyd, however, associates Todd's life with the expression of identity, and its formative factors, more than with nationality as such. Like Fergus Lamont in Robin Jenkins's novel, it is a relationship with an absent mother which complicates psychology, more than dislike of the father. Whether the idea of 'mother equals Scotland' is an interpretation that *The New Confessions* can bear is another matter. In his best books, Jenkins is a more overtly Scottish novelist, if also a various and well-travelled one. Compared to Jenkins, Boyd seems coincidentally Scots, half-hidden, nationality emerging as a fact to try and escape, often in situations associated with menace, fear and violence.

Todd, for example, a bomb-thrower in a Public Schools Battalion of the South Oxfordshire Light Infantry, finds his company attached to a Bantam outfit of the fictitious Grampian Highlanders. It is an opportunity to indulge in passages of caricature not far from the German description of small Scottish soldiers as Poison Dwarfs. One of the worst of them rejoices in the anyone-for-tennis name of Tangueray – a fisherman from Stonehaven. 'He insisted I was English and I was tired of remonstrating. I became a symbol of the dark genetic conspiracy that had contrived to render him small.' Thieves, killers, stunted wee brutes, they are said to speak like this: ' "Gonnae get youse, cunt, see'f ah doant, right inna fuckin spine. Palaryse yü. Die in paaaaayne!" That sort of thing.' That sort of thing probably has its origins in an observed or actual disagreeable encounter, and it would whitewash Scottish or any other nationality to claim that nasty little people do not exist and make odious threats to those perceived as posh, tall, English, or in other ways alleged to be objectionable. Anxious repetition of the same or very similar motifs adds up to a worrying picture of Boyd (or his characters) fearful or perplexed before the grimmer aspects of nationality and its deprivations.

How people speak, however, ought not to be as uniformly dire, odious and caricatured as Boyd renders it. But the fascination strikes deep. Todd, for example, goes to the assistance of an Ulsterman sinking in the mud of a shell crater.

> 'You English? I can't see very well.' He has a strong Ulster accent.
>
> 'I'm Scottish, actually . . . but it doesn't matter.'
>
> 'Get me out of here, pal, will you? I'm going down.'
>
> *Doyn* he pronounces it.[4]

It hardly seems a suitable moment for the observation of accent or nationality. (Massie and Frame, too, refer regularly to how people speak when their accents depart from a supposed norm.) Into the horrors of trench warfare and no-man's-land, Boyd introduces a grotesque social comedy which, while effective in its own terms, suggests also that at such moments his comic strengths serve to twist the expectations of decorum and realism. He enjoys hectic tempos, broad comic strokes, catastrophes and embarrassments.

Fictional cartooning is often the result, as in the scene where Todd arranges to spend the night with a whore from Leith as part of his divorce strategems. The night is spent in The Harry Lauder Temperance Hotel, with Senga, who complains about a walk on the beach, saying: 'I cannae walk inna sond, wi' these shuze'. During the Second World War, Todd, by now a newsreel journalist, is ambushed by Scottish paratroopers in the south of France and seriously wounded. 'Sorry, Yank. We thought youse was Gerries inna fuckin Merc. Onyboady hurt?'

As a representative of Boyd's Scotsmen, John James Todd travels far, directs films, becomes implicated in the Hollywood trials, and carries his portable, life-sifting introspection, his constant autobiographical patterning, and it is not for nothing that he is obsessed with his part-namesake Jean-Jacques Rousseau. He is pursued by his own life, by its similarities with Rousseau's, and it is a life in which a homecoming can solve nothing.

Deracination and spiritual homelessness, as well as the opinions and perspectives of a minority within a broadly-defined society, suggest themselves as authentic subjects for a certain kind of Scottish writer. Boyd's diasporic background and subsequent education might be as valid as any other kind of Scottish experience. It is just this kind of chasing after a national 'authenticity', however, which is so distasteful, especially at a time when an inclusive notion of Scottishness would serve better the cultural and political dilemmas of the country than those wilful narrowings of the social focus on actual accents in writing, and social reflection, which are encouraged by the political climate. While this belief in the desirability of more inclusive definitions might seem self-defeatingly generous, it is not one that has been devised for the purpose of evading a critical grasp on what these writers actually say about Scotland, or do not say, or what seem to be the underlying attitudes to their points of view. Part of the trouble was created by the rise of MacDiarmid's Scottish Renaissance movement. From the 1920s on, an invaluable and, at times, inspirational reminder of Scottishness has pervaded every aspect of cultural life. MacDiarmid's biases, however, introduced complications from which the novel in particular has suffered ever since. One consequence of MacDiarmid's impact has been that Scott, Stevenson, Barrie, Buchan and Linklater have been endowed with a dismissed prestige for reasons which owe little to aesthetic considerations and rather a lot to a notion of what constitutes a 'sound' Scottish writer. Never mind critical and popular *success* outside Scotland, *comprehension* in the English-speaking world seems to set up the sort of antipathy of which any critic ought to be wary when dealing with contemporary works which confound the standards by which indigenousness is measured. Special pleading is not the point here. What is being indicated is a state of affairs which, if the general critical climate is anything to go by, has created the hunch that it is impossible to appreciate novels by James Kelman *and* William Boyd, or Alasdair Gray *and* Allan Massie, or William McIlvanney *and* Ronald Frame. Nor is it anything like so simple as a contest of the experimental and imaginative with straightforward, old-fashioned narrative. What has been set up is a limiting idea and practice which constitutes an orthodoxy. To be absolutely plain and clear, Boyd, Massie and Frame are not working-class in origin or in political affiliation. It is in danger of becoming more than an antiquated but a disabling handicap in Scottish fiction, and literature as a whole, that its writers, critics and readership could fall for a vision of society which cannot exist without an act of cultural or actual exclusion. What is to be done with Scottish writers who refuse to subscribe to the average pieties of socialism, dialect, poverty, Glasgow, Edinburgh, small-town life, rural predicaments or nationalism? No more pertinent question of Scottish writing could be asked. A question more to the point of Scottish life in general could not be asked, if, that is, there is a width of mind willing to *include* rather than dismiss the nature of the country and those who live here, or, in the case of William Boyd, those who do not.

Scottish fiction represents these questions more vividly than it might have been given credit for. Allan Massie is well known through his writing as a political columnist for *The Sunday Times* and elsewhere as being on the right wing of the Scottish political spectrum. As far as the native literary intelligentsia goes, Massie is maverick and at odds with the political tendency of the country. In a climate which welcomes (deservedly) novels and stories by Gray, Kelman and McIlvanney, Massie's subjects and convictions can look heretical, an impression he shares with Boyd and Ronald Frame. However, they have arrived at this unstable prestige by different routes.

It is partly a matter of style, and of literary allegiances and affinities. Scottishness is secondary to Boyd, whose comic mode seems almost directly connected to predecessors like Waugh and Amis. Nationality is more important to Massie. His narrators are often allowed to snipe at local topics with a snappy abandon which issues from both diminished identity and an awareness of being less than significant. Matthew Arnold's line 'This strange disease of modern life' crops up in *The Last Peacock* (1980) and *One Night in Winter* (1984), Massie's most explicitly Scottish novels, with the exception of *The Hanging Tree* (1990) – 'a romance of the fifteenth century' at the centre of which, however, is the idea of 'anglicisation' as a means to the improvement of life. Unionist despair haunts the two earlier novels – 'the fatigue of the north and of the flesh' – as well as a rattled displacement of self and a hankering after an allegedly uncomplicated, 'premodern' yesteryear. 'In England friends mock my Scots accent. Here I'm shoved into the gutter as a bloody Englishman', Dallas says in *One Night in Winter* to the working-class Alick, who has been misled by an accent. 'Dinosaurs and dodos,' Colin says in *The Last Peacock*,

> we'd be that anywhere, but it's even worse when we have a stake in a piddling place like this. Oh yes, I was brought up to despise nationality, except the British cardboard J. Arthur Rank variety . . .[5]

Later in the same book, there is this exchange:

> 'Why do you always feel guilty in Scotland?'
> 'Why do you ask? Don't you?'
> 'I don't often think about Scotland.'
> 'But you are Scots?'
> 'Oh yes.'
> 'Doesn't that answer your question?'
> 'Does it?'
> 'I don't know. I can't stand almost anything that manifests itself as Scots. Tartan and this beer, and Billy Connolly and Morningside and hard men and football supporters . . .'
> 'Well, who can . . . I mean that's not the whole of Scotland . . .'
> 'No, but . . . it's terrible to feel ashamed of your family.'
>
> (*TLP*, 158–9)

It can read as if Massie's characters are tired of the purposes to which their author is putting them. Exhaustion, however, is what Massie evokes in these novels, even if it can take the forms of mania, rancid energy, momentary fits of brilliance, alcohol, and the lucidity of self-examination seen against a psychological background of belonging to a country but being seriously out of step with its contemporary disposition. 'What about people like me?' Dallas asks himself in *One Night in Winter* after a conversation with the nationalist Gavin Gregory:

> What of the remnants of the landed gentry? A ridiculous question; just as well he hadn't asked it, even of a clown like wee Gavin. He had no land; the word gentleman was a social joke. And yet, and yet, for Dallas and a few others, it was still there. He felt himself to be different. He didn't, however he might pretend to Cambridge chums, belong to the aristocracy; yet even that wasn't quite absurd. His position wasn't so dissimilar. Noblesse, however petite, did oblige. Loyalties were confused. He was certainly Scottish. Apart from a French great-grandmother he had no ancestor who was anything else. The family didn't even have much tradition of Empire service to confuse matters by substituting a primary loyalty to the idea of Britain. Did it all come down to education and class awareness? For the fact was that, while he would have insisted to anyone that Scotland was an entity, yes a nation, he wasn't terribly impressed by the concept of nationality; and he couldn't take the idea of a Scottish state seriously. That was an old song, long ended, sold down the river.[6]

As far as recent fiction in Scotland is concerned, Massie's initiating perspective is exceptional, perhaps even unique, and, in its own terms, astute. He explores a minority whose power and prominence have waned to such an extent that its surviving representatives can see themselves as 'white settlers' despite sharing the same nationality as the 'natives'. While the pathos of this exposed class is unmistakable, its dilemma is clinically and unsentimentally anatomised. It is a class accused of being 'quislings' by the nationalist minister of the Kirk, Gregory. Its older members recommend the younger, such as Dallas, to get out while the door is still open. Ebenezer advises Dallas:

> Of course a political framework would retain a few – but how many? Ireland is governed by grocers. The men of energy on whom the vitality of a society depends would still take wing; the world is for the big battalions. Small countries cannot withstand it, especially when they are not protected by the barrier of a different language. Their geographical fate determines their nature. You won't stay in Scotland, Dallas. For all the protestations of clowns like Mr Gregory and men of exuberant but ill-directed will like Fraser, Scotland will grow ever less Scottish and ever less stimulating; we live in a withered culture. Sounds of energy are the energy of the death-rattle. The Union may not have been the end of an auld sang, but it led us into the last verse. (*ONW*, 112)

Eloquent, perhaps also contrived, Ebenezer's dispiriting analysis stands as an extreme point of view stemming from despondency as well as resentment. Massie's historical acumen is adequate to the task of showing a section of society pushed to the side of time by change. Crumbling mansions, overgrown paths, relentlessly encroaching rhododendrons, exhausted power, the separating silk threads of a bell-pull – in these two novels, Massie describes the fragility of status, the impermanence of privilege and supremacy. Both books are soured elegies for something larger than a way of life which has turned decrepit.

Historical zest breaks down in the depiction of characters against whom Massie's gentry defines its ethos and discovers unedifying contemporaneity. Fraser Donnelly, for example, a California-influenced nationalist, liberationist, sexual entrepreneur and businessman, is simply overdrawn; his broad, up-tempo speech, his coarseness, his disgustingness, are all part of a savage satire of the new. Although no-one need doubt that in an open cultural and political scene those with a capacity for using people will do so, this particular character seems loaded with Massie's negative opinion. Donnelly seems to possess *all* the energetic Scottish vices with nothing to redeem them other than a charmless, offensive wit of a sort with which the Scottish mentality is all-too-infatuated. As a result, Donnelly looms as a massive caricature, calculated to load too much in favour of Dallas and the past which he represents. It could be salutary to remember that it was probably the awful likes of Donnelly (but without the Irish name) who kicked off the wealth and power that set up the withered dynasties that have ended in the likes of Dallas. Mansie Niven, too, a Tory MP who appears in both novels, is a caricature – but this might be forgivable. What, after all, is Sir Nicholas Fairbairn?

At times, Massie can seem a historian working in fiction. It is a quality he shares with another Tory novelist, John Buchan. *Augustus* (1986) and *Tiberius* (1990) immerse themselves in studies of absolute power, its burdens and responsibilities, the anguish of the private life in a public world, and the vulnerability of power to sexual scandal. Some of Massie's best prose will be found there. His writing assumes its natural poise when separated from the necessity to reproduce Scots dialogue, which, especially in *One Night in Winter*, is superficially 'of the ear' rather than a speech intuitively understood by him, or which he can use in a way that avoids condescension.

Virtuous writing is more apparent in *The Death of Men* (1981), *A Question of Loyalties* (1989) and, spasmodically, *The Sins of the Father*

(1991). The first of these spectates on the psychology of terrorism. Clever as well as serious in its use of the political thriller genre, Massie's imagination is appropriate to narrative spoken by, for example, Raimundo, a Prufrockian dilettante, charming, cynical and too elegant ever to be entirely bewildered. Raimundo's brother, Corrado Dusa, is kidnapped along lines that parallel the fate of Aldo Moro; and Massie explores this political family with insight and real experience of Italy and its political climate. Novelistic daring is demonstrated by a willingness to tell part of the story through the mind of Tomaso, one of the kidnappers. Easy enough in a superficial thriller, in a novel with obvious literary claims a contrast between assassinated and assassin sets up a demanding area within which to work and still hope for balance and irony, to say nothing of as great a degree of disinterestedness as a writer can bear to part with. In novels which exist to evoke recent history, most readers will always be alert to the detection of an author's point of view. Even-handed fair play seems the first bargain that should be struck between a writer of fictionalised recent events and his material, while departures from it into the writer's judgemental-tending decisions have to be seen to be deserved by the pressures forced on the writer by his characters, what they do, and what is done to them. Absolute disinterestedness might not be impossible, but it is unlikely that readers will expect it. What may well be anticipated is evidence of that preliminary bargain, from the grace of which it is probable that the writer will fall – fall, that is, from a purer, aesthetic realm into the topicality of irresistible conviction, which the reader might not share.

In *The Death of Men*, Christopher, an expatriate English journalist in Rome, says: 'There is no difference between ignorance and wilful innocence'. Well-turned aphorisms litter Massie's writing. They crop up like bravura moments of silver-tongued, polished prose. Worldly, eloquent, like agents of the *ancien régime*, in his Scottish novels his aphoristic bent can look raffish and significantly displaced, or as resistant outcrops of style scornful of dialect. They are more at home in *A Question of Loyalties*. Massie's 'old Europeans' are much given to them. Over the past few decades, it has become noticeable that aphoristic sentences are a hallmark of prose by writers whose political opinions are of the Right. Simon Raven and Peter Vansittart are two examples, and there are signs of it in Kingsley Amis's books too. If an aphorism can be considered as a single thought encapsulated in no more than two (but preferably only one) brief sentences conspicuous for a witty balance of parts, then it can be seen – gesturally, at least – as a momentary *display* of style, self-consciously directed at the reader. Few sentences tend more to self-aware stylishness than aphorisms and epigrams. They also underline a writer's willingness, eagerness even, to reveal an ironic temper as well as a distrust of the more functional, modish or less traditional styles of the day. It is not too much to claim that they can be read as keys to a writer's personality. They indicate an ethical foundation of which a writer (or a character) feels secure.

Massie is fond of nutshell sentences. They are a necessary part of his lucidity and ironic overview. At times, they can be lyrical and extended:

> Stretched out on the rough ground below the tree, listening to the myriad of little sounds, which only deepened the silence that was the background to their music, it was possible to imagine that there was no such thing as History.
>
> But in my father's study History was all too present.[7]

The 'author' of that perception is Etienne de Balafré recalling a visit to his grandmother in the Provençal château which he will inherit. Brought up in England and South Africa, having left France with his English mother in 1939 at the age of nine, Etienne's father, Lucien – whose history the novel unravels with astute helpings of information discreetly revealed and structured – is remembered by some as a French hero and patriot, and, by a majority, as a traitor and collaborator who served as an under-secretary in the Vichy government. Europe's terror, fury, pathos, contradictions and ironies attract Massie in *A Question of Loyalties* with what can seem a mischievous humanity. His exposures of upheavals in emotive choices and loyalties within a nationality and its patriotism can make the tremors within our own look feeble, petty and underdisclosed. While that might be the intention, it seems equally feasible that Massie is aware of the predicament of those who, like himself, support a Union between Scotland and England which historical forces have tended to loosen, and point the movement of history in what looks like a different direction. Etienne's view of his father is that he was 'pompous, ridiculous, yet somehow decent'. It is that decency which is the source of most of the irony. As an older man, for example, Etienne, in Geneva, visited by a young Canadian interested in his father's career, points to a spot where a Reformation martyr was burned. 'He was burned by a heretic, Calvin, on account of heresy.' Double flaws within fallible history are what warm Massie to his work. Special pleading of a right-wing nature is not always absent; but in this case it is redeemed by the elegiac dignity of an approach to a period of time marked by its vengeful negation of understanding. 'History is written from then to now, but understood back to front', Massie has Etienne write. Implicated in that (again, aphoristic) remark is the possibility that, in a design of *mutual* errors, it is only those of the defeated which are shown to be without excuse.

'He who overcomes himself is divine', wrote the German historian Leopold von Ranke. 'Most see their ruin before their eyes; but they go into it.' As a novel of quest, discovery, putting pieces together, *A Question of Loyalties* is nicely evoked by Ranke's wise but disheartening remark. It is especially true when the book's concern with fascism is kept in mind. Lucien's mentality is informed by obedience to a patriotic sense of duty rather than fascism; but perhaps it ought to be clearer than Massie makes out that patriotism and fascism are equally liable to enlistment in the powerful forces which dictatorial government can manipulate for ends which, in retrospect, seem calculated to make time go wrong, and, as a result, introduce evil as an allegedly inevitable category in human behaviour, which has to be confronted – even if belatedly.

Massie can seem to enjoy anguished historical complexities, subtleties and ironies, *for their own sake*. It could be the temperamental pleasure of a gifted historian-in-fiction. Or it could be more tactical: a matter of choice, or decision, which sees History as the transcendence of what actually happened – why, when, where, by whom and for what reasons events were perpetrated; on whom, with what results, and at what cost. He does not neglect these issues so much as subordinate them to the entanglements of personality with public, national and private life. It can create a mood of generalised pessimism from which there seems no way out. Loyalties, courses of action and decisions are seen as contingent on fortuitous circumstances. Had Lucien not met his prewar German friend Rupert, for instance, then his destination in 1940 might have been Bordeaux and constructive flight to Britain and the Free French instead of Vichy and 'the long chain of misery, betrayal, revenge'. Rupert becomes a conspirator in the Stauffenberg plot. Lucien could have betrayed him and others under torture. Postponed resistance, some good deeds along the way, and a character at no point tarnished by wickedness, merely with what history considers mistakes, introduce valour to Lucien's story: irony's spanner twisting the nut as tight as it will go, or a right-wing historian having it both ways.

Similar methods are followed in the less accomplished *The Sins of the Father*. The ironical dilemma here is that Eli Czinner, a German Jew living in Argentina, was in the 1930s a major participant in Schacht's Ministry of Economics and hence the economic renewal of Nazi Germany. His daughter is in love with Franz Schmidt, son of a German-Argentinian engineer who is revealed as Kestner, a former SS officer and war criminal whose voice is recognised by the blind Eli. The 'sins' of the title are made to work both ways, on both fathers. But despite some insightful passages, and the suspense of gradually-released information – Czinner's speech to the Israeli court is written with admirable ethical agility and brilliance – the novel bogs down in its own unravelling, elaborate plot. 'Nothing coheres', says the Israeli intellectual Luke. 'And yet we are obliged to behave as if that wasn't so.' Again, that snappy, epigrammatic urge in Massie's prose; but here it begins to suffer from fatigue, while the effort to work in as much irony as possible starts to look predictable. Luke's wife, for example, says, reporting on what Israeli papers say of her husband's acquaintanceship with Kestner's son: 'The implication is that he doesn't give a damn for what the Jewish people have suffered because he is a rootless cosmopolitan with an American wife and now with Nazi friends. It stinks.' 'Rootless cosmopolitan' was the pejorative phrase used by Nazis to accuse Jewish intellectuals of being disqualified from German culture. In this context it seems a willed ironic replica, connected with the belief of a character in *A Question of Loyalties* that History does not repeat itself; people repeat History. People do, and sometimes against the grain, but here it is less challenging than cheap. Although confident with his difficult material, the final impression is that subjects like the Holocaust, German guilt (or lack of it), Jewish revenge, and contemporary Israel, are liable to overwhelm any novelist without a more literal stake in them other than a 'sense of history' and a prose style capable of traditional perfections.

William Boyd has written next to nothing about contemporary Scotland: the circumstances of his background would seem to preclude it. Two of Massie's novels deal interestingly with a marginalised Scottish gentry, but his more ambitious work tackles the ironies of Roman and recent European history (even if *A Question of Loyalties* suggests a Scottish Unionist predicament, and, for that matter, given the vast presence of patriotism in that novel, Nationalist dilemmas as well). Although far more indigenous than Boyd, Ronald Frame's specifically Scottish work is sparse (short stories, one of them, 'Paris', reworked as a TV play) when compared with the astounding as well as remarkably extensive *Englishness* of such big books as *Sandmouth People* (1987), *Penelope's Hat* (1989) and *Bluette* (1990).

A point suggests itself: a certain kind of Scottish literary gift, with its personal roots in middle-class life or the caste above it, will find its horizons narrowed by inexperience of the wider social scene, whether urban or rural. How a large number of Scots actually speak and behave will in all likelihood be rendered condescendingly or subjected to distortion. It works two ways. Inexperience of middle-class Scotland tends to exclude middle- and upper-class characters from fiction by writers like James Kelman and William McIlvanney. And is the 'ear' of writers like these *entirely* 'disinterested'? Or could there be pointing-up of accent and dialect, a shade or two of exaggeration as part of the purpose of making a point or exploiting 'material'? Lurking behind this, a larger problem poses itself. It was stated neatly as long ago as 1904 in 'The Scot of Fiction', an essay in Jane Findlater's *Stones from a Glass House* (1904). After discussing the 'savage caricature' of Brown's *The House With the Green Shutters*, she continued:

> It is almost ridiculous to turn, by way of contrast, to Mr Barrie's *Window in Thrums*. Thrums is indeed the antithesis of Barbie to an extent that falsifies the one picture or the other as we choose to accept them; they cannot both be true.[8]

Daring? Yes. Critics were braver then. Findlater meant that neither portrait was true, that both Brown's and Barrie's visions of Scottish life departed from reality. Nor has this issue been settled. Almost ninety years on, Scottish fiction *still* seems an unresolved and contentious area divided in a sectarian manner by class affiliations, in which a political perspective is practically demanded by the shaping climate of an unordered nationalism and a correspondingly deranged realism.

Frame's first novel, *Winter Journey* (1984), is set in London, Czechoslovakia, Austria and Greece. It introduces his distinctive, remarkable and also tantalising imaginative voice, which, even when not the first-person feminine singular, usually identifies itself with Frame's opposite gender. Boyd's first-person (for example, in some sections of *Brazzaville Beach*) can look like an avoidance of prose's aesthetic dimension. Of these three novelists, Frame is the most self-consciously artistic. His dedication to style, however, is also sartorial, with major sidelines in domestic architecture, furniture, wallpaper and *objets d'art*. His expertise in women's clothing is practically profound. In the first three pages of *Winter Journey*, he gives us 'Worth perfume', a 'Sulka suede glove' and a 'Rayne shoe'. His eye for a Hartnell dress or a Simpson's blazer is unflagging, but he is much more than a novelist of the wardrobe and the dressing-table. A hedonistic tragedian, his writing shimmers with the by-products of brittle affluence and expensive tastes. These, though, are part of the stories he tells.

'History is also what is personal to you', Annoele says towards the end of Frame's first novel. Compassionate but unsentimental immersion in his characters, stories, and in a created England, is Frame's primary distinction. In an introduction to his TV play *Paris* (1987), he wrote:

> I don't write to make political points, or to be circumstantially 'relevant' in the social sense. The best I can hope for, how I justify myself, is to try to induce an awareness of what merits our

> sympathy and understanding in lives that may otherwise appear utterly distinct and apart from our own. The purpose is as wide – but, I trust, not as vague or abstract – as (ahem!) 'Humanity'.[9]

Instead of relevance – and there could be a whimsical defence of the inconsequential hiding in those inverted commas and that 'ahem' – Frame's fiction relies on emotional and ethical accuracy within invented territory. *Winter Journey*, for example, takes the form of a first-person narrative told by Annoele, during which she graduates from girlhood to maturity. That is, the book exists in the present tense of Annoele's telling of her story. Minimal use of the *he said/she said* conventions of dialogue help to set up the narrative as a sequence of flashbacks in which the frame momentarily hazes and trembles before clearing into the vivid past remembered. An only child, Annoele evokes herself as a knowing but also innocent daughter whose father's glamour was subsidised by the sale of state secrets, and whose mother's elegance and infidelity were underwritten by treason. If anything mars Frame's writing, it is his fey perfectionism in the precise details which are necessary to it. Privilege and its vulnerable foundations are exposed by the book, however, and there are moments of what Massie calls 'violent truth'. Annoele's reprehensible parents, for example, are extreme cases of selfishness and self-regarding detachment from the average standards of responsibility. A 'scene' in a posh hotel restaurant reduces the story to its starkest outline, as does another in a car, which crashes, with the death of the mother and disfigurement of the father. Disappearances, changes of identity, the stepping out of reality and into imaginative or created life, recur in Frame's work, and it is tempting to see an elusive Scottish syndrome in these attempted invisibilities – the self-aware *making-up* of a double into whose body a real person steps and then walks away. It could be an extreme imaginative gesture, or it could show Frame giving the slip to historical Scottish pressures for which he has little patience, and, perhaps, no feelings of responsibility whatsoever.

Fantasy, or some other mood tending equally to beg the reader's indulgence, would fail to describe Frame's imagination. Nearer the mark, perhaps, is his evident relish of fictitiousness. *Penelope's Hat*, for example, sets up a range of questions concerning fiction's relationship to lived experience (or what is made of it). Much of this emerges through Penelope Milne, who is also a novelist. By the end of the book, it becomes clear that *Penelope's Hat* is by Penelope Milne, and that the convention of a discovered, edited manuscript has been cunningly and cleverly delayed. Fictitious autobiography composed by a hand other than that (of course) of the imaginary author suggests fiction-within-fiction or a doubled fictitiousness. At one and the same time, Frame's art destabilises fiction while rejoicing in the liberties of storytelling and invention. Neither fiction nor the imagination on which it depends is subverted. Both are re-examined. Imagination is presented over the leisurely but intense scale of his novels. As Penelope exemplifies in *Penelope's Hat*, and as Catherine discovers in *Bluette*, imagination is a protective quality of mind, an 'only defence against the callous business of the world'.

An aesthetic resourcefulness such as Frame's seems to have its origins in so un-Scottish a temperamental preference as literary hedonism. Implicated as it is with vulnerable but strong women characters, it amounts to what must be a unique imaginative wager made by a male Scottish writer. Also, it seems easy to connect this instinctive or deliberate trait with the emphasis he places on imagination, pretence and his perceptions of half-real moments of existence, blurrings of reality and, in general, some sustained passages of prose lyricism. It could appear to be a highly ambiguous approach to fiction. What succeeds in fixing it to the page (other than thoughtful prose) is painstaking reconstructions of the past. Wartime London, for instance, is evoked in part of *Penelope's Hat*. Some of it, inevitably, illustrates the book's sartorial fascinations. Significant, fateful millinery traipses through the book, like a bobbing, hatted head in a crowd, constantly changing headgear – the cream pagoda hat, the burgundy velvet side-beret, the boater, the white plush turban, the ochre cartwheel, the black grosgrain beret, etc. (all quoted, of course). It can seem quirky, perhaps even kinky, or dotty; but it might be the result of a controlled eccentricity. Precise details of past fashions gleaned by research for the sake of authenticity are a relatively small but very significant part of it. Frame is saying something 'serious' about clothes and how they reflect personality and mood, their role in the *imaginative* presentation of individual temperaments. Yet it is also something 'light'. Dress is seen as a profound levity and a superficial expression of a person's deepest beliefs of her most intimate self and her ambitions. A sentence like this, however, can read like an exercise in winsome inconsequentiality:

> She laid out pair after pair of shoes from their boxes, all signed by Ferragamo, which might have been a lesson in the history of the woman's fine shoe in the twentieth century.[10]

Rarely, if ever, does one of Frame's principal characters purchase an item of clothing off a high-street peg. There is a valiant defiance to Frame's commitment to elegance-at-all-costs. Individual self-assessments, in the form of appearances, contest the worst of history. Attire challenges bombing. Consider, for example, the description of Mrs Christopher Sykes:

> on her bicycle rides about London on Government business she wore a mustard wool suit with a draped, buttoned skirt run up by her dressmaker, a Pole called Madame Przeworska. Cecil Beaton, photographing a Digby Morton suit in the ruins of the Temple, assured them that 'Fashion is indestructible'. More practically, a Dereta camel winter coat cost only fifteen coupons. While so many women had to stick to the three-inch regulation length for hair, they learned from illustrations how to tie theirs into a net turban, so it could be hidden under their hats. (*PH*, 214)

At one level, as information, it is extremely interesting. Those fondly-specified details, however, suggest an imagination willing to risk the pornographic in its close-ups, and the epicene in its justifications. Similarly, a fastidious ear for accents and an overall sensory awareness of symptoms of social class – these recur frequently in *Penelope's Hat* and elsewhere in Frame's writing – can make the antennae twitch as if in the presence of prissiness. Despite a double first and two sporting blues, one character from Penelope's past is said to have 'hailed from a Birmingham suburb, although none of it might have been guessed'. Earlier, the disgusting Jardine is described as

> a small, hunched Scotsman of sixty or so, with a goatee beard and a lazy eye and a proliferation of couthy burrs in his speech. He smelt of mothballs, and rumour had it that when he was in his room . . . his tweed suit stayed in the wardrobe while he walked about or sat in his flannel vest and combinations. (*PH*, 102)

Frame's impersonation of classic English 'respectability' is virtually complete. *Sandmouth People*, *A Woman of Judah* (1987), *Bluette* and many of his short stories bear witness to his fictional border-crossing. The implication would seem to be that, in order to create the conditions under which his imagination can enjoy the freedom it deserves, he has been obliged to disregard his nationality and the kind of writing expected of it. Frame confronts language in a way which makes 'Englishness' look unavoidable, whether we think of prose, subjects, characters or locations. The implication is that 'Englishness' is actually what he enjoys exemplifying. Although distinctly unfashionable, it is also distinctive: after all, Frame has written novels and stories which are accomplished and ingenious as well as provocative and exciting in what they say about fiction itself.

To consider Frame, Massie and Boyd together, while bearing in mind the vernacular energies of other recent fiction, is to expose the obvious divisions in Scottish writing. Were they only a matter of language, social class and political belief, then the problem would be easier to resolve. Hefty aesthetic issues are also implicated, and it is these which are neglected when criticism proves vulnerable to deflection by political desire. Frame, for example, is instinctively elusive when it comes to 'relevance': his recreated English times and settings might amount to imaginative space, an other-where and other-time, less important for their 'Englishness' than as fictitious habitats freed from topicality. In contriving their own deaths or disappearances, or assumptions of other identities altogether (a vanishing act which happens three times in *Penelope's Hat*), Frame can be seen to risk his own invisibility or disenfranchisement in Scottish letters. What he is saying might not be 'about' Scotland, but it reflects his work's departure from such Scottish inhibitions as resistance to pleasure, suspicion of the graceful and the elegant, and, above all, a distrust of the fictitious. It is possible to see Frame's priorities as passively opposed to the vernacular impulse in other Scottish writing. In the context of recent Scottish fiction as a whole, what he shares with Massie and Boyd (perhaps also with Muriel Spark) is a divergent mischief, an insistence on the imagination's freedom from the nationality whose constraints might even have encouraged the necessity of making that choice.

NOTES

1. William Boyd, *School Ties* (London: Hamish Hamilton, 1985), Introduction, pp. 17–18.
2. William Boyd, *An Ice-Cream War* (London: Hamish Hamilton, 1982), p. 288. Subsequent references are to this edition.
3. William Boyd, *A Good Man in Africa* (London: Hamish Hamilton, 1981; reprinted Harmondsworth: Penguin, 1982), p. 14. Subsequent references are to the Penguin edition.
4. William Boyd, *The New Confessions* (London: Hamish Hamilton, 1987), p. 120.
5. Allan Massie, *The Last Peacock* (London: Bodley Head, 198[illegible]), pp. 111–12. Subsequent references are to this edition.
6. Allan Massie, *One Night in Winter* (London: Bodley Head, 1984), pp. 87–8. Subsequent references are to this edition.
7. Allan Massie, *A Question of Loyalties* (London: Bodley Head, 1989), p. 54.
8. Jane Findlater, *Stones from a Glass House* (London: James Nisbet & Co., 1904), p. 104.
9. Ronald Frame, *Paris* (London: Faber & Faber, 1987), Foreword, p. xii.
10. Ronald Frame, *Penelope's Hat* (1989; reprinted London: Hodder & Stoughton/Sceptre, 1990), p. 209. Subsequent references are to this edition.

Twelve

Listening to the Women Talk

Carol Anderson

The placing of women writers together in one chapter begs some questions. There is, surely, a danger of ghettoising women; there is a real danger, too, of 'tokenism'. It can also be argued that just because writers are female does not necessarily mean they feel themselves to have anything much in common. Some writers are interested in femaleness, and write about women quite self-consciously. Others are not and do not: their imagination is taken up with other things, though, of course, it can be countered that femininity may be there unconsciously. Writing about women does not necessarily make a writer 'feminist', either, and indeed what 'feminist' means is itself open to discussion. Debates rage on in some quarters about 'feminine' language and related issues: the search for gender-specific writing-traits is fraught with difficulties.[1] Is it, then, useful to group women writers together?

Many women who write do share some kinds of common experience, whether self-conscious or not, because of their gender and existing social structures, and such writers can sometimes be seen to explore common themes in their fiction. It can be illuminating to consider these themes, as well as the various narrative strategies which the writers adopt. It is also significant that there has been recently in Scotland a burgeoning of female talent, although it would be false to see this as springing from nowhere: there have long been Scottish women writers, many of them very good indeed, if not always noticed and applauded by influential critics. There is a strong case for arguing that there is a women's tradition in our literature, not entirely separate from writing by men, but with its own qualities, and unduly neglected. This tradition should be highlighted and considered in its own right, as well as integrated into the more general view of our traditions.

It is not easy, however, particularly when considering contemporary fiction, to decide which writers should be foregrounded. There is still shamefully little written about some very good and well-established writers such as Elspeth Davie and Naomi Mitchison. Besides the very gifted Janice Galloway, who is discussed elsewhere in this volume, there are also many other young women publishing both fiction and poetry and creating a strong impression with their work. Among the many interesting novels appearing in recent years, there are Margaret Elphinstone's distinctive and haunting *The Incomer* (1987) and *A Sparrow's Flight* (1990); several novels by Alison Fell, including *Every Move You Make* (1984); Sian Hayton's *Cells of Knowledge* (1989); and Candia McWilliam's *A Case of Knives* (1988) and *A Little Stranger* (1989). There are, of course, certain problems in defining 'Scottish' writing; not all these writers live in Scotland, and a number of others might or might not be included according to the view one has of what constitutes 'Scottishness' in literature: the excellent Shena Mackay, for example, as well as Sara Maitland and Anne Fine. Even Angela Carter attributed her feeling of being somewhat 'outside' English society to the fact that she had a Scottish father.[2] Are any or all of these 'Scottish writers'? There are no easy answers, and it would seem desirable to keep issues of definition open and alive.

The three writers I have chosen for discussion here are not perhaps the most obvious grouping: Jessie Kesson (b. 1916), Emma Tennant (b. 1937) and Sharman Macdonald (b. 1951). Some sense of the achievement of these three writers may be suggested through discussion of a novel by each of them. No value judgement is intended in respect to those writers omitted, although I believe that the writers under consideration here deserve more attention than they have received. Their differences illustrate the diversity of writing by Scottish women, its achievement and its potential; yet there are ways in which these three apparently disparate writers may share common ground.

The experience of exclusion or marginalisation, and the sense of being a divided self, are strongly present in some Scottish writing.[3] If male Scottish authors have had to contend with difficulties generated in part by a problematic relationship to national identity, language and literary tradition, for Scottish women this experience is compounded by gender. Women have been marginalised in most areas of society, as well as in terms of cultural tradition, and have had to struggle for a sense of self.[4] Against this background, we may see the interest of some women writers, including the three discussed here, in the experience of social and internal conflict and in life at the margins. These writers are all concerned to some degree with issues of gender; with specifically female experience; and with the exploration of female subjectivity and the difficulties which women face in society.

An especially interesting comparison for Scottish fiction might be made with writing by women in other countries where issues of cultural identity are particularly significant. Writing about fiction by Canadian women writers, Coral Ann Howalls notes

> their urge to shift the emphasis and so throw the storyline of traditional structures of authority open to question. Shifts and questionings involve disruption, which is a common characteristic of all these fictions.[5]

She goes on to describe other features of the fiction discussed, including shifts into fantasy, indeterminacy and open-endedness. The work of the Scottish writers considered here also challenges novelistic conventions – in ways that several recent critics[6] have seen, like Howalls, as typical of women's writing – reshaping expectations and countering traditional realism with subversive uses of tradition. Intertextuality may be seen as a feature of the novels examined here: previous literary texts, songs, myths, fairytales and folk culture are all used to explore, among other things, gender roles, and to challenge the established social order. All the texts looked at might also be described as 'interrogative', engaging readers in the construction of their meaning, and inviting plural reading.[7]

Many of the narrative features described here are similar to those found in postmodernist writing more generally. According to Julia Kristeva, a woman is 'an eternal dissident in relation to social and political consensus, in exile from power . . .',[8] and, taking up Kristeva's idea of the experimental writer as another form of 'dissident', some critics comment on the shared impetus of women and experimentalists 'towards marginalization and indefinition; they are in a condition of "exile" from a centred identity of meaning and its claims to a totalized law or truth'.[9] The three writers discussed here, Kesson, Tennant and Macdonald, all live in physical 'exile' from Scotland – all three live in London. Like other women decentred in one way, they may strive for a place nearer power in another. Excluded for so long, female voices speak, not 'authoritatively', but eloquently, from (beyond) the margins of Scottish society. We should listen to them.

Jessie Kesson's novel *Another Time, Another Place* (1983) is not the earliest of the novels looked at here, but she is the oldest of the writers, and appears to represent an older tradition. Yet this novel, like Kesson's other fiction, is subtly subversive of convention, both social and literary. One of its most disconcerting features is that its female protagonist is nameless: she is merely 'the young woman' throughout.

Such a strategy is unexpected in fiction, especially sustained over a full-length work, and brings some of the power and dignity of ballad to the novel. The quality of anonymity evokes the folk tradition which haunts the novel through songs and rhymes, suggesting that the character may be read as both an individual and a universal, timeless figure.

However, the reader is also challenged to question and define her or his relationship to the character, and to a text in which issues of power and identity are raised, being both drawn in to share the inner thoughts and feelings of the character, and yet never fully allowed to know her because of her namelessness. In the oral tradition, to know someone's name is to have power over them:[10] here, the reader is never allowed to grasp the identity of the protagonist, who thus remains in the last analysis unknowable. The argument that woman is 'something that cannot be represented, something that is not said, something above and beyond nomenclatures and ideologies'[11] is relevant, too, to a text concerned with femininity and female experience.

The nameless woman is searching for a sense of her own identity, in a context which denies her power. The unnamed third term of the title 'Another Time, Another Place, is hinted at near the beginning (my italics):

> it still took her unaware to be addressed by her recently acquired married title, still took her time to respond to it, as if those who uttered it spoke to *another person*, a different person from the one she knew herself to be.[12]

Kesson suggests the ways in which women are traditionally defined by society and themselves: throughout the novel, the woman struggles not only with the constraints of her time and place, but also with the role of 'another person', the role of married woman.

The passage just quoted is followed by one of the many snatches of rhyme that interweave the text:

> If no one ever marries me
> And I don't see why they should
> They say that I'm not pretty
> And I'm very seldom good
>
> (p. 7)

The protagonist immediately applies the rhyme to her own experience: 'But someone *had* married her, though she hadn't got used to that either'. The woman's own story apparently has 'closure', but the last words imply a sense of unease with her present state. Interestingly, too, the snatch of rhyme starts 'If . . .' but is left unfinished. There is, therefore, a hint at open-endedness. The novel explores the young woman's 'want', in the senses of both lack and desire, her attempts at self-definition in a context which denies her options, and her search for fulfilment, stunted and denied yet never entirely crushed.

The novel's opening implies a negative 'end' of the woman's story: 'There would be no gathering in of the corn today'. The harvest, traditional symbol of fertility, is not to be completed. Indeed, the novel emphasises loss, lack, denial and incompleteness in the lives of all the women in the community. Female experience in this context seems bleak; it is not surprising that while there are links between the women in the community, the young woman cannot fully find a sense of self through identification with them. She seeks selfhood – 'her image, reflected in the looking-glass above the sink, gazed back at her' (p. 15) – but finds herself both inside and outside the community of women, the rural community, and that of the incomer Italian prisoners with whom she also identifies herself in some ways, since they represent for her the qualities repressed by those around her, and many of the things lacking in her own life. Inside a marriage and yet distanced from it by the pressures of her own youthful and insistent sexuality and emotional longing, she dreams of a desert island where she might escape with the Italian Paolo (p. 62). Ironically, the island is in a sense there in her life, only it is not as she imagined. Rather, she finds herself on the island on which Crusoe was marooned (p. 63), alone and isolated.

Physically trapped by the 'stand still order' at the end of the novel, and by the limitations of her life as a woman (p. 66), the novel offers no conventional 'happy ever after' conclusion for its protagonist: 'No Roma. No Napoli. So this was what it was like to be a prisoner' (p. 91). Like Joanna Bannerman in Catherine Carswell's *Open the Door!* (1920), the young woman must acknowledge that Romantic Italy offers no true escape. Just as she recognises that a leisurely rural life is an illusion created by seeing things from a distance (p. 64), so she must understand the illusion of romance, built on the desire to be seen by the male gaze, and to be desired.

But if the woman remains in some ways deprived and alienated, there are also glimmers of hope, or at least of 'openness'. 'Small miracles' punctuate the novel. The myth of Persephone (also taken up by Emma Tennant in *Alice Fell*, 1980) is a reminder of Hades, but also of growth and life (p. 84); the negative opening, the postponed harvest, does not necessarily mean eternal darkness. At the end, the young woman is reconciled with her estranged friend, Elspeth, who may be bitter and repressed but who is also a woman of dignity and independent spirit. The last image of the novel is the miniature ship made for the young woman by the Italians, an image of romance and escape now offered only in imagination. The young woman may not have found romantic love; there is, though, some emotional succour in this symbol of their real affection for her. She has also acquired a name, 'Dina', given to her by the Italians, who never knew either her own name or the community name for her:

> 'Wifie', the general title of the Cottar Row touched both her mind and her mouth with irony. Wifie. Luigi would never have found the Italian word for that in his dictionary. (p. 94).

She has, at least, escaped, in however limited a way, the confining terms of her own community.

Compressed and understated, this slim, enjoyable novel says much about the difficulties for a young woman facing her world. It hints at the repressed power of female sexuality – 'There was something nocturnal in her. Atavistic. Something that had never had a chance' (p. 26) – implied, too, through imagery of fire. Speaking through its silences as well as its words, the novel also addresses problems of communication and the limits of language – examined, for example, in the young woman's relationship with the Italians. Kesson may write of life in rural Scotland, but her themes and narrative techniques demand that she be seen as an innovator who uses tradition for her own ends.

Kesson seems at least to be well known in Scotland, and there are signs of growing interest in her work. Emma Tennant, on the other hand, although well established and widely published south of the Border, has barely been considered in the context of Scottish Literature. True, she lives in London, but she regularly insists in interviews on the importance to her of her Scottish childhood and the influence on her of Scottish writers, especially James Hogg and R. L. Stevenson.[13] Significantly, the other influences on her which she notes are 'Latin American, Marquez, of course. But above all East European, particularly Bruno Schultz.'[14] Her own writing shows a sense of distance from Establishment English society, and her achievement certainly does not seem to lie in the field of the 'traditional English novel', although she admires that form.[15] Sensitive to social divisions of various kinds, she is an acute critic of inequality, of what she calls 'an increasingly divided society'.[16] She explores this society and its divisions in various non-realist modes, including fantasy, allegory and science fiction.

In a number of her novels, she presents the corruption of a class-ridden society through examination of the aristocracy or upper middle classes, taking traditional forms such as the country house novel, and undermining them from within, as she does, for instance, in *The Last of the Country House Murders* (1974), which employs humour, parody and pastiche. My main concern here, however, is to look at a novel which demonstrates her particular interest in two other kinds of 'division' relating to Scottishness and femininity. Tennant herself has made a number of statements about her own sense of identity, suggesting that 'the concept of the split personality is particularly appealing to Scottish writers because the doubleness of national identity has been there for so long'.[17] In *The Bad Sister*, Tennant takes on a structure and themes suggested by the Scottish writer James Hogg's *The Private Memoirs and Confessions of a Justified Sinner* (1824), which uses the motif of the double and ideas of division; but her novel also specifically explores the experience of 'division' suffered by many women in contemporary society.

The novel opens with references to the mysterious deaths of a father and daughter, the Dalzells of the Scottish Borders (the action moves between the Borders and London). As in Hogg's novel, the 'Editor' is a fictionalised persona who comments on the Dalzell murders:

> It now seems possible to understand these odd killings a little better, and it may protect the health of our society if we learn to do so. They are not, after all, isolated instances – murder by middle-class female urban guerillas is ever on the increase in the West – yet it is also the case that 'Jane' may not fit into that category of person.[18]

The anxiety about female power and the desire to 'categorise' hint here, however, subtly, at a certain frame of mind and attitudes, more fully illustrated in the final section of the novel.

Moreover, within the framework of this first part of the novel are still other (male) narratives: a shortish letter from one Luke Saighton, and then the account of Stephen, the young clergyman whose vision of the female commune, 'the women's house', as being like the 'front parlour of a grim Victorian brothel' (p. 123) must be read in context. Viewed with suspicion by the Editor as somewhat 'liberal', he is, we later learn from Jane Wild's narrative, also viewed with some sense of distance by her. None of the opening narratives, in fact, offers the reader a secure position from which to read the longest part of the novel, Jane Wild's narrative, which brings its own challenges. However, the first part of the novel does foreshadow the ambiguities to come, hinting at its own duplicity and themes of duality. Jane, the unacknowledged, illegitimate daughter of Dalzell by a poor Irish shop assistant, is the supposed killer of both her father and her half-sister, the more privileged Ishbel. From the perspective of Stephen, the young clergyman, she is a woman 'in two minds' (p. 26), torn by her radical upbringing and temperament and her desire for peace.

Like Robert Wringhim's in Hogg's novel, Jane's narrative is in the first person, allowing exploration of her subjectivity, and creating a living sense of 'division'. Jane seems to be uncertain of her identity, seeking another self through different clothes: for instance, she also cuts off her 'blonde' hair. It is dyed; Jane is actually dark, in contrast with her rich, 'lucky' sister Ishbel, a natural blonde like her socially-favoured mother. Tennant here is pursuing the division between pairs of sisters, blonde and dark, that can be traced back to Walter Scott. Jane Wild might be proclaiming, like Maggie Tulliver in *The Mill on the Floss*, that she wants to avenge Scott's passionate, outcast heroines, 'all the dark unhappy ones',[19] rejecting the more conventional, socially-constructed aspects of femininity suggested by 'blondeness'.

Jane is apparently internally 'divided' and uncertain; she is also haunted by a series of doubles, not only her sister Ishbel but also Miranda, 'the other woman' whom she believes her lover to be seeing. If doubleness is a feature of the book, however, it is a doubleness that splinters further, as if Tennant, like Hélène Cixous and Catherine Clément, is unpicking binary oppositions to reveal plurality.[20] Where the novel's title suggests a single split, the fiction itself presents more than one 'bad sister'. In a powerful and disorientating sequence at the heart of the novel, the reader moves with Jane Wild along a city street that metamorphoses into a rural landscape: indistinctly, as if one reality coexists with another, and with no explanation, Jane has 'become', it seems, a character called 'Jeanne', a servant in a big house, looking for her sister Marie. At the end of the sequence, the two women lie together: 'There in the concealing grass, I searched her face anxiously. She was my sister, all my dark sisters' (p. 68). The place of 'Jeanne and Marie' as servants echoes elements in Jane's own life, as does the image of the big house, but the reader has to work towards the full significance of this passage. Are these figures merely projections of Jane's troubled mind? Tennant's comments on identity, following Stevenson, would seem relevant here:

> I do believe that in any one moment there are about 150 things going on inside a person. People were shocked by *Jekyll and Hyde*, but one of the things that meant a lot to me was Stevenson's comment that it was just the beginning: 'every human being is a polity of innumerable and incongruous denizens'.[21]

Like Hogg's novel and Stevenson's later novella, *The Bad Sister* questions the nature of identity, challenging the idea of the 'unified' self, and in particular exploring the question of 'selfhood' for women, the pressures on female subjectivity.

Tennant has suggested one important area of ideas in this complex novel with her references to Virginia Woolf and the difficulties for a woman writer in finding a 'muse', 'because if the muse is female there are then two unpleasantly warring women in the same breast'.[22] An analysis chiming with one offered elsewhere by Tennant herself is put, in this novel, into the mouth of one of the 'dark sisters', Meg, leader of the female commune: she identifies 'the root of the wrongs of society – the suppression of masculinity in women and of femininity in men' (p. 28). Jane fitfully glimpses a male Muse, who comes to her in moments of vision, brought apparently by Meg, who claims kinship with him (pp. 85, 100–1). Meg herself seems to be associated with female creativity, as suggested by the relationship between her and Jane's friend Gala.

She is also associated with the subconscious, the 'world below the surface' (p. 73). Although she represents something damaging and distortive, akin to the power of extreme Calvinism in Hogg's novel, she is a complex figure, for repression of a woman's 'wild side' – with its creative aspect – is, after all, also dangerous: 'if we had no shadows we couldn't be alive' (p. 118). There are contradictory forces at work on the female subject: Tennant herself has commented that 'The important split which makes this wild person is only there because of the necessity to conform'.[23] Jane is under powerful social pressures, and both Jane and Meg may be read in the context of a society which attempts to categorise and repress, but only produces further divisions and disruption. Jane is an outsider; so is Meg, but she is nevertheless a part of, a product of, this society. Meg is, in a sense, merely the shadow side of conventional society. Tennant widely examines the social forces at work on a woman. Jane's narrative opens with her anxiety to 'become another person', and the imagery suggests the sense she has of her present role:

> As I walked on I could feel myself falling apart. I was in a frenzy of impatience to become another person. My rump was soft and divided under my clinging silk dress and men photographers would have it divide: ripe, ready for a mouthful to be taken out.
>
> My legs were thin and perched in high-heeled sandals . . . (p. 33)

Here, imagery of woman as food, reminiscent of ideas in Margaret Atwood's *The Edible Woman*, suggests that women are objects packaged for a consumer society. Food – Sunday lunch, for example (p. 44) – is also something prepared by women; women shop for food, too, at the supermarket.

> In the dark corners of the boxes, the still unwrapped portions, under the Free Gift Offer, lies the forgotten past. The women pull

> and tear at the little white worms of paper that make the wadding. Then the box lies open and shallow. It has revealed nothing at all. (p. 56)

Women's search for self, for identity, for meaningfulness, is shown as at once encouraged and thwarted in this consumer society.

Jane's sense of herself, in the opening passage of the novel, as an object for a photographer is also picked up in several ways and developed thematically. Jane, we are told, worked as a film critic, and Tony, her boyfriend, 'was in the film world' (p. 42). The role of the media is suggested, in many ways, as contributing to the pressures experienced by Jane. Such analysis of the novel, however, does not communicate the almost surreal power of Jane's narrative, with its dislocations and passages of intense symbolic suggestiveness. Through Jane, the reader is drawn in to a rich textual experience, 'a wild ride through the night' (p. 96). Clearly, the name 'wild' is significant: it is shared by all the women in the commune, as if signifying the 'wild zone' that is female experience. Tennant uses its connotations elsewhere in her work; *Wild Nights*, for instance, takes its title from a poem by Emily Dickinson. Names and other allusions in her work contribute to the dense texture of her fiction. *The Bad Sister* indicates its literary connections through an epigraph from Wordsworth, one which hints not only at the theme of doubleness but also at the 'Scottish' dimension, for it is 'Yarrow Unvisited'. The name, 'Meg', may echo Scott's 'wild' women in *The Heart of Midlothian* and *Guy Mannering*. The name of Jane's 'rival', Miranda, evokes *The Tempest* (p. 150), and when Jane imagines Tony with Miranda, she thinks:

> Miranda . . . ah, Miranda . . . I would call Taranta! . . . and what could she do but obey me, she the woman in a sexual hysterical frenzy, the spider-bitten woman trembling and shaking in the poison of her wants. (p. 161)

Here the name Miranda may also echo a poem, 'Tarantella', by Hilaire Belloc. The tarantella is an Italian dance, said to be performed as antidote to the bite of the tarantula spider; it is discussed by Hélène Cixous and Catherine Clément (in *The Newly Born Woman*) as a female ritual, an interlude of female 'orgasmic freedom'.

Another reference is to Conrad's novel *Chance*, which is to be made into a film by Tony's company. Jane's attitude is significant:

> poor Flora, whose life was recounted by three men, all equally determined on her helplessness and fragility. If she had had power, she would have turned their words into meaningless gossip by taking matters into her own hands and doing something

> so unacceptable they would have been unable to recount it. (pp. 106–7)

The ironies here are reminiscent of Hogg: like his narrator, the 'Sinner' Robert Wringhim, the speaker here is pitifully unaware of her own lack of power. Yet Jane, unlike Flora, does recount her own story, and the narrative as a whole does, of course, deal with 'something unacceptable': female unhappiness, violence, madness, the dark shadow side of society and of social images. By references to a male version of a woman's life, Tennant draws attention to the alternative nature of her own text.

It is also significant that Jane's narrative is prefaced by a poem from Marina Tsvetayeva, a poem in translation. The idea of 'translation' is one that haunts the novel: as Jane reflects, 'Translated! . . . that was what was happening to me. I was being translated into another state' (p. 116). It has been suggested that Freud used the term 'Übersetzung', or translation, to describe transposing all the hard work of the unconscious. Wordplay and challenging puns have their place in a text which explores the unconscious and which is, moreover, implicitly critical of the 'received' use of language; like Fay Weldon, for instance, Tennant is acute in her observation of the tired social uses of words to mask realities, as when, for instance, Jane thinks: 'an IUD like a computer gadget lay inside me, with a thin cord for removal if I "decided to start a family" ' (p. 50).

Comparing and contrasting herself with Angela Carter, Tennant has said that in writing she likes to 'plunder':

> I feel the point of writing for a woman is to take, magpie-like, anything they please from anywhere, and produce a subversive text out of the scraps; out of patriarchal or any kind of material they can get in their beaks.[24]

In *The Bad Sister*, Tennant has created a 'subversive' text, taking ideas and 'scraps' from various sources, yet forging something that conveys strongly her own particular and insistent concerns. A novel ostensibly 'about' duality, its rich plurality demands much of the reader, but also offers much.

The Scottish 'scraps' surface elsewhere in Tennant's by now considerable body of fiction. Stevenson's subversive *Dr Jekyll and Mr Hyde* (1886) is used to Tennant's own ends in *Two Women of London* (1989), and Stevenson is also mentioned in *The Magic Drum* (1989), a novel which features 'doubling' with the characters of Catherine and Katerina, and Katerina and Muriel; it also has a structure reminiscent of Hogg or Stevenson, with its somewhat dislocated diary form framed by other fragmentary material, apparently factual statements and newspaper reports. Similarly, *Queen of Stones* (1983) achieves an effect of authenticity through use of newspaper accounts and psychoanalysts' reports. *The House of Hospitalities* (1987) also has an epigraph from another Scot, J. M. Barrie. The vein of 'fantasy' which Tennant mines so powerfully in *The Bad Sister* is explored again, rather differently, in *Wild Nights* (1979), where the location is – although never explicitly so – a fantastic Scotland of the mind. Scotland is not merely a trope for the imagination, though it seems to play such a role for Tennant: her use of Scottish literary traditions is so fertile and powerful that one can only applaud and look forward to her next move.

Tennant's work is often troubling. The title of Sharman Macdonald's 1986 novel *The Beast* likewise sets up expectations of disturbing content – a horror story or a tale of sexual violence – but it actually refers to something innocuous, a yogurt culture, given as a gift.

> 'Why do you call it a beast?' said Jade.
>
> 'It's alive, isn't it? said Naomi. 'It grows'.[25]

The disparity between the connotations of the title and the mundane, even bathetic, reality which it denotes is echoed in other ways in a text which explores the gulf between appearance and reality, material circumstances and dreams. In *The Beast*, 'the culture' suggests not only yogurt but also a cultural milieu, the world inhabited by a group of thirty-something adults each in their own ways frustrated, still dreaming of their youth, longing for fulfilment. The novel evokes a middle-class world of Hampstead delicatessens, herbal tea and stripped-pine shops, as well as a more challenging urban scene, the London of crowded Underground, marginalised people, not enough money. There is another dimension, too, that interweaves the material world: these people's dreams and fantasies.

Unlike the ones by Kesson and Tennant already discussed, this novel does not have a female subject as its main focus; rather, it is interesting for the way in which narrative perspective is dispersed, encouraging the reader to gain sympathy for each of the characters and to share in the emotional and sexual longings and fantasies that underlie their exterior lives, whether male or female. Although Naomi is, as her husband reminds her, grey-haired, 'an ordinary woman' (p. 23), the reader shares her rich fantasy life, with her dreams of other possible selves, such as 'Sarah Jane, curly hair pulled back, tendrils escaping wild, black eyes flashing' (p. 27), a gypsy-like figure. In the course of the warm summer day, picnicking in the park, physically and emotionally frustrated, she couples with a man she meets and hardly knows; in her vision, he is 'the gypsy man', the romantic lover of her dreams, who will give her the baby she desires.

The novel is comic and entertaining, yet interrogates traditional gender roles, too. There is something gypsy-like in the fantasy life of Naomi's husband, John, as well, for all his apparent obsession with the mundane need to save money. He sees Naomi and himself as 'vagabonds with a desire for order' (p. 26). Just as we glimpse the less attractive reality that lies beneath the exterior of the 'gypsy man', so we catch, with sympathy, a glimpse of the anxieties that lie beneath John's irascible front: 'I do the ironing. My son's best friend's mother called me domesticated and she didn't mean it kindly. Unmanly, that's me' (p. 25). His combat trousers are the costume of a man insecure in his status, unemployed and working at home; he is daunted by a 'young lion' of an adolescent on the tube going home (p. 110). We see him attempt to live a revivifying fantasy of love for a woman 'not his wife' (as it is put by another character) on this 'day of conquests' (p. 26), but it ends with his realisation of his need for Naomi.

Open to the reader, too, are the insecurities of physically-imperfect Roger, with his dwindling hair and his 'fat man's soul' (p. 122), embarrassed by his bodily functions and his 'lack of wit' (p. 50). Where John dreams of 'conquests', Roger dreams of chivalry; driving his BMW, Roger 'set his charger prancing to the task. His cool hands grasped the controls of his great grey steed' (p. 43).

Fairytale and myth dominate the characters' fantasy lives and are woven into the narrative itself, illustrating something explored by both Kesson and Tennant, the role of symbolic systems in human subjectivity. *The Beast* employs traditional fairy stories but undercuts conventional readings of them. The effects are often incongruous, both amusing and unsettling for the reader: Roger and his beautiful, physically perfect wife Jade are embodiments of 'Beauty and the Beast', but Jade is a modern beauty who buys her potions from the Body Shop. John kisses a sleeping au pair girl, awakening a sleeping beauty to a very angry and messy reality (she shits with fright), and Jade, too, is a kind of sleeping beauty, being sexually unawakened.

Yet if *The Beast* is a novel which encourages questioning, it is also very importantly a novel of celebration and affirmation. The two couples, Roger and Jade, and Naomi and John and their child Laurie, emerge in the course of a day spent together to tentative, partial understandings of what they want and can have in life. The importance of giving and receiving is signified by the gift of the Beast. Significantly, it has reached Jade by a complex route:

> My Chinese working companion gave me the culture, the beast. She used to live in Switzerland. The beast came from Russia. Really. A dissident got out. Some such thing. He brought the

beast with him. Didn't bring much but he brought that. It grows, you see. (p. 68)

The beast's cosmopolitan, eastern and 'dissident' origins, and its power to grow, are suggestive of the novel's own celebration of the marginal, the offbeat, the eccentric and the culturally diverse.

The novel charts 'magical encounters' that, despite their mundane setting, never entirely lose a slightly surreal or dreamlike quality: the very ordinary is shown to be enchanted or enchanting. Naomi's and John's son – usually referred to as just 'the boy' – *is* an 'ordinary boy', yet also 'stunningly beautiful, this ordinary boy' (p. 40). Roger, by the end, has entered fully the imaginative world of the boy and decided he wants a child himself, providing the novel with some of its most comically effective and touching moments, such as when he buys the boy no fewer than six 'Draculas' (ice lollies) and then stands with them melting in his hands.

Macdonald also charts and celebrates unlikely partnerships and collusions, such as Naomi's affinity with the young Muslim in the grocer shop, or the Scottish butcher who flirts with her. If Scotland enters the narrative, it is along with other marginalised cultures, as something 'real' in this society, yet a kind of trope, too, for imaginative otherness in the lives of the characters. Beautiful, frigid Jade, who has never had an orgasm, is 'enamoured of Jasmine, a Jewish girl from Edinburgh, who wanted to be a comedienne' (p. 109), a character suggesting several kinds of marginalisation, yet implied as powerful and enriching. The multicultural reality of British society is thus evoked, and used, too, to illustrate the persistence of Romantic longings in the characters: it is not merely incidental that the book which Jade lends to Naomi is *The Far Pavilions* (p. 106). That does not mean, however, that the novel enshrines the notion of Romantic escape.

The novel's ending offers both Romantic hope and a very modern kind of uncertainty. Naomi may well be, as she hopes, pregnant, but will it be by her husband or by 'the gypsy man'? Roger has learnt that he wants a child, and that he needs to lose weight; but what does the ending imply about his wife, Jade, who transmutes into plain (or is it Holy?) Mary, and has her first orgasm, but has it alone? The conclusion seems affirmative, on the whole, as the characters fall asleep, smiling, and 'the yogurt beast bubbled and smiled' (p. 128), but the book as a whole is too witty and delicately balanced to be accused of falling into a sentimental rounding-off. Rather, it is open-ended.

Sharman Macdonald has published only one other novel to date (*Night Night*, 1988), but deserves to be recognised as a considerable talent in drama as well as fiction. In Scotland, she is still discussed remarkably little, despite the success of her play *When I was a Girl I used to Scream and Shout* (1984), although, like Tennant, she acknowledges the significance to her of her Scottish background:

> Tale-telling in Scotland has developed into a fine art. Whether that's a Celtic trait, a Gaelic trait or what I don't know, but certainly the vocal tradition is very, very strong. It's true of the American South as well – maybe it comes from sitting on porches in the evening light spinning yarns. The same kind of thing happened in my grandmother's kitchen or when the women were talking – I remember that magic thing of listening to the women talk as they told stories of death, disaster and dire destruction, always with laughter in them.[26]

The tale-telling tradition is alive in the work of the writers discussed here, who combine in such diverse and creative ways the serious and the comic, the questioning and the life-affirming.

Kesson, Tennant and Macdonald are only three from among many deserving wider attention. Besides those mentioned earlier, there are numerous other talented women whose fiction might be considered: Moira Burgess, Janet Caird, Margaret D'Ambrosio, Joan Lingard and Agnes Owens, among others, are all interesting in their different ways. There has been some excellent work in the short-story form, too, with the award-winning collection by A. L. Kennedy, *Night Geometry and the Garscadden Trains*, and Dilys Rose's fine and rightly-praised *Our Lady of the Pickpockets*. The Polygon anthologies of writing by Scottish women reflect much activity and talent, most recently *Meantime*, as do women's contributions to literary magazines such as *New Writing Scotland*, *Chapman* and others. It will never again, I hope, be possible to see the Scottish literary tradition as a male province.

NOTES

1. The kinds of debate alluded to here are present in much feminist writing, particularly among French writers such as Hélène Cixous, Luce Irigaray and Julia Kristeva.
2. Flora Alexander, *Contemporary Women Novelists* (London: Edward Arnold, 1989), p. 76.
3. Works suggestive of this would include James Hogg's *Private Memoirs and Confessions of a Justified Sinner* (1824), R. L. Stevenson's *The Strange Case of Dr Jekyll and Mr Hyde* (1886), and non-fiction works such as R. D. Laing's *The Divided Self* (1960) and Karl Miller's *Doubles: Studies in Literary History* (1985).
4. For discussion of the problems of subjectivity for women, see for instance Catherine Belsey, 'Constructing the Subject: Deconstructing the Text' in *Feminist Criticism and Social Change: Sex, Class and Race in Literature and Culture*, ed. Judith Newton and Deborah

Rosenfelt (New York and London: Methuen, 1985), pp. 45–64. For specific discussion of the Scottish situation, see Joy Hendry, 'The Double Knot in the Peeny' in *In other Words: Writing as a Feminist*, ed. Gail Chester and Sigrid Nielsen (London: Hutchinson, 1987), and 'Twentieth-Century Women's Writing: The Nest of Singing Birds' in *The History of Scottish Literature* vol. 4: *The Twentieth Century*, ed. Cairns Craig (Aberdeen: Aberdeen University Press, 1987), pp. 291–309.

5. Coral Ann Howalls, *Private and Fictional Words: Canadian Women Novelists of the 1970s and 1980s* (London and New York: Methuen, 1987), p. 13.
6. See, for example, Maggie Humm, *Border Traffic: Strategies of Contemporary Women Writers* (Manchester: Manchester University Press, 1981) and Patricia Waugh, *Feminine Fictions: Revisiting the Postmodern* (London: Routledge, 1989).
7. For explanation and discussion of these terms, see Catherine Belsey, *Critical Practice* (London: Methuen, 1980; reprinted London and New York: Routledge, 1991). See especially Chapter 4.
8. Julia Kristeva, in *Polylogue* (Paris: Seuil, 1977), p. 159, quoted in 'Talking about *Polylogue*' in *French Feminist Thought: A Reader*, ed. Toril Moi (Oxford: Basil Blackwell, 1987), p. 113.
9. Thomas Docherty, 'Postmodern Characterization: The Ethics of Alterity', in *Postmodernism and Contemporary Fiction*, ed. Edmund J. Smyth (London: Batsford, 1991), pp. 187–8.
10. Walter Ong, *Orality and Literacy: The Technologizing of the Word* (1982; reprinted London: Routledge, 1990), pp. 32–3.
11. Julia Kristeva, from 'La femme, ce n'est jamais ça' (Woman can never be defined), an interview by 'psychoanalysis and politics' in *Tel Quel*, Autumn 1974, reprinted in *New French Feminisms*, ed. Elaine Marks and Isabelle de Courtivron (Brighton: Harvester Press, 1980), p. 137.
12. Jessie Kesson, *Another Time, Another Place* (London: Chatto & Windus/The Hogarth Press, 1983). Subsequent references are to this edition.
13. Interviews with Tennant include John Haffenden, *Novelists in Interview* (London: Methuen, 1985), pp. 281–304; Olga Kenyon, *Women Writers Talk* (Oxford: Lennard Publishing, 1989), pp. 173–187; 'Margaret Atwood in Conversation with Emma Tennant' in *Women's Review*, 21 July 1987, pp. 8–10.
14. Kenyon, p. 181.
15. Haffenden, p. 293.
16. Kenyon, p. 177.
17. Haffenden, p. 292.
18. Emma Tennant, *The Bad Sister* (London: Victor Gollancz, 1978; reprinted London: Faber and Faber, 1989), p. 11. Subsequent references are to the Faber edition.
19. George Eliot, *The Mill on the Floss*, 3 vols (Edinburgh and London: William Blackwood, 1860), vol. II, p. 266.

20. See, for example, 'Sorties, Out and Out, Attacks/Ways Out/Forays' in Hélène Cixous and Catherine Clément. *The Newly Born Woman*, trans. Betsy Wing (Manchester: Manchester University Press, 1987, pp. 63–131, first published in France as *Le Jeune Née*, 1975).
21. Haffenden, p. 289. Further references are to this interview.
22. Ibid., p. 292.
23. Ibid., p. 293.
24. Kenyon, p. 176.
25. Sharman Macdonald, *The Beast* (London and Glasgow: William Collins, 1986; reprinted London: Fontana, 1987), p. 39. Subsequent references are to the Fontana edition.
26. 'Speaking Mother Tongues', Sharman Macdonald interviewed by Sabine Durrant, *The Independent*, 9 January 1991, p. 14.

Thirteen

Gnawing the Mammoth: History, Class and Politics in the Modern Scottish and Welsh Novel

Christopher Harvie

> 'Does your novel have a title?' Llewellyn asked.
>
> 'Something like, "Whatever happened to Jerusalem", with an exclamation mark.'
>
> 'You don't mean that, of course.'
>
> 'All right, what about "Arrows of Desire"?'
>
> 'So it's all about the crumbling of ideals. The young hero seduced by fame and the good life, abandoning responsibilities. Meanwhile back in his home town the pinched faces of the unemployed hang over their bowls of thin gruel in the soup kitchens. He's a poor lost soul, the tiresome git, and makes a pilgrimage of rediscovery – self-regeneration by sharing the poverty of the noble proles he left behind. But it's too late. He forgot the golden rule. Never Go Back. They shun him in the streets. They *stone* him in the streets. But there's this old flame he put in the family way when he was the hope of the valley – it's got to be set in Wales, this – and now she's grey and withered. She alone befriends him and takes him to her bed. The roof falls in just as he's giving her one.'[1]

This caricature of the postwar British political novel seems the right place to begin. It is from *Mid-Century Men* (1982) by Arthur Hopcraft, one of the few novels worth reading in a genre now as decrepit as its subject matter, but once both commentary and convention within the 'theatre of politics', from Disraeli to Joyce Cary.[2]

'It's got to be set in Wales.' Hopcraft's clichés are based on Howard Spring's *Fame is the Spur* (1940) and the 1950s parliamentary novels of Maurice Edelman. Both were Cardiff men; Spring's family were Irish and Edelman's Russian Jewish, representative – along with Orcadian Eric Linklater (born in Barry) and Norwegian Roald Dahl (born in

Cowbridge) – of 'cosmopolitan South Wales' at its zenith. Spring and Edelman dealt with 'British' politics, centred on Westminster, with only a marginal, stereotyped Welsh presence. Richard Hughes's remarkable *The Human Predicament* (1961, 1973) took off from Wales to explore the psychosis of interwar Europe. By contrast, a sequence about the greatest of all Welsh politicians, David Lloyd George – Joyce Cary's *Chester Nimmo* trilogy (1953–5), which has claims to be the last great British political novel – was written by an Oxford-based Anglo-Irishman and set in Devon.

The 'matter of Wales' is less precise than 'the matter of Scotland'. Borders seem to matter more than the nation. The very fact that Wales is, in Dennis Balsom's model, 'divisible into three parts' – Y Fro Cymraeg, Welsh Wales and British Wales – reinforces this. Yet, in this, class remains fundamental and also unsettling: not the 'layer cake of fine class distinctions' which Ralf Dahrendorf sees as stabilising English society, but not the activism of the class-conscious proletariat either.[3]

In Welsh nationalism, this dialectic penetrates to the bone. At Machynlleth in September 1989, Dafydd Elis Thomas, representing a Welsh identity surfing, so to speak, down the waves of historical and economic change, came up against R. S. Thomas's discourse of Wales as the epic of the *gwerin*, but one facing annihilation with the threat to the language. Frustrated Marxists confront pessimistic nationalists: Gwyn Alfie Williams's *When Was Wales?* versus Emyr Humphreys's *The Taliesin Tradition*. This conflict made the front page of the *Daily Post* and the *Western Mail*. In Scotland, Professor Alan Peacock, when appointed chairman of the Scottish Arts Council in 1986, confessed that the notion of any Scottish literary revival was news to him.

Literature is politics in Wales in a way in which it is not in Scotland. A few years ago, the Welsh equivalent to *A Scots Quair* would have been *How Green Was My Valley* (1939), well-crafted, Dylan-Thomas-and-water illiberal hokum which could reduce Aberdare miners in the 1960s to tears[4] – much less likely in these days of Welsh-language television. But Scotland still has a bulky commercial literary output, much of it semi-political or historical in subject matter. Dorothy Dunnett, Nigel Tranter, Alastair MacLean and George MacDonald Fraser are at its (rather traditional) upper end, until recently deftly exploited by Collins in Glasgow. A new commercial order might be discernible in the phenomenon of 'Alastair McClone'; the risible 'Scottish' element in Jeffrey Archer's *First Among Equals* (1984); Mrs Rupert Murdoch's everyday stories about media tycoons; and the truly appalling *Elite* (1989) by Helen Liddell, former Secretary of the Scottish Council of the

Labour Party. But this strengthens the argument that tackling the novel of politics means tackling the politics of cultural production.

The Scottish equivalent to the Machynlleth confrontation was the struggle over 'Glasgow: European City of Culture' between Scottish urban radicals and the 'bourgeois regionalism' which had brought Glasgow to European notice. Alasdair Gray, Liz Lochhead, Agnes Owens, James Kelman etc. had their own idea of a small-scale socialist *polis* and an order of media which would allow 'folk on low incomes' to talk to one another. The range of experience and opinion which they represented was far beyond that of, say, the Dublin suburban novel – Roddy Doyle's Rabbite books. This suggests that the attempt to mediate between MacDiarmid and Gibbon and A. J. Cronin and the Broons might yet prove successful.[5]

The goal of Alasdair Gray's 'Scottish Co-operative Wholesale Republic' – autonomous rather than nationalist – is one that the *Blaid* formulated long ago, though the Scots reader-and-writership has been formed by both industrialisation and a complicated history and civil society. Why is it presently richer than Wales, and far richer than the English provinces, in those elements of individuality through which the novel bursts into its own identity?[6] To answer this means examining the way in which the imaginative portrayal of politics and class was in the past related both to actual change and to its enclosure by the 'rationale' of print capitalism and civil society.

Scots political fiction was always 'extraparliamentary'; its 'theatre of politics' both intimate and cosmic, with a satire, irony and obliquity which were turned on the individual's ideological and psychological involvement with the political. Galt, Scott and Hogg did not just comment on but were also *part* of Scotland's 'willed' modernisation; this impulse transformed itself into the 'popular print capitalism' of Victorian newspaper novels. Peacock – maybe – apart, there was no Welsh equivalent until the Kailyard, which promoted pietistic kitsch and Sunday-school goody-books, ripping off Bunyan and Scottish or Welsh rural society. The counterattack – out of Ibsen, Wells and the Russians – was devastating right along the Celtic line: J. M. Synge and the young Joyce, George Douglas Brown, MacDougall Hay, Caradoc Evans; but this vertiginous consciousness was based on wobbly industrial foundations.

World War I turned economic development sour and destroyed communities; Ramsay MacDonald's 'ethical socialism' did not work. Post-Versailles nationalism and communism became rival heirs; while Plaid Cymru and the National Party of Scotland were being formed in

1925 and 1928 respectively, the CPGB was learning to love the directives of the Kremlin. In the mid-1930s, quite suddenly – although perhaps deriving some inspiration from Scots writers like James Welsh and Joe Corrie – came the Welsh Mining Novel: Jack Jones, Gwyn Jones, Lewis Jones and the young Gwyn Thomas, not to mention *How Green Was My Valley*, Alexander Cordell, Howard Spring and so on in the 1940s and 1950s; A. J. Cronin, Nigel Tranter, Alastair MacLean and more, many more, provided a Scottish accompaniment. After the difficult and authentic came the crafted and commercial.

This seemed to subdue native literary imagination, but in Scotland activity has now regained the volubility of the early 1800s. If current Scottish politics has a slogan, it must be Alasdair Gray's 'Work as if you were living in the early days of a better nation', which comes from the cover of *Unlikely Stories, Mostly* (1983) and reappears in the climax – in every sense of the term – of his *1982, Janine*.[7] Both hiatus and sudden flowering have to be explained.

In 'The Body in the Kitbag', a seminal essay of the 1980s, Cairns Craig, whose *The History of Scottish Literature* (1987–9) is itself a cultural marker, wrote that the Scots predicament was, currently, that of being 'history-less'. His image came from a story in Alan Sharp's neo-Gibbonian *A Green Tree in Gedde* (1964): a Scots soldier's fear of leaving his community leads him first to incarcerate himself in his kitchen and then to kill himself by getting into a kitbag, attaching its drawstring to the ceiling and rolling off the table.[8] Scotland, by losing – or rather failing to trace – its history in the nineteenth century, had become agoraphobic: it was terrified of resuming contact with great economic and social projects. The referendum of 1979 seemed to have us clambering into the kitbag.

In fact, it did the opposite. The politicians retreated, the writers – academic and imaginative – advanced. The impact of the gaining of S4C cannot be underestimated: if the Welsh, after the referendum, could do *that* . . . The Scots came rather quickly to realise, through the research which was filling in the great lacuna of industrialising Scotland, that their working-class culture *has always needed* the 'ideal types' of fiction, however unconventional – satire, morality, imaginative autobiography, newspaper serials. 'If a city hasn't been used by an artist not even the inhabitants live there imaginatively' – Gray again, in *Lanark*. Fiction has dissolved into history and present politics. More importantly, using another Gray symbol, it has drawn its own maps.[9]

Are such maps necessary? Orthodox Marxism regarded class-consciousness as sufficient. But neither country's political resources –

whether class-formation or nationalism – were straightforward, and the social structures created by the dialogue of these and the productive process are distinctive. Wales was divided by the language, which has its own clerisy and collectivity. After the 1930s, a remarkable but chronologically restricted Anglo-Welsh politico-literary output showed how class, nonconformity and elements of the *gwerin* ideology could produce a socalist literature. But, through Richard Llewellyn and A. J. Cronin (again!), these ingredients also created an instant industrial Kailyard. The 'Red Clyde' literature of the 1930s – by Davie Kirkwood, Tom Bell, Willie Gallacher and James Barke – was in some ways a comparable movement, and also implied a wider claim to *represent* Scotland. But its outcome was a flow into British politics: Ewan Tavendale leading his hunger-marchers south in *Grey Granite* (1934); Jennie Lee in *Tomorrow is a New Day* (1939) bidding farewell to the mining *gemeinschaft* of West Fife and marrying Aneurin Bevan; Edwin Muir rejecting the whole nationalist literary project in *Scott and Scotland* (1936).

In fact, Scotland and Wales were about as different as any two working-class societies could be. In Wales, mining and metal-processing were supreme: over 250,000 employees in 1910, against 132,000 in Scotland, while heavy engineering and shipbuilding were less important (91,000 to 231,000). Wales was a 'feeder' economy to English industrial districts, with a specialised directive Anglophone bourgeoisie. Scotland was really a miniature of the whole British economy. Class could also divide. The West Central Scottish skilled working class was sixty to seventy per cent of the male labour force. Riveters, patternmakers, boilermakers and engineers were distinct from the 'labour aristocracy' of England or Edinburgh, having continuity with the rural craftsmen, cottars and farm workers, and much of their fierce independence.[10] 'My class was earning its living in sweat,' Gibbon's Chris Colquhoun tells an unemployed man in *Grey Granite*, 'while yours was lying down with a whine in the dirt.'[11] Welsh rural-urban continuity replaced the struggle on the land with the collier-coalowner battle. But the consciousness of being *embodied* in the creation of something of great beauty – such as a ship or locomotive – which is bound to be destroyed is different from the coalmining experience.

Cosmopolitan Wales was an 'immigration' culture with the miners and railwaymen at its centre, in small, semi-rural communities. Its people lived somewhere: Meadow Prospect, Pandy, Glanyrafon. Scotland was the opposite, subject to rapid and wholesale urbanisation in which 'nothing endured but change'. Children continuously left the working class – for middle-class positions, for futures in Canada or New

Zealand. Clydesiders lived in a city which was always in flux – from linen to textiles to engineering to ships to banks and offices; from cottage to slum tenement to housing scheme to thirty-storey point block.

The result was a practical juxtaposition of the real and the incredible. Pride in craft has persisted in journalism and among Grierson's successors in documentary, but also in the ironic sculptures of George Wylie – his straw locomotive, his metal 'paper boat' portending Gwyn Alfie Williams's 'b-biggest bloody industrial heritage trail in Europe'. In Alasdair Gray's *Lanark* (1981), there is an anti-Glasgow called the Institute hundreds of feet underground. This is a fantasy. In reality, thousands of Glasgow people live hundreds of feet in the air. Disappearance and transformation are inherently part of Scottish working-class experience. Up to now, half the Scottish population has been all but invisible.

The Scottish and Welsh clerisies were distinctive. The Welsh-speakers lodged themselves in academia and the media, areas which in Scotland were subject to English colonisation. Yet Scots who went south remained Scots, whereas many South Welsh – from Edelman and Spring to Michael Heseltine and Geoffrey Howe – assimilated effortlessly. English commercial writers, such as Kingsley Amis and Bernard Levin, were allowed to insult the Welsh. They were much more circumspect about the Scots.

The crucial and enduring Anglo-Scots paradigm was John Buchan, publisher, public servant, politician, spy. His type was better at marketing nationalism of a rather high-Tory, Jacobite sort (Eric Linklater, Compton Mackenzie, at first glance Neil Gunn) than the undisciplined communism of Grassic Gibbon and MacDiarmid, yet he never wholly entered English society. As 'people's remembrancer', Buchan needed a Scottish resonance: only there would he find 'a seat by the fire and a special chunk of mammoth'.[12]

In Wales, political nationalism was and (unlike in Scotland) remains culture-based. Kate Roberts and T. Rowland Hughes tackled the same sort of theme as Gibbon, but were marginalised by the destruction of the war, the depression, the decline of the language and nonconformity, not to mention the hostility to the industrial order of Plaid Cymru's leader Saunders Lewis as dramatist, novelist and critic. While Neil Gunn almost attained a cognate role in Scottish politics, helping to create the SNP in 1933–4 but then choosing to stay in the background, Lewis and his allies, by sheer force of personality, imprinted themselves on *Blaid* policies. When the Welsh mining novel came in – just as the

Scots started to flag – it was a vehicle promoted in aid of the 'British' *gemeinschaft* of the Popular Front. It did not urge revolution, still less national independence along Lewis's Catholic conservative lines.[13]

From the 1940s to the 1970s, a Conservative party doctrine of 'central autonomy' preserved such regional peculiarities, just like T.S. Eliot's recipe in *Notes towards the Definition of Culture* (1947). This tolerance underlies Cary's *Chester Nimmo* and the plays of John Arden after 1956. Cary subsumes Lloyd George into the British nonconformist radical experience, and Arden reopens 'the matter of Britain' in *The Island of the Mighty* (1961) and *Armstrong's Last Goodnight* (1963). In Wales, there is uncertainty. Raymond Williams's careful attempt to extend his 'border country' from Abergavenny to Cambridge ('by measuring the distance, we come home') was coupled with the project in *Culture and Society* (1958) to replace Eliot with a left-wing interpretation of the British *gemeinschaft*.[14]

But the left was unfriendly to national identity. The socialist epiphany over which Edwin Muir had agonised in a novel like *Poor Tom* (1934) seemed embodied in Aneurin Bevan: a resolute anti-devolutionist whose name was talismanic in the Labour party anywhere. 'Britain' did not, however, take up this Jacobin opportunity. In J. D. Scott's *The End of an Old Song* (1954), a 'lad o' pairts' smashes his way out of Kingisbyres, a Jacobite-Mackenzieite epitome of Scots history, but rejects Britain as fainéant; his future lies, like that of Scott himself, in America. In Wales, more tragically, Gwyn Thomas's baroque, internationalist pessimism made its own accommodation with the British literary world, to be marketed in *Punch* as a proletarian P. G. Wodehouse.[15] Tolerance came out of lassitude, not enterprise.

With Gwyn Thomas and Raymond Williams, Emyr Humphreys and Richard Hughes, the Wales of the 1960s was articulate. A Welsh 'reader-and-writership', anglophone but national, was being built up.[16] During this period, the Scots were either silent or cryptic. As Glenda Norquay observed, the 'Calvinist convention' of the time – 'the obsession with the dream of transcendence' – seemed to usher the active hero, and the active author, Robin Jenkins, Alan Sharp, James Kennaway, out of the country.[17]

The Scottish and Welsh literary 'professions' were predominantly 'amateur', part of the state-sector middle class: teachers, academics, journalists and broadcasters, activists in various bodies receiving Arts Council subsidies. The alternative, the market-forces-driven Anglo-Scottish littérateur, diminished with the steady transfer of mass-market publishing southwards.

This sapped one area of ambiguity, seen in several Scottish instances and in the notable Welsh one of Raymond Williams: the distance between 'Cambridge' and 'home'. Allan Massie, a leading realist and deeply 'political' novelist, still bears its traces. Massie's subjects take on a European conspectus: the kidnapping and murder of Aldo Moro in *The Death of Men* (1981), Vichy France in *A Question of Loyalties* (1988). He has also intervened frequently in Scottish politics, moving from fringe devolution in the 1970s to embattled Unionism in the 1980s. Too serious ever to become a Scottish Auberon Waugh, and apparently devoted to his uncomfortable Scottish location – what would have happened had he gone to London like Clive James? – his one encounter with contemporary Scotland was *One Night in Winter*, published by Cape in 1984.

Massie confesses a debt to Buchan, and one thinks, though only momentarily, of *Castle Gay* (1932). But the tone is elegiac, the attitude to nationalism dismissive. Massie's narrator, Dallas Graham, returns to his family mansion in Kincardineshire and joins the louche entourage of a rising SNP politician called Fraser Donnelly. Donnelly, a haulage contractor, represents the new enterprise culture (though John Gourlay, too, was thus occupied). A monster of the permissive age, sexually voracious, he is killed off by his wife while in flagrante. As a handy Marxist friend assures Graham, Donnelly is what small nationalism would turn out to be: nasty, brutish and Scots.

Ultimately, *One Night in Winter* is mechanically derivative where not melodramatic: Lampedusa, Anthony Powell and John Fowles leave their prints on too many episodes. Only the final section, when Graham, now an antique dealer in London, tries to make contact with Donnelly's widow/murderess, conveys a sense of individual experience. Massie's point may indeed be that real life can only be lived away from the Scottish phantasmagoria; but delineating the Scottish situation – even if only to reject it – requires greater empathy.

Bewilderment rather than exhaustion is implied in another, more fricative 'Buchanite': James Kennaway in *Tunes of Glory* (1956) and *The Bells of Shoreditch* (1963). In the latter, which Kennaway based on the alleged 'Bank-Rate Leak' of 1957, Stella MacNaughton, kept from being too much a Chris Guthrie by a sexuality which is the more compelling for being implied, sublimates her ILP politics in an affair with a London merchant banker. She writes to her cousin George, about her husband:

> With Glasgow people like you, and me, politics is a part of life, isn't it. It's life, from hot tears in a corner to a Sunday outing with some ridiculous flag, Sister Anna and the rest – but not for

> Andrew. With him politics is a thing apart. You could drop an atomic bomb on Berlin and he would still have to pretend he's been to vote.

Ultimately, Stella cannot disentangle politics from sex: 'the old magnet thing, felt hard and strong and low, dreamt about, hated, loved, all the rest . . .'[18] Coupling with Sarson is for her both necessary – getting to the centre of power – and a betrayal: of principle, marriage, the idea of a just society. The symbolism of *The Bells of Shoreditch* shows Kennaway uncomfortable with his early Unionism, a fecund uncertainty which remained, tragically, undeveloped.

'Cambridge' also haunts Stuart Hood's *The Upper Hand* (1987), in the intertwined careers of Colin Elphinstone, an aristocratic Scot who becomes a Soviet agent in the 1930s, and John Melville, the son of the local Free Church minister, who observes him as a government agent. Melville versus Elphinstone suggests Edwin Muir's image of Scottish stasis, the confrontation of Calvinism and cultivation: 'But Knox and Melville clapped their preaching palms/ And bundled all the harvesters away'. The emergence of Scot after Scot from the intestines of British Intelligence and the BBC reflects that division of the Scots psyche on which R. D. Laing, Karl Miller and John Herdman have commented, but ultimately produces a curiously parochial atmosphere: the Kailyard – or the gossip of Barbie's 'bodies' – rendered on a global scale.[19]

The constellation of media, patriotism and 'intelligence' also attracted two of the principal cultural historians of the New Left – Scottish and Welsh – into writing their own 'theoretical histories'. In David Craig's *The Rebels and the Hostage* (1978), a group of young radicals, based on the Baeder-Meinhof gang and the Angry Brigade, kidnaps a senior civil servant and is tracked down by the authorities, cheated and killed. The interest here is as much in the attempt to control media coverage as in the relationships of captors, captured and pursuers. The reader's last images – of the shooting of the rebels and their hostage – are carried by the portable TV which has been their link with the outside.

The comparison is obvious enough with the later fiction of Raymond Williams, particularly *Loyalties* (1985), where the solidarity of the Welsh mining community is contrasted with the communist elitism of another agent, Sir Norman Braose. The name here is interesting, as it was the Norman Baron de Braose who set up the infamous 'night of the long knives' at Abergavenny Castle in 1176 in which the retainers of the Welsh king were surprised at a peaceable dinner and slain. 'Braose *bradwr*' – 'Braose the traitor': Williams gives the game away right from the beginning to his Welsh compatriots; the English are kept guessing.

The problem with nearly all Williams's fiction, after the early and effective *Border Country* (1960), is that obscurity of style seems to mask simple and over-unproblematic loyalties. Politics, in the sense of transaction and manoeuvre, scarcely figures. Perhaps this is inseparable from Williams's own 'frontier' position: his search for community. He had to revise *Border Country* seven times before publication, and this shows in the empathy – not automatic but carefully crafted – which he has for a highly 'politicised' figure like Morgan Rosser, whose class-identity is qualified by his business and council career but reified again by his capacity for friendship. The Matthew Price of *Border Country*, confronted with the almost choking intimacy of a working-class, nonconformist Welsh community, is more believable than the conscious 'scientist' of the latter novels. As with Ewan Tavendale at the end of *Grey Granite*, we feel that Matthew, however 'right' he is, has moved away from the environment which gave him strength.

A similar underlying pessimism can be seen in Emyr Humphreys's remarkable *roman fleuve* which started out as *Land of the Living* and is now called, more soberly, *Bonds of Attachment*. Humphreys's first volume, *National Winner* (1971), is disappointing, a novel of the Melvyn Bragg/Raymond Williams mediacentric type: the two sons of a Welsh poet attempt to work out their own emotional problems in parallel with investigating the reasons for their father's death. But then, in a series of beautifully-crafted social tragicomedies, Humphreys centred the series on John Cilydd Jones's widow, Amy Parry, producing someone closer to Stella MacNaughton than to Chris Guthrie, though calculatedly less attractive. Amy's progress, from her childhood as the adopted daughter of a Welsh-speaking Methodist radical in a North Wales quarry village, to her marriage to John Cilydd, one of the generation around Saunders Lewis, then her desertion of Welsh nationalism for British Labourism, provides a perceptive 'realist' commentary on the course of Welsh identity in this century, to which no parallel exists in Scotland. Its symbolism is also unhopeful. Neither of Amy's boys is by Cilydd: the elder is adopted, Cilydd's son by her friend Enid Prydderch, who died in childbirth; the other is by Pen Lewis, a barely-fictionalised Lewis Jones, who goes off to die in Spain.

Amy is less than admirable, but she is a survivor, and in her seems to reside a Welsh *geist*: 'The central figure had to be a woman. Wales would have disappeared long ago if it had depended on men.'[20] Humphreys's position is, however, challenged by critics who regard him as illegitimately blending the myths of 'tribal' discourse with the 'industrial' evolution of the South Wales working class, recapturing the past for a tiny Welsh-speaking elite. As with Anthony Powell, the civility of the discourse may be used to sell us a deeply conservative interpretation.[21]

I think this underestimates Humphreys's liberalism – his enthusiasm for Saunders Lewis never led him to deprecate the philosophical strength of nonconformity – his skill in characterisation, and his ultimate pessimism. A much more convincing successor to Saunders Lewis – in anti-industrial Catholic conviction, medievalism and 'European' moralism – would be the Orcadian George Mackay Brown in *Greenvoe* (1972) and *Magnus* (1973). But both Humphreys and Scotland's 'neo-Calvinists' in the 1960s were limited by the novel as the 'history' of a national, public-sector bourgeoisie, threatened with betrayal or rampant materialism when action moved to the political centre. Hence the central symbol of the journalist or the spy, not the participative politician; or of the country as woman, whether 'White Goddess' or passive endurer. Retrospection, moreover, seemed unavoidable where the cards were always stacked against the local; where the initiative always rested with 'the greater herd and the great machines'.

Such fiction runs the threat of being pigeonholed by the market: Eng. Lit. and its restrictive readership at one end; 'MacCloning' at the other. Humphreys and Williams, as much as Hood and Massie, show overall 'pessimism of the intellect'. The phrase is from Antonio Gramsci, Sardinian, communist, cultural theorist, a portentous figure in both countries.[22] Scott, Galt and Hogg likewise saw that the future was moving away from them, and grand political gestures making it move even faster, yet exploited this predicament through a discourse of masterly scope and originality. Does the present 'break up of Britain' offer a similar, but more positive, opportunity?

The work that best fits this point of balance is Robin Jenkins's *Fergus Lamont*, which appeared in the fateful year of 1979, a biography of a twentieth-century nationalist littérateur unrooted in 'real' politics. Fergus has elements of MacDiarmid, Compton Mackenzie and Muir, and is conman and fantasist, willing participant in the Kailyard. That he manages to find fulfilment with his avatar, the practical, pipe-smoking Kirstie, on a Hebridean island, suggests that human potential lies not in Anglo-Scottish 'glittering prizes' but in liberating the potential for delight inhering in ordinary people: a return in some ways to the philosophy of Neil Gunn's moral fables. On the other hand, Fergus is a Galtian 'theoretical historian' in the Balwhidder, Pawkie, Jobbry succession, and indicates new and hopeful departures in narrative and structure.

Such opportunities stress the second part of the Gramsci phrase – 'optimism of the will'. Once the citizen – no less than the intellectual – has made sense of his *total* social position, his relation to the structures by which power and ideology are exercised, he can act – particularly when the structures of politics are themselves in flux. What we call 'postmodernism', in the Scottish context also incorporating 'premodernism', locates the Scottish experience by breaking down the isolation of the text – as well as that of the individual – to let in the audience, the ideology and the productive mechanism. Only of limited effect in London, with several English-language cultures pouring in on it, this revelation is vital in a resource-starved province, where our texts must provide some sort of shelter for our own consciousness.[23]

If Scottish involvement in party politics has usually diminished nation and individual, Scottish involvement with print-capitalism is almost vertiginous: Scott's incredible leap into the historical novel *and* the cheap books business; the newspaper serialists subverting the notion of the Victorian novel as a high-price bourgeois neighbourhood.[24] Even Robertson Nicoll and Buchan made classic literature available to the likes of Caradoc Evans, Muir and MacDiarmid, in a mass enlightenment aimed at the boarding-school pupil-teacher and the office worker, which compares very well with the Marie Corelli/Charles Garvice/William Le Queux rubbish which the English lower middle class was being fed. This was a Scoto-Welsh project. Robert Owen, of Newtown and New Lanark, Sir Henry Jones, Tom Jones and Emrys Hughes came north. *Y Traethodydd* always kept its eye on Edinburgh. Keir Hardie and MacDiarmid were part of 'cosmopolitan South Wales'. John Grierson's influence continues to lie long over S4C.[25]

The blossoming of this in Scottish fiction is the work of the 1980s, but its roots lie somewhat earlier in the drama. John Arden wrote that the revival of Sir David Lindsay's *The Three Estates* in Edinburgh in 1948 was a revelation to him: he did not have to read the theory of Brecht; he could see already how it functioned.[26] In the 1970s, political argument and entertainment were further fused to praxis by John McGrath and in particular by *The Cheviot, the Stag and the Black, Black Oil*, whose tour of the Highlands in 1973 awoke the Scots to the issue of oil, influencing consciousness and action. The drama had a cognate importance to Alasdair Gray, long before *Lanark* made its appearance, and the central episode of *1982, Janine* is McLeish's transformation through lighting effects of the essentially Galt-and-Barrie 'Scotchman on the make' entertainment of *McGrotty and Ludmilla* (1990) into cosmic drama.[27]

Old-style politics, taken neat, makes the people of *Lanark* change into dragons. Thus dehumanised, they get eaten, which is as good a place as any to begin. Kurt Wittig, Douglas Gifford and Rory Watson believe that the Scottish novel must be realistic; it must also be fantastic, overdriven, grotesque: our old friend the antisyzygy again. As James Kelman puts it: 'Getting rid of that standard third-party narrative voice is getting rid of the whole value system'. We walk back along the tracks, trying to find the relevant set of points, and we find them – like so much else – in Thomas Carlyle.[28]

Carlyle presents the Enlightenment, in which his own loyalties lay, with its principle of an eternal pattern in human relationships, heaved towards chaos by the French and industrial revolutions. Escape came through reading the signs, existentially grasping and modelling reality. Carlyle leads directly to the *Communist Manifesto*. Through his influence on Disraeli, he is behind the English political novel, which dissipates the crisis of the 1840s by fusing the theatre of politics to the 'layer-cake of fine class distinctions'. But he also brings in myth and language: the doomed priest in the wood, the enchantress, the bard. He revivifies that division between the rational and the fantastic. The files of *Y Traethodydd*, the early career of Lloyd George, show him little less influential in Wales but – significantly – as an English writer. He is the great signpainter, and when we interpret his legacy we dissolve literature into political action.

Sartor Resartus lurks throughout *Lanark* and *1982, Janine*; Carlyle himself surfaces in Frederic Lindsay's *Brond* (1983), a complex elliptic thriller whose masochistic, imperturbable magus – a South African agent, an MI5 man, the devil, God? – seems the 'eternal nay' personified. References to Northern Ireland – the Scottish Mrs Rochester, locked up in the west wing of our consciousness – remind us of the line in 'Characteristics': 'civilisation as the "thin crust" over the cauldron', and its subsequent provenance in Disraeli, Wells, Buchan and Le Carré. Carlyle, through his modern interpreters, conveys the sense that Scotland is a place where the intimate can disturb – destructively – if not interpreted with imagination and sensitivity.

'The interpreter's house' – a symbol from one 'great overlapper', John Bunyan, amplified by a second, John Buchan – can provide us, in closing, with a map of the concerns of our new political fiction. 'Premature postmodernism' gives a 'theoretical history' which works its way out from the *gestalt* of the individual in society, and from the most intimate of politics. The Victorians were uninformative about sex, in a society as deeply repressed as the Scots. A Carlyle pamphlet, never completed, was on 'Phallus-worship', written against the sentimental eroticism of George Sand: 'Unhappy generation of the world, which has no marching-standards but these two: a Phallus and a moneybag'.[30] When Stevenson was regretting such sublimation at the end of his own life, J. G. Frazer was assembling that huge compendium *The Golden Bough* on the persistence of myth and ritual in what Eliot, his disciple, defined as human: 'birth, copulation and death'.

In the Scottish tradition, the male-female relationship is more than sexual, it is both religious and rational: Goethe's 'Das ewige-weibliche zieht uns hinan'. The most serious Scottish treatment in Scottish fiction of the Enlightenment agenda – and the *Faust* motif – is also 'a sado-masochistic fantasy set inside the head of an ageing inspector of security installations'. God appears during a typographical orgasm also involving alcoholism, attempted suicide and clothes-fetishism. *1982, Janine* is unlikely to figure in many sermons, but Gray's politics force us to reconsider not only male sexuality but also the metaphysical roots of religion and politics.[31]

Sex ought to be an intimate and generous politics. MacDiarmid's *Drunk Man* sees this as having continuity with the politically orgasmic: the crucified rose blossoming and withering in the General Strike. This stands opposed to the power-sex of Kennaway's *Bells of Shoreditch* and McLeish's pornography, or that didactic nudity in Grassic Gibbon, where Ewan Tavendale and his girlfriend couple in the cause of diffusionism, like naked hunters before they died of clothes and agriculture.

'There's more enterprise', Gray seems to agree with Yeats, 'in walking naked'. In Lanark you are lucky to have skin: Dragonhide can turn you into a tasty mollusc. Jock McLeish and his fantasy lover Janine end *1982, Janine* spiritually naked, and the book's only illustration – McLeish delicately poised *as* acrobat – is also a nude, suggesting da Vinci or William Blake. This is a nakedness of equality and vulnerability, not of *Playboy* exploitation – not far from *Sartor Resartus* or, perhaps, from Gwyn Alfie Williams's vivid ending to *When Was Wales?*: 'my people and no mean people, who have for a millennium and a half lived in them as a Welsh people, are now nothing but a naked people under an acid rain'.[32]

From the naked individual, the 'conjectural history' of the Enlightenment takes us to the family and its ideology. Sentimentalised by Burns in 'A Cottar's Saturday Night', the Scots family was still like a diminished clan, as D. H. Lawrence described it in *The First Lady Chatterley*: something peculiarly enveloping which mimicked society, rather than something stemming from sex.[33] In *Lanark*, the parents of the asthmatic Thaw torture him out of affection and ignorance, not alienation or hatred. 'Sympathy' – out of Adam Smith – subsists, although its consequences can be bizarre. The same choking solidarity exists in Grassic Gibbon, where John Guthrie, whose sexual urges destroy his wife and whose temper drives his sons abroad, still forces his daughter's and our political sympathy. The Morgans in *How Green Was My Valley* are an exaggerated version of sensitively-drawn families in Gwyn Thomas, Lewis Jones or Raymond Williams, where the father-figures are variously sorrowful-comic, epic-heroic, or dignified epitomes of class-solidarity.[34]

The Scottish or Welsh continuum of experience between working- and middle-class life may be cemented by the fact that education does not mean separation; the young man or woman has got to negotiate the family. Such families need not be happy – Humphreys's title *Bonds of Attachment* seems to denote relationships through which affection can crush and deform. But could a Scots or Welsh author emulate Nicholas Jenkins in Anthony Powell's *Dance to the Music of Time* (1951–75), who tells us nothing about his wife or children? In Scotland or Wales, family is a part of a geographical and political community; in England, such families as matter are part of an established social/landed/professional order, and the ingestion into it of the provincial bourgeoisie may account for the weakness of contemporary English regional culture.

'From Milne's Bar to the Absolute Idea and back': God – either created or interpreted – necessarily persists where metaphysics is still concerned with his existence, and the language of the Bible, and the possibility of divine immanence within the just society, still penetrate. Such preoccupations lapsed in the 1940–80 period, landing us back on what Carlyle, referring to the elitism of David Hume and Adam Smith, called 'the flat continuous threshing-floor of logic'. To replace the openness of 'common-sense' philosophy with the pedantry of logical positivism was no great gain.[35]

'Common sense' plays a more ambiguous part in James Kelman, a writer hounded by the constrictions of poverty and place. In *A Disaffection* (1989), Patrick Doyle reaches a socialist epiphany of sorts when talking to his brother's children about the pipes that he has constructed into a musical instrument:

> Naw kids I'm no kidding, it was an urge, like a magic spell had befallen me. It was as if these two pipes themselves were calling out to me to come on and play me come on and play me, so I lifted one up and what I did I just, okay, blew into it, and out came this long and deep sound that made me think of scores and scores of years, and generations and generations and generations of people

> all down through the ages, and this tune – not exactly a tune, more of a sound, the one kind of long sound that you could occasionally just pause from doing, then start again as if ye hadni stopped at all except when you came to the very end of it you would know about the pauses you did, they would all be a part of it. It was really really beautiful weans and it made me think of magic. I'm no kidding ye on. Magic.[36]

We seem to be very close to that mysticism that MacDiarmid also achieved in 'A Glass of Pure Water' – 'an imperceptible movement/ and a sound like talking to God', though Doyle's Utopia is unachieved and ultimately hopeless.

To reach this stage is to realise what has not been mentioned. Working from accepted definitions of political fiction towards new and more inclusive ones, one finds oneself confronted by women writers who have more right to be there than many mentioned up to now. A politics of sexuality and family must grant Catherine Carswell, Muriel Spark and Naomi Mitchison priority. The only Scottish writer to concern herself deeply with Northern Ireland has been Joan Lingard. For my money there is, in Agnes Owens's desperate cases, a greater sense of the energies of human decency than in James Kelman's thoughtful but self-pitying fall guys, just as Suzie Kettles, in John Byrne's remarkable *Tutti-Frutti*, likewise provided a way out of the swamp in which the 'rock of ageism' micropolitics of the Majestics had landed them.[37] And what do we make of the fact that the two cleverest feminist writers on politics – Fay Weldon and Zoe Fairbairns – went to St Andrews? More than we make of that university's reputation as a Thatcherite nursery? I hope so.

The path back to a 'people's enlightenment' both politicises a Scottish identity and creates linkages between Scotland, Wales and Ireland. 'By measuring the distance, we come home': Raymond Williams was in *Culture and Society* the rediscoverer of the radical Carlyle as well as the sensitive archaeologist of what 'home' means – above all in *Border Country*. The tradition of social criticism which he detected runs in Scottish channels, via Patrick Geddes, the disciple of Carlyle and Ruskin, nearly the last pope of religious positivism (botanist, regional planner, psychologist, and Celtic and Indian nationalist), to MacDiarmid and Gray.

Geddes tried to plan for Dublin, and believed that such reforms would have obviated the causes of the Easter Rising. He influenced the rise of sociology in Wales, which has, particularly through its influence on Leopold Kohr, taken on a European significance. His concept of 'synergy' – an equilibrium occurring at a high rate of intellectual activity – is not just the opposite of the schizophrenia traditionally ascribed to the Scots. It is also demonstrated – potentially – by Jock McLeish, and actually, in William Boyd's *The New Confessions* (1987), by John James Todd, a frenetic dealer in a new technology which he packs with the ideas of the Enlightenment. Will such synergy follow in Wales? I think so, when writers locate themselves relative to their pasts, as well as to a present of unemployment, tourism, retirement homes and the tension between the perils of Wales and the precipitate decline of the British state.[38]

This could also end in Carlylean confusion: too many people trying to do too much with too few resources, while the metropolitan Rolls-Royce sweeps along the paths they have cleared, en route to the bank. In the 1930s, London publishers and literary editors policed the 'renaissance' and got MacDiarmid sent off, regardless of his talent, instead promoting the no better behaved but more manageable Dylan Thomas.[39] Regionalism may be 'in' for one decade, then 'out'. But new print technology now makes literature of quality cheap, without the overheads of the big London outfits. Wales's métier seems at the moment to run in history, poetry and film rather than in the novel, but the message of 'theoretical history' seems to be that it doesn't matter in what mode you write, provided you keep up a dialogue with the people around you. The writer, whether historian, playwright or novelist, is back at the communal fire, gnawing his mammoth-meat.

NOTES

1. Arthur Hopcraft, *Mid-Century Men* (London: Hamish Hamilton, 1982), p. 224.
2. See Christopher Harvie, *The Centre of Things: Political Fiction in Britain from Disraeli to the Present* (London: Unwin Hyman, 1991).
3. Denis Balsom, 'The Three-Wales Model' in John Osmond, ed., *The National Question Again* (Llandysul: Gomer Press, 1985), pp. 1–17; Ralf Dahrendorf, *On Britain* (BBC 1983), p. 55.
4. *Planet* 73, February/March 1989, p. 15.
5. Roddy Doyle, *The Commitments*, *The Van* (London: Heinemann/Minerva, 1988 and 1991).
6. If this group has a manifesto, it is Alasdair Gray's 'Postscript' to Agnes Owens, *Gentlemen of the West* (1985; Harmondsworth: Penguin, 1986), pp. 129–41.
7. Op. cit. (1984; Penguin, 1985), p. 185 (about halfway down and on the left . . .).
8. Art. cit., in *Cencrastus* no 1, Autumn 1979, pp. 18–23.

9. Gray, op. cit. (1982), pp. 243, 560; for a conspectus view of where the 1980s got us, see Craig Beveridge and Ronnie Turnbull, *The Eclipse of Scottish Culture* (Edinburgh: Polygon, 1988).
10. See the essays by W. Knox, J. Treble, C. T. Harvie and Graham Walker in W. Hamish Fraser and R. J. Morris, eds, *People and Society in Scotland*, vol. 2, *1830–1914* (Edinburgh: John Donald, 1990).
11. Op. cit. (Jarrolds, 1934), p. 25.
12. Janet Adam Smith, *John Buchan* (1965; Oxford: OUP, 1985), p. 251; and see the present writer's 'Second Thoughts of a Scotsman on the Make' in *The Scottish Historical Review*, vol. LXX, 1: no 188: April 1991.
13. For Scotland, see Jack Brand, *The National Movement in Scotland* (London: Routledge, 1978), pp. 102, 217; on Saunders Lewis, the case for the prosecution is put by Gwyn A. Williams, *When Was Wales?*, pp. 278–87; for the defence, see Bruce Griffiths, *Saunders Lewis* (Cardiff: University of Wales Press, 1979), pp. 20ff.
14. For the theory of this, see Jim Bulpitt, 'Conservatism, Unionism and the Problem of Territorial Management' in Peter Madgwick and Richard Rose, *The Territorian Dimension in United Kingdom Politics* (London: Macmillan, 1982), pp. 139–76.
15. See Dai Smith, *Wales! Wales?* (London: Allen and Unwin, 1984), esp. chapter 6.
16. See Tony Bianchi, 'R. S. Thomas and his Readers' in Tony Curtis, ed., *Wales: the Imagined Nation* (Bridgend: Poetry Wales Press, 1986), pp. 69–96.
17. Glenda Norquay, 'Four Novelists of the 1950s and 1960s' in Cairns Craig, ed., op. cit., *The History of Scottish Literature*, vol. 4, *The Twentieth Century* (Aberdeen: Aberdeen University Press, 1987), pp. 259–76.
18. Kennaway, op. cit., pp. 71, 78, and see Trevor Royle, *James and Jim* (Edinburgh: Mainstream, 1983), pp. 39ff.
19. R. D. Laing, *The Divided Self* (1965; Harmondsworth: Penguin, 1987); Karl Miller, *Doubles, Studies in Literary History* (Oxford: OUP, 1988); John Herdman, *The Double in Victorian Fiction* (London: Macmillan, 1990).
20. Humphreys, interview in *New Welsh Review*, no 2 (Autumn 1988), p. 9.
21. See Dai Smith in *Planet* 89, December 1991.
22. Gramsci was first translated by Hamish Henderson, and has been written about by Gwyn A. Williams; a film on his life was made for Channel 4 in 1988 by the 'Scottish' team of Tom Nairn, Mike Alexander and John Sessions.
23. See Beat Witschi, *Glasgow Urban Writing and Post-Modernism: the Fiction of Alasdair Gray* (Frankfurt: Peter Lang, 1991).
24. See John Sutherland, *Victorian Novelists and Publishers* (Oxford: OUP, 1980), and William Donaldson, *Popular Literature in Victorian Scotland* (Aberdeen: Aberdeen University Press, 1986).

25. For the background to this, see my Sir John Rhys Lecture, 'The *Werin* and the Folk' (London: British Academy, 1992).
26. Malcolm Page, *Arden on File* (London: Methuen, 1985), p. 78.
27. Gray, *1982, Janine*, pp. 221–92.
28. See Kurt Wittig, *The Scottish Tradition in Literature* (Edinburgh: Oliver and Boyd, 1961); and the essays by Douglas Gifford and Roderick Watson in *The History of Scottish Literature*, vol. III, *The Nineteenth Century* (Aberdeen: Aberdeen University Press, 1989).
29. See Harvie, *Centre of Things*, pp. 22–6.
30. See Fred Kaplan, *Thomas Carlyle* (Cambridge: CUP, 1983), pp. 332–3.
31. See the essays in Robert Crawford and Thom Nairn, eds, *The Arts of Alasdair Gray* (Edinburgh: Polygon, 1991).
32. Williams, op. cit., p. 305.
33. This argument has been explicitly made by Emmanuel Todd in *The Explanation of Ideology: Family Structures and Social Systems* (Oxford: Blackwell, 1985).
34. For Richard Llewellyn, see the essays in *Planet* 76, 1989.
35. The importance of philosophy as a central organising principle is firmly lodged in the work of George Davie; see in particular his references to John Anderson in *The Crisis of the Democratic Intellect* (Edinburgh: Polygon, 1983), and see Beveridge and Turnbull, op. cit., passim.
36. Kelman, *A Disaffection* (London: Secker and Warburg, 1989), pp. 288–9.
37. See Bert Wright, '*Tutti-Frutti*: Sex, Violence and Enlightenment' in *Radical Scotland*, no 27, June/July 1987, pp. 24–5.
38. 'The Institute' in *Lanark* (pp. 57–8) uses classic Geddesian technology in its projection of the surrounding landscape on its underground walls by a camera obscura similar in principle to the one he built at the top of his Outlook Tower.
39. Both Caradoc Evans and Hugh MacDiarmid suffered this fate. See John Harris, *Fury Never Leaves Us* (Poetry Wales Press, 1984); and Alan Bold, *Hugh MacDiarmid* (London: John Murray, 1988).

Fourteen

Image and Text: Fiction on Film

Ian Spring

It cannot be said that the premier novels of the last twenty years have made a particularly notable contribution to the (limited) film and television production of this country. The difficulty of acquiring funding for film production in Scotland has been well documented by Ian Lockerbie and John Caughie, among others. Fortunately, some recent support from the Scottish Film Council and the Scottish Film Production Fund, and the involvement of Scottish film-makers with, for example, the British Film Institute and the National Film and Television School (and also some European agencies), has led to a small but developing Scottish film movement.

However, within the period 1970–90, we can genuinely identify only around thirty to thirty-five feature films (depending on the exact criteria we employ) that deal with Scotland or Scottish issues to any extent. Of these, a comparatively small amount are truly Scottish productions with Scottish directors.[1] Some years have been comparatively productive, e.g. 1983 with *Local Hero*; *Another Time, Another Place*; and *Living Apart Together*; and 1989 with *Silent Scream*; *Venus Peter*; and *Play Me Something*; while others, such as 1977 and 1988, have produced a complete blank.

As far as filmed versions of recent Scottish novels go, it is only possible to identify three unqualified candidates: *Another Time, Another Place*, adapted from the novel of the same name by Jessie Kesson and released in 1983; *Venus Peter*, adapted from the novel *A Twelvemonth and a Day* by Christopher Rush and released in 1989; and *The Big Man*, from William McIlvanney's novel of that name in 1990. Stretching our definition, however, we might consider *Dreaming*, a film based on the short story of the same name by McIlvanney; the television serialisation of *Brond*, Frederic Lindsay's detective novel set in Glasgow; or the television adaptation of *A Sense of Freedom* by Jimmy Boyle and the film version of *Silent Scream* based on the writings of Larry Winters, both of these emanating from the writings of inmates of Barlinnie's Special Unit.

Perhaps of as much interest as these texts are the films of contemporary novels that have *not* been made. However, more of that later. For the moment, I want to consider briefly what we might learn from the three major projects listed above.

Another Time, Another Place is a partly nostalgic, partly romantic realist novel written in the early 1980s by Jessie Kesson. Because of the nature either of the writing or of the author (Jessie Kesson was born in 1914), however, it is often felt to belong to an earlier period. The novel is set in wartime rural Scotland and concerns a farmer's wife's tragic affair with an Italian prisoner of war working on the land. The film version, directed by Michael Radford, is a conventional romantic realist adaptation – rather like the television versions of Grassic Gibbon's *A Scots Quair* trilogy – which was generally well-received, praised for its visual qualities and for the strong performance in the leading role from Phyllis Logan.

The following account of the film, in Forsyth Hardy's comprehensive but rather uncritical account of the Scottish film industry, *Film in Scotland*, exemplifies one point of view in which the visual aspects of the film, notably the Black Isle landscape, contribute to the perceived realism:

> One of its many virtues was the sensitive rendering of the countryside and the farming year: the low hills rising from the waterside; the sowing of the grain, its ripening, harvesting and the threshing in the farmyard dominated by the noisy, smoky steam engine; the potato planting and the precisely turned furrows; the singling and the eventual picking of the turnips; a midnight carving at the farm. All of this activity, so distinct a part of the Scottish farming scene and here essential to the development of the story, was photographed over the changing seasons with great skill by Roger Deakins so that the film, if incidentally, was a unique record, as faithful and comprehensive as any documentary.[2]

There are quite clearly, however, some weaknesses in this approach. The supposed documentary intentions of the film are not an issue (it is a feature of the fictions of the periphery that a spurious documentary function is often ascribed to them, in much the same way that the limiting discourse of social realism is often used to impose constraints upon working-class urban fictions). Also, the 'essential' link between the landscape and farming imagery and the development of the narrative will be recognised by those familiar with the Scottish novel as a metaphoric technique that equates sexuality with nature, and therefore landscape, most notably in Grassic Gibbon's *A Scots Quair*. Essentially, however, Hardy's commentary comes from a literary discourse of film criticism in which the connection between narrative and the nature of the film's *mise en scène* are seen as unproblematic.

At the other extreme to this approach, for example, is Connie Balides's interesting essay on the film in which she applies contemporary film theory relating to issues of specularity – notably Laura Mulvey's influential concept of 'the look'. The two stages of her argument are basically as follows: first, while the film purports to a female perspective, the editing and the *mise en scène* are constructed to 'take away' the dominant specularity of the female character and replace this with another version of the male gaze. Second, the film trivialises issues of violence against women (there is a crucial rape scene) and dwells on the regressive nature of Scottish sexual repression:

> the film deals with the issue of Scotland at the expense of the woman . . . while appearing to present the woman's story from her point of view [it] makes the same mistakes as dominant cinema in the place it gives to the woman.[3]

Whether or not one approves of this sort of close textual reading of the film, it is a good example of how film criticism can offer a perspective on the very filmic qualities of an adaptation of a novel that conventional literary criticism cannot. John Brown, formerly of the Scottish Film Council and a screenwriter himself, has adopted an interesting perspective on Scottish film. Taking Leslie Fiedler's classic study of American literature *Love and Death in the American Novel* as an examplar, he looks at how Scottish film reflects particularly national, social and sexual repressions in a manner that is reminiscent of some literary criticism. His verdict on *Another Time, Another Place* is as follows:

> All the resonances, social, historical, religious which could have been thematically gathered around the Janey/Luigi relationship and used to explode *Another Time, Another Place* out of its comfortable resemblance to standard romantic fiction and into an anatomy of the way Scottish society constructs community and masculinity – all the resonances are there, but undeveloped.[4]

Similar textual and contextual issues to those applied to *Another Time, Another Place* could also be applied to *Venus Peter*, directed by Ian Sellar.

What makes *Venus Peter* of particular interest is that we have an account by Christopher Rush, on whose novel *A Twelvemonth and a Day*

(1985) the film is based, of its genesis and his own development of the screenplay from the book:

> The book has, in fact, no strong story line in terms of plot and must have seemed even to the most intrepid filmmaker to be little more than a series of disconnected impressions. To go for 'time' as the plot connector would be impracticable in terms of an eight-week shooting programme and yet I could not envisage the story torn from its seasonal context. To show the boy narrator of the book ageing visibly in the course of the film would call for two young boy actors who would look reasonably alike – not an idea to be courted if it could be avoided, and yet the keystone of the project involved growing up and out of childhood. The closer the inspection the greater seemed the impracticability of making a film out of this book.[5]

The article details the necessary changes to the plot of the book required for the film adaptation: adding characters, combining characters, change of location, collapsing of timescale, and the slight but important reconstruction of the ending – 'for Ian Sellar the unwritten chapter of *Twelvemonth* had to show itself in the smile on Peter's face just as the film ends'.[6]

Rush's conclusion is as follows:

> reading a book and seeing a film are two entirely different experiences and *Venus Peter* goes off on voyages of its own that do not concern the book. For one thing the book is highly inclusive: it simply contains everything that I could remember. The film is much more selective and in that sense more artistic than the book, since art is ultimately a selection from reality. Where *Venus Peter* perhaps succeeds more emphatically than *Twelvemonth* is in its presentation of two distinct levels of experience: the realistic and the poetic. I believe that *Twelvemonth* is wholly submerged in its own poetry. *Venus Peter*, on the other hand, shows a boy of heightened sensibilities experiencing poetic fantasies, while all around him is a world of hard economic fact, a world falling apart.[7]

In fact, this film constitutes one of the very few examples of authors of Scottish fictional works being involved at all in the film or television adaptation of their own work, and, for that reason, it does seem that *Venus Peter* evokes many of the same thoughts and reactions as the novel on which it based. However, some of the crucial critical apparatus of film studies could also be applied to the film, notably with regard to questions of perspective. Similarly, the elements of sexual repression and a morbidly elegiac strain that are often said to typify Scottish literature can be examined in the structure of the film itself.

The sort of approaches at which I am hinting come, I think, in two forms. First, there are structuralist approaches to film theory that are primarily textual and concerned with questions of spectatorship – in, for example, the work of Laura Mulvey or Stephen Heath. Correlative to these approaches, there is work in narrative theory (often based on literary criticism) that is concerned with questions of perspective. As mentioned Connie Balides's article on *Another Time, Another Place* is a good example of this kind of approach. Second, there is criticism largely based on discourse theory which is contextual. The key figures in this area are Michel Foucault, Franz Fanon and Edward Said. Although none of these writers concerns himself with the area of representations of Scotland, their work has been widely applied. Craig Beveridge and Ronald Turnbull,[8] for example, take Franz Fanon's concept of Inferiorism (developed with reference to the French colonisation of Africa) and apply it to the Scottish situation. A similar theory, Jack Goody's anthropological model, the Grand Dichotomy, has been applied in various forms to Scottish culture, notably by Malcolm Chapman in his excellent *The Gaelic Vision in Scottish Culture*[9] and – of particular interest to the subject of this chapter – by Colin McArthur[10] in various writings on Scottish film. In its various forms, this model states that peripheral cultures are represented as a sort of mirror image of the core culture representing them. The characteristics that this engenders constitute a sort of hegemony that then forms a consciousness or restricted mental universe that the peripheral culture inhabits. Colin McArthur applies this in general to Scottish film culture to show that a body of Scottish films employ regressive characteristics relating to Scots and Scotland that function to disable political debate and narrowly define national identity even when, through romanticism or sentimentality, they are presented as superficially appealing.

McArthur's argument, strongly political in essence, has attracted some opposition but still remains the clearest and most rigorously-defined critical position with regard to Scottish film. Obviously, these ideas could be applied to a critical reading of both *Another Time, Another Place* and *Venus Peter*. They can also be applied to another body of texts about Scotland that deal with specifically urban mythologies.

One of the most abiding mythologies in representations of urban Scotland is the mythology of the Hard Man. Familiar to Scots of the last two generations at least, the Hard Man is the city cognoscente. He is tougher, wiser, more calculating than the rest. This enables him to survive in a society that is impoverished, squalid, sordid and ruthless.

The Hard Man need not be physically imposing – in some versions he is the 'Wee Hard Man' – but in William McIlvanney's novel, and the film adaptation of the same title, directed by David Leland, he is *The Big Man*.

The Hard Man mythology is, of course, a particularly potent form of inferiorist discourse in which the characteristics of the peripheral culture are not exactly the opposite of the core culture, but instead a carefully delineated perversion of them. The Hard Man may be a 'winner' in the sense of exhibiting and benefiting from the supposedly progressive characteristics that typify western capitalist culture, but his victory is really Pyrrhic – enacted on a stage that is only a netherland of the real world, condemned by oppression to remain apart from it. The most substantial realisation of this mythology comes in the tightly-structued television dramas of Peter McDougall – notably *Just Another Saturday* and *Just a Boy's Game* – as well as his television adaptation of Jimmy Boyle's autobiographical *A Sense of Freedom*.

William McIlvanney's novels have successfully compressed much of this urban mythology (derived partly in opposition to the earlier 'urban Kailyard' school, for example the novels of George Blake) and have proved highly successful. One notable offspring of his work has been the tremendously successful television series, *Taggart*, whose leading character, a hybrid of the Hard Man, a tough, cynical, hard-bitten policeman on the right side of the law, clearly seems to be based on McIlvanney's Laidlaw, from the novel of that name, although the programme's producers consistently deny any connection.

The filming of McIlvanney's novel *The Big Man* (1985) was, however, of great interest as an attempt to translate Scottish popular fiction into the British popular film tradition – almost an imitation of Hollywood. The seriousness of the project was demonstrated quite early on by a typically insensitive decision to cast an Irishman and an Englishwoman – Liam Neeson and Joanne Whalley-Kilmer – in the main parts. *The Big Man* was panned by the critics – somewhat unfairly, as it cannot be said that any particular part of the film is especially bad. In general, however, the film fails to match either the atmosphere (the constructed post-industrial landscape seems somehow sanitised in the film) or the complexity of motivation of McIlvanney's novel.

The film is based on two contrasting maxims – a simplification of McIlvanney's more subtle novel – stated outright in the film: 'out of pain comes glory' and 'if you can't fight for the right reason, keep your hands in your pockets'. However, the main point of Denny's fist-fight in *The Big Man* is seen to be as a sublimation of the 'real fight' – the fight to keep the local pits open that has unfortunately failed. In the novel, despite some dubious myth-making and sentimentality, McIlvanney does manage to evoke a real sense of community that is realised as an almost subconscious feeling at the end of the book. The film lays this on far too thickly. At the end, the people of Scoular's community, Thornbank ('it's not Disneyland', we are told, thoughtfully), gather together as one body to oppose, passively, the crooked bookie Matt Mason. In another scene, the unemployed miner Danny runs through the town to cheers; later, they all turn out to support him, waving lion rampants and playing 'Campbeltown Loch, I wish you were whisky' – with, significantly, a union banner in the background.

In the end, *The Big Man*, on film, fails to satisfy. It is a bit like *Rocky* out of *Gregory's Girl*, mixing two genres. Unlike the novel, the film fails to find a coherent market because, perhaps, it does not stick closely enough to the urban mythologies that inform McIlvanney's most popular work. A much smaller-budget film, *Dreaming*, based on a McIlvanney short story, stole the plaudits from *The Big Man* in the year of its release.

If space allowed, it would be worth discussing the television adaptation of Frederic Lindsay's novel *Brond*, directed by Michael Caton-Jones – in many ways a much more successful urban thriller than *The Big Man* – and John Byrne's highly-rated television series *Tutti-Frutti* as alternative urban mythologies. Also David Hayman's directorial debut, *Silent Scream*, based on the posthumous writings of Larry Winters who died in the Barlinnie Special Unit, is an impressive and subtle exploration of violence, psychosis and fantasy. However, to conclude, I would like to take another tack.

The selection of texts here is rather too limited to draw any general conclusions about the translation of the contemporary Scottish novel into film, and it would also be fairly futile here (even if interesting in its own right) simply to analyse the structure of each of these film texts in turn with a view, perhaps, to assessing the comparative success, in qualitative terms, of each. This would not reveal very much about the wider issue of what the contemporary Scottish novel has to offer contemporary Scottish film – or vice versa. Instead, I would suggest the importance of another issue: the extent to which strategies applied both in literary studies and in film and television studies may enhance our understanding of a variety of texts. I have outlined some of these strategies above, and would further suggest that they could be applied to future film texts, along with the interesting new work being done in areas such as national identity and institutional determinants of textual production. I shall now address some of the same issues in a rather contrary manner, not by considering the limited texts on hand, but by considering some significant absences.

The first of these absences concerns those film versions of Scottish novels that *have not yet been made*. As I write this, I believe that there are plans to film Iain Banks's flawed but powerful first novel *The Wasp Factory* (1984). For some time, there has also been eager anticipation of the film version of Alasdair Gray's epic novel *Lanark* (in my own opinion, *the* great Scottish novel of the second half of this century). I think it is safe to say that both these novels offer great visual potential to the film-maker. *The Wasp Factory* offers the imaginative metaphor from which it takes its title and the disturbing and cruel internalised imagery of the narrative rather than the almost incidental correlatives of the location – the north-west of Scotland. *Lanark*, on the other hand, is a highly descriptive novel, and much has been made of Gray's background as a visual artist and the contribution of his work in this area to the novel. To my mind, the crucial factor in understanding *Lanark* is Gray's use of perspective, which is innovative and various. At times, the descriptive elements of *Lanark* are traditionally focalised, from a single, unitary point of view; at times, versions of an alternative, fragmented perspective appear, notably in the final sections of the book. Similarly, the narrative plays with the use of perspective, moving, on occasions, towards and away from the point of view of the eponymous Lanark. This aspect of Gray's writing clearly derives from his painting and has been commented on by, among others, Cairns Craig and Edwin Morgan.[11] Alasdair Gray's own storyboard, an interesting work in its own right, has been serialised in *The Scottish Book Collector*. The film version of *Lanark* is eagerly awaited.

Without labouring this point, then, it appears that elements of both these novels offer a rich visual potential to a film-maker. The fact that they are both, to some extent, fantasy (although in Banks's case this may be not quite clear), rather than the fairly standard realist novels from which earlier film versions are derived, also seems to offer a challenge to film-makers. It is interesting, also, that Banks is untypical of Scottish authors in that his work is derived from genre fiction – notably from science fiction, which he still writes. Like John Byrne, his work reflects the influence of international popular culture on the Scottish consciousness. (Twenty years ago, this might have been enough to exclude them from the elitist canon of Scottish literature!) While looking forward to these two forthcoming productions, I would also lament the absence of film versions of the brilliant short stories of Alan Spence, and his recent novel, *The Magic Flute* (1990).

The second absence, however, cannot easily be remedied. There is a notable body of Scottish fiction that has been highly acclaimed lately from which films cannot be made – or at least not without some considerable difficulty. The most obvious example is the work of James Kelman. Other writers who have to some extent followed in his footsteps include Janice Galloway, whose *The Trick is to Keep Breathing* (1989) is, to be glib, a sort of feminist version of Kelman's *A Disaffection* (1989). Both deal with psychotic or neurotic schoolteachers in the West of Scotland whose breakdown under a variety of personal and social pressures is meticulously related. Both employ interior monologue to some extent, and both have limited narrative development. This type of supposedly socialist realist fiction, heavily laden with colloquial rhetoric and short on plot, has been very popular in this country and is produced very skilfully by Kelman and Galloway (although less so by some imitators). It is interestingly at odds with developments in fiction in other countries in which forms of both fantasy and pastiche genre fiction seem popular. For example, Kelman and Galloway do not sell in the United States, where both Alasdair Gray and Charles Palliser, author of *The Quincunx* (1989), are very popular. It would take a brave and imaginative film-maker to translate any of this body of work into film, although some of the short stories of Kelman and Galloway – those with slightly less unrelenting moroseness and fewer elements of the surreal – might offer possibilities.

Setting aside the paradoxical category of 'films made from books that *should* be Scottish' (of which the film version of Bernard MacLaverty's *Cal* (1983) is perhaps the best example), the third significant area of absence is that of films *not* made from books. This category, of course, constitutes the major part of Scottish film production over the period in question.

Of those films that may seem to have a 'literary flavour' although not directly deriving from literary texts, a couple stand out. First, there is Bill Douglas's much-acclaimed trilogy of short films, *My Childhood*, *My Ain Folk* and *My Way Home*. These intense, auteuristic films have been cited by Andrew Noble[12] and others as giving the lie to Colin McArthur's critique of Scottish film production, based on discourses such as tartanry, Kailyard and Clydesideism. They are certainly individual and fascinating films, but I suspect they may owe more to a Scottish fictional tradition of the 'poisoned childhood', typified by writers such as Alan Sharp and even Christopher Rush, than their staunch supporters might like to admit. Second, several commentators, including McArthur and Philip Schlesinger,[13] Professor of Film and

Media Studies at Stirling University, have seen Tim Neat's award-winning *Play Me Something*, based on a short story by John Berger, as a new, innovative breed of internationalist (in the best sense) Scottish film. *Play Me Something* employs a literary – or rather oral – style of comparatively straightforward storytelling with a complex style of partly montage editing that works within a distinct hierarchy of discourse. It is, however, very much filmic in its construction, blending varieties of narration, rather than the single omniscient voice of the classic realist or modernist novel.

The two projects discussed above are, however, exceptions to the rule. In fact, the most prominent school of Scottish film – and the most prolific and successful – has, to my mind, arisen directly in opposition to the Hard Man mythology described above. I have elsewhere described this body of texts, typified by the highly popular films of Bill Forsyth, in terms of its opposition to this structure:

> In these and other films . . . the hard man stereotype is turned on its head. If, in the established schema, the hard man exists in a totally malevolent world, vicious, unyielding, an underworld populated only by the lowest of the low, in which he can survive only by divesting himself of all human frailty, compassion, misgivings or childish misconceptions, then the structure of these films is exactly the opposite – the world is almost totally benevolent and weaknesses and even criminal acts go unpunished, redemption is always available, the future is always rosy. The survivors are hardly hard-bitten but underdeveloped, childlike adults with foibles, inadequacies, illusions – in fact, *soft men*.[14]

Within this category I would place, with varying degrees of precision, all the Forsyth films set in Scotland: *That Sinking Feeling*, *Gregory's Girl*, *Local Hero* and *Comfort and Joy*; Charles Gormley's *Living Apart Together* and *Heavenly Pursuits*; Cary Parker's *The Girl in the Picture*; and lastly Michael Hoffman's *Restless Natives*, which is in some ways the epitome of the genre.

Without commenting further, and with no intended attempt at denigration, I would simply note that this most successful and popular brand of Scottish film over the last twenty years, if translated back to an imaginary fictional correlative, would constitute a body of novels not for adults, but for children.

NOTES

1. See Janet McBain, 'Scotland in Feature Film: A Filmography' in Eddie Dick, ed., *From Limelight to Satellite: A Scottish Film Book* (London: British Film Institute, 1990). It is particularly interesting

that, whereas the literary world has generally extended the stated or tacit criteria for inclusion in the body of Scottish writing over the last few years (cf. book prizes, etc.), this, the first substantial filmography, is rather limited and content-based in this respect – 'Scots "authorship" alone is not necessarily enough to warrant inclusion. The content has to reflect some aspect of "Scottishness" ' (ibid., p. 233).

2. Forsyth Hardy, *Scotland in Film* (Edinburgh: Edinburgh University Press, 1990), p. 188.
3. Connie Balides, '*Another Time, Another Place* . . . Another Male View?', *Cencrastus*, no 16 (Spring 1984), pp. 37–40, p. 40.
4. John Brown, 'Land Beyond Brigadoon', *Sight and Sound*, vol. 53, no 1 (Winter 1983/84), 40–6, p. 45.
5. Christopher Rush, '*Venus Peter*: from Pictures to Pictures' in Eddie Dick, ed., *From Limelight to Satellite: A Scottish Film Book* (London: British Film Institute, 1990), p. 117.
6. Ibid., p. 132.
7. Ibid., pp. 127–8.
8. Craig Beveridge and Ronald Turnbull, *The Eclipse of Scottish Culture* (Edinburgh: Polygon, 1989).
9. Malcolm Chapman, *The Gaelic Vision in Scottish Culture* (London: Croom Helm, 1978).
10. Most notably in Colin McArthur, ed., *Scotch Reels* (London: British Film Institute, 1982), and in various articles in the journal *Cencrastus*.
11. Cairns Craig, 'Going Down to Hell is Easy: *Lanark*, Realism and the Limits of the Imagination', and Edwin Morgan, 'Gray and Glasgow', both in Robert Crawford and Thom Nairn, eds, *The Arts of Alasdair Gray* (Edinburgh: Edinburgh University Press, 1991).
12. Andrew Noble, 'Bill Douglas's Trilogy', in Eddie Dick, ed., *From Limelight to Satellite: A Scottish Film Book*, pp. 149–50.
13. See Philip Schlesinger, 'Scotland, Europe and Identity' in Eddie Dick, ed., *From Limelight to Satellite: A Scottish Film Book*.
14. Ian Spring, *Phantom Village: The Myth of the New Glasgow* (Edinburgh: Polygon, 1990).

Fifteen

Voices in Empty Houses: The Novel of Damaged Identity

Gavin Wallace

THE SCOTTISH MALAISE?

> . . . all you've got to do is follow some people around and look at their existence for 24 hours, and it will be horror. It will just be horror.[1]

James Kelman's Beckettian blueprint for the worthwhile Scottish novel may appear depressingly simple, if not simply depressing. While he may oversimplify the complex artistry through which his minimalism is made convincing, it is a nihilistic summary relevant to many Scottish novels other than Kelman's own. A substantial majority of the most significant novels, in fact, published since the 1970s comprise a catalogue of Kelman's 'horror' in its range of constituent complaints: the spiritual and material deprivations of unemployment and decaying communities; failures to find – or accept – self-fulfilment in education, work, emotional relationships; inarticulacy and alienation escaped through alcoholism; destructive mental instability; the paralysing hyper-awareness of class and cultural differentiation; crippling incapacities to give love, or to receive it. Even the more affirmative Scottish novelists feel unable to evade the imperative nature of such themes; many of the most respected novels to have appeared since Gray's *Lanark* (1981) embrace all of them at once. The Scottish novel continues to build upon an already spectacular tradition of despair.

As Tom Leonard's poem puts it, there is 'nuthnlik disperr'[2] to keep you going, and there is no despair like Scottish despair better calculated to throttle the most innocent of affections: hence James Kelman's grimly logical and literal refinement of the condition into *dis*affection. Disaffection not only keeps the Scottish novel going – it seems positively in love with it. In English novels, the deranged, the desperate, the neurotic and the variously addicted might provide the odd deviant diversion to emphasise the reassuring normality of everything else. In Scottish novels, they are narrators and protagonists, rarely, if ever, fully in control of their existences, and morbidly aware of the fact. The literary revival of the 1970s succeeded in the compellingly imaginative depiction of Scotland as the one country best designed to drive anyone with the faintest glimmer of an imagination quietly insane, or as far away as possible to become more noisily so. The continuing revival of the 1980s has given the trend a further twist: the successful search for a self-confident and distinctive 'Scottish voice' has inspired a school of novels notable for their fluency in anatomising the introverted torments of self-inflicted silences.

Paradox and contradiction of this kind is nothing new in Scottish letters, of course. Whether conscious or unconscious, for better or for worse, duality, division and fracture persist as the prevailing creative and critical tools in Scotland. That the antisyzygy fast approaching its centenary sizzles still is a source of concern and puzzlement to newer, younger critics, but it would be difficult to deny the continuing relevance of the fundamental issues of contradictoriness and paradox to the Scottish imagination. They underline, for example, Douglas Gifford's celebrated diagnosis of the fictional revival of the 1970s as characterised by the 'juxtaposition of international ideas with an introverted sense of place'.[3] Scottish culture may have become increasingly cosmopolitan *and* extravert since the 1970s, but Gifford's acute sense of an inherent antithesis in Scottish fiction is just as valid for the 1980s. There is a new cultural identity celebrated in recent Scottish fiction, but an identity whose instability and claustrophobic intimacy with psychological maiming writers inevitably deplore, yet appear incapable of forsaking; an insufferable burden that cannot be shaken off.

The symptoms of this malaise have become sufficiently institutionalised in literature to oblige a younger writer like the poet Pat Morrissey to conclude a biographical self-introduction with the wry disclaimer that, despite being one himself, he is '*not* currently working on a novel about a Scottish school-teacher suffering a mental breakdown'.[4] The classroom has above all become the symbolic clinic for indigenous angst. Critics faced with a corpus of texts which must often be seen to comprise an extended series of psychiatric case-notes rather than a thriving literary tradition have not been reluctant to acknowledge the prevalence of this oppressive mood of disenchantment either. Bob Tait and Isobel Murray concede: 'there is no dodging the fact that most of our novelists find very little to cheer about', while adding the important qualification that 'so often the writing is so obviously not that of cheerless people, nor is it fundamentally about cheerless people'.[5] Encouraged by his more objective vantage point, there is a sense of puzzlement in the German critic Peter Zenzinger's conclusion to his recent survey of contemporary fiction that

> contemporary life as depicted by Scottish writers has very few alluring traits . . . all the zest has gone out of life, all prospect of a better future has withered. This complaint is familiar enough in all industrialized countries, and yet the extreme bitterness with which it is uttered in Scottish writing is remarkable.[6]

He is careful to list a series of individual sociological, political and cultural factors – such as deindustrialisation and the Calvinist heritage – which might account for the Scots' propensity to imbue universal preoccupations with the sourness of indigenous disenchantment, but his obvious perplexity should be seen as worrying.

The extraliterary factors which Zenzinger lists have themselves become the object of much-needed intellectual analysis and reappraisal in Scotland over the past ten years in an efflorescence of original critical thought which has contributed to a thorough reconstruction of Scotland's sense of itself, which in turn has impinged dramatically upon the reflection of Scotland in her literature. Many outdated maps have been redrawn to reveal the nation's paradoxical perspective on its own historical identity; the disabling nature of distorting national stereotypes; the tracts of historical experience previously marginalised or buried, especially that of the working class; the undermining effect of inherently anglocentric modes of interpreting Scottish culture; the potential of a new Scottish feminist consciousness. Common to the emergence of these and many other new configurations is a preoccupation with the varying degrees to which the prevalent features of Scottish identity owe their origins – and in some cases their continuing dynamic – to the country's anomalous predicament of stateless nationhood within a larger political arrangement in which varying degrees of internal colonisation, both covert and overt, continue to operate.

There exists, then, a wider intellectual framework within which the consistent preoccupation of novelists with the symptoms of a tangibly Scottish malaise makes perfect sense as a set of urgent sociological imperatives. Foregrounding such identifiably 'social' themes is equally the concern of the increasing number of Scottish novels which have challenged the limits of realist modes of narrative through excursions into fantasy or postmodern techniques. Whether depicted as the familiarly real or the disturbingly strange, however, there exists a real danger – as Zenzinger perhaps implies – that in this fictional landscape barren of hope a new myth can be seen slouching towards Scotland to be born, in the form of a grey and morose beast prone to lengthy fits of self-pity. Ironically, the understandable 'bitterness' with peculiarly Scottish woes might prove dangerously appealing to those very purveyors of cultural defeatism and perpetrators of the 'inferiorist' reflex whose manoeuvres recent revisionary critics have so successfully exposed, showing them to amount to an undermining ideology which has contributed to the complexity of such woes in the first place. Fracture, disintegration and damaged identity may continue to be convincingly demonstrated as ineluctable features of the society and culture which Scottish fiction seeks to understand. It might equally be argued, however, that such motifs have become entrenched as readily identifiable and assimilable literary tropes which, despite their continued creative appeal, may have not only outlived their function, but also become the internalised submission to a condition in which the Scottish imagination will eventually colonise itself.[7]

The way out of such an impasse may lie not in how novelists write in Scotland, but how critics in Scotland write about writers. Despite diverging emphases, 'Scottishness' remains the logically acceptable criterion for assessing Scottish literature, in reality a multiple series of criteria incapable of synthesis, and all ultimately dependent on highly subjective interpretive practices. The very absence, of course, of stable critical parameters in itself mirrors a culture renowned for its volatile self-questioning, and continues to guarantee a literature possibly unique in richness and diversity. Despite numerous innovative attempts throughout the 1980s, systematic theories which have sought to place the nature of Scottish creativity within wider intellectual paradigms have been slow to catch on, suggesting that the intricacy of the country's cultural and social infrastructures must inevitably frustrate all such totalising perspectives, however exciting or challenging.

As Francis Russell Hart discovered in 1978, the concluding 'theory' to which his survey of the Scottish novel enticingly led could progress no further beyond mere tentative 'notes towards'. His difficulties persist. Criticism of fiction – increasingly perceptive and extensive though it is – still tends towards a *culturally* orientated method of interpretation in which novels are diagnosed as symptoms of a wider 'identity problem' which must, by definition, remain notoriously difficult to define and prone to prejudicial pleading. There is nothing inherently wrong with such an approach; indeed, within the intractable anomalies of Scottish culture, it may remain a necessary one. It has produced, however, a prevailing critical orthodoxy in which extrinsic factors (history, politics, class) figure prominently at the expense of intrinsic ones (form, structure, narrative): recurring *formal* patterns within Scottish fiction which, properly considered, might encourage a more sharply-defined and coherent reading of cultural self-expression to emerge. As Cairns Craig, one of the few Scottish critics who has sought precisely this kind of enlarging of parameters for the Scottish novel in practice, has suggested, 'we still have to establish . . . what kind of inner dialectic of the development of the form . . . is characteristic of Scotland'.[8]

FINDING A VOICE

One such crucial neglected characteristic of the 'inner dialectic' of the development of the Scottish novel is the matter of *voice*. From Francis Russell Hart onwards, it has become a critical commonplace that the most significant creative dilemma facing the Scottish novelist is the question of narrative voice, and how far this can faithfully reflect the realities of several forms of non-English Scottish speech and syntax without unduly limiting the writer's potential audience. Satisfactorily sustained creative solutions to the problem are rare. Lewis Grassic Gibbon and James Kelman remain the two exemplars in adapting and internalising the cadences of dialect forms so that they become effective modes of narration in themselves and an equally effective means of escape from the traditional compromise of balancing omniscient English narrative with dialogue in various forms of Scots. The polarity between Kelman and McIlvanney is illustrative here. In the nihilistic labyrinths of repetition of Kelman's minimalist monologues, narrative no longer renders but enacts; enacts the entire complex of socioeconomic and psycholinguistic pressures which define and debase the conscious and subconscious lives of his characters. In McIlvanney's more traditional naturalistic aesthetic, there is a constant war between an at times baroquely oversophisticated literary English narrative voice and an equally sophisticated urban Scots dialogue. This creates not the contradiction or weakness that some critics have suggested, but an attempted reconciliation between two antithetical sets of cultural values – standard English uniformity as opposed to individual Scottish community – forced into an equivalence in which they articulate *for each other*.

Both novelists are articulating correspondingly extreme solutions which are inseparable from the cultural predicament out of which they write. Linguistic fissure, whether boldly reproduced by McIlvanney or radically challenged by Kelman, is not a reality confined to matters of narrative method and presentation, but the source of an inarticulacy both mythical and real which has become a central thematic preoccupation of Scottish fiction since the 1970s. Failed struggles to articulate an adequate sense of self-identity have gradually come to form the twisted, broken heart of the Scottish novel's grim fascination with damaged identity: the familiar aching cry of the strangled Scottish voice. Douglas Gifford has rightly located the recurrent urgency of a shared thematic concern with

> the debasement of character and language and the failure to find a *voice* which will connect with the aspirant's dreams and confused sense of self . . .
>
> The gap between local and perhaps debased dialect and formal English is a part of the problem. But the failure to find a self-confident register of expression, style, *voice* matters so much more.[9]

Significantly, the affliction suggested here is as much an external impasse impeding the formal and stylistic choices facing the novelist as an internal one suffered by the characters whom they depict. What Gifford pinpoints is precisely that recurring 'inner dialectic of the development of the form' at which Cairns Craig hinted, a dialectic which emerges in those recent central novels which perpetrate the tradition of damaged identity as one between the *voiced* and the *unvoiced*. Viewed in accordance with this internal pattern, it is possible to suggest that the sense of negativity and despair which has become synonymous with Scottish fiction is less of a regressive reflex than has been supposed.

Indeed, the directions which such novels appear to be taking would suggest that, rather than the *failure* to find a voice, the process being envisaged is – with varying degrees of confidence – the successful *retrieval* of one. As possibly the first extended interior monologue in Scottish fiction, Alasdair Gray's *1982, Janine* represents an appropriate starting point. Centred on the conflicting inner voices of its crumbling, alcoholic narrator Jock McLeish, Gray's narrative method of the 'self-inciting vocative' – which he claims to have taken from a short story by Brian McCabe – is one with suitably Scottish connotations, explored in the chronic duality between the self-indulgence of the hero in sexual fantasies and his intensifying self-laceration with the misery and loss to which sex and alcohol must finally yield in candid self-appraisal. It is above all the escape from the solipsism of the unvoiced which Jock so desperately seeks; or, rather, from the cacophony of the unvoiced 'Ministry of Voices' of the climactic Chapter 11 in which Jock's final breakdown and suicide attempt are rendered as a spectacular explosion of typographical psychobabble, finally dissolving into the white noise of several blank pages of unconsciousness.

The subsequent cathartic reappraisal of Jock's failed life – its agonies and betrayals symbolising those of Scotland's history – culminates in his most appropriately poignant memory: defending a fellow pupil from appalling punishment for his *speech defect* at the hands of the insanely Calvinist teacher, Mad Hislop. Jock's recounting of his intervention, which precipitates Hislop's capitulation to his dangerous mental inadequacy, unleashes Jock from his own 'insane' repression to embrace a new-found hermaphrodite identity – 'O Janine, my silly soul, come to me now'. His imaginary erotic heroine's body having acquired a mind, Jock is ready to acquire something for himself of equal significance:

> Footsteps in corridor.
> KNOCK KNOCK.
> A woman's voice.
> 'Eight-fifteen Mr McLeish. Breakfast is being served till nine.'
>
> My voice.
> 'All right'.[10]

The novel closes with the sound of two voices, a woman's and a (new?) man's, an enactment of the reconciliation between Jock's previously disjunct masculine and feminine selves, while the two apparently banal but portentous final words 'All right' – in many ways the equivalent of the 'Yes' which closes *Ulysses* in tacit affirmation – remain the only words in Jock's entire narrative directly signified as spoken in the present. A superficial speech act becomes first symptom of release from Jock's damaged past into the promise of a future – 'I will not do nothing' – which can be articulated, a future which may prove far from 'all right' but, it is implied, perhaps no longer all wrong.

A similar pattern is inscribed in the progress of Joy Stone in Janice Galloway's *The Trick is to Keep Breathing* (1989), in many ways a novel which serves as the perfect analogue to Gray's as an exploration of psychological collapse from a feminine perspective. Solipsistic entrapment in inarticulacy and confused internalised voices failing to find utterance are Galloway's urgent concerns, though particularly focused by her sensitivity to areas of female experience alternately marginalised and besieged by an entrenched male value system. In this way, the anxieties with specifically Scottish inhibitions accentuated by Gray and Kelman – the two influences most evident in Galloway's writing – are both extended and qualified in a powerful statement about the regressively masculine values inscribed in Scottish society and culture.

Joy Stone is seen to suffer even more acutely than Jock McLeish from an inarticulable grief and a voice from which she remains dissociated. Even when it tries to speak, it is a voice repeatedly drowned out by a sinister chorus of louder, external ones – those of insensitive psychiatric opinion, of authoritarian employers, of exploitative women's journalism – which conspire to eradicate her emotional claim on the memory of her dead lover, another woman's husband, and compound her own self-inflicted guilt. Even in moments of seemingly candid confession, her voice does not belong to her:

> I had to trust my mouth. I closed my eyes and the mouth said
>
> My mother walked into the sea.
>
> I remember the voice: chiselled as crystal. Cold as a razor. I hadn't known it would start like this but then I was redundant. The voice didn't need me. It didn't even like me. I let the story come out in this disembodied glass voice and listened, out of harm's way in the corner of the room.[11]

Not until Joy can learn to 'trust her mouth' and to tell her pain to herself as well as others – by fully reliving the trauma of her lover's death – can she escape from the 'corner of the room' in which the novel's opening finds her trapped, literally and symbolically. By the novel's end, only her 'shadow' will be seen there. Reconciliation between mind and voice and the rediscovery of selfhood entails a multiple forgiveness – of her lover for dying, of the society incapable of understanding female solitude and grief, of herself for failing to accept a death because it is 'unsayable'.

> I take another mouthful of whisky, slide my finger on the volume control. Waves rippling through the headphones. And something else.
>
> The human voice. I listen watching the coloured lights, fanning like sea anemones over the ceiling, till the music stops.
>
> A click and tape whirring into silence at the end of the reel.
>
> The voice is still there.
>
> I forgive you.
>
> I hear it quite distinctly, my own voice in the empty house.
>
> I forgive you.
>
> Nobody needs to know I said it. Nobody needs to know. (*TKB*, 235)

The final 'trick' of *The Trick is to Keep Breathing* is the narrator's 'voice in the empty house': both the novel itself, providing the woman's voice long absent from the house of Scottish fiction, and the narrator's implied retrieval of her selfhood through the speech releasing the individual from the silence of the solipsistic past, become the nightmare of an eternal present, into a future which is considerably more ambiguous than in the case of Jock McLeish. Precisely for whom Joy's voice is meant nobody is supposed to know, while 'everybody' has been told. A secret is something you tell one person at a time.

ESCAPING THE MALAISE

Gray and Galloway have substantially enriched the Scottish novel's forensic fascination with the problematics of identity. In their correspondingly candid dissections of Scottish stereotypes of gender, experimental approaches to narrative, but above all in their compassionate gestures towards liberating their protagonists from the failures to win articulacy and self-esteem familiar from many previous Scottish novels, they also point significantly towards a new emancipation from the obsessive restrictions of the past. Encouragingly, theirs is not an isolated attempt to offer new visions of this particular old nightmare, nor the first. Longer-established in the literary scene since the 1970s, Brian McCabe and Ron Butlin are two of Scotland's finest poets and short-story writers (still mysteriously underrated), both of whom have produced first novels of considerable quality which – in radically different ways – suggest even clearer and more constructive escape routes from the Scottish malaise. McCabe's *The Other McCoy* (1990) and Butlin's *The Sound of My Voice* (1987) between them compromise subtle and ingenious reworkings of traditional tropes of duality, inarticulacy and psychic damage. Equally ambitious novels such as Robert Alan Jamieson's *A Day at the Office* (1991) and Andrew Greig's *Electric Brae* (1992) – which reveal an intriguing fascination with ever-shifting layers of temporality, disparate narrative personae and challenging polyphonic structures – confirm that the Scottish literary imagination is exploring newly-enabling, exciting and more affirmative directions.

By creating a Scottish comic novel with such obvious commitment to its subject matter, *The Other McCoy* is a significant achievement in its own right. As Tait and Murray observe, Scottish fiction is rarely the product of cheerless minds, but, though Scotland excels in comic writing, the discreetly optimistic impulses connoted by the comic genre have repeatedly proved alien to a fretful and embittered fictional tradition. Scottish comic novels are not trusted, and, when one considers the apparent flippancy – and enduring popularity – of the genial, Tory, Anglo-Scottish school of Highland humour typified by some of Linklater's inferior productions and Compton Mackenzie's series of farces, this is hardly surprising.[12] Those major novels by Linklater where exuberant comedy and farce totter dangerously on the verge of darkness have proved most amenable to the Scottish spirit.

The Other McCoy is reminiscent, in fact, of Linklater at his undoubted best in this mode in *Magnus Merriman* (1934), with its mock-heroic and teasingly ironic interweaving of authentic and unauthentic 'Scottishness'. In its playful strategies for demythologising the familiar Scottish 'divided self' as further distorted in the context of the grim Thatcherite 1980s, McCabe's novel is in many ways the counterpart of Linklater's wilfully ambivalent portrayal of Scotland's Nationalist and Renaissance 1930s, though discernibly gloomier in tone and emphasis. A carefully and economically plotted black comedy, anatomising the time-honoured pilgrimage of its anti-hero to the nadir of native self-abasement and back during the national self-abasement of New Year, the novel boasts a surprising compression and reworking of the traditional motifs of internal division, inarticulacy and alcoholism. All the sorry symptoms of Scotland as 'a state of mind', or a country with a permanent spiritual hangover, are identifiable from the novel's opening 'morning after':

> It was the last day of the year.
>
> Patrick McCoy, an unemployed comedian, awoke with a bad hangover. The kind of hangover it was difficult not to take personally. He wondered what he'd done to deserve it. It had lasted all the previous day, butting him on the forehead, slipping its chiv into his liver and twisting, booting him in the gut and making his bladder lurch. Now here it was again. He shuddered. He sweated. He held on for dear life to his coat, which was doubling as a blanket because of the freezing cold.[13]

McCabe injects much-needed vitality into the now anaemic-seeming antisyzygy by having his hero impaled and split not on the piercing contradictions of MacDiarmid's thistle, but on a more banal and kitsch equivalent, the dismally triumphalist slogan of bogus authenticity 'the real McCoy' with which endless comic postcards, music-hall routines and whisky commercials have sanctified their myths of ersatz virile Scottishness. Caught between his elusive, inarticulable 'Real McCoy' and the comedian's repertory of mimicking mendacious 'Others', Pat has only an overcoat borrowed from Gogol to which to cling as he struggles to make sense of a purgatorial urban Scotland, disfigured by the selfish materialism of the 1980s, as it prepares for the annual infernal debauch of 'the last day of the year'. To complete the novel's subtle schema of intertextual echo and wry reworking of Scottish existential motifs, Pat is also until the novel's dénouement unwittingly a Dead Soul himself, a throwaway drunken joke ('All his jokes had a knack of turning against him in the end') about suicidal intentions having backfired to the extent that all his friends, girlfriend Yvonne included (who may be carrying his child), believe the rumour that he is dead.

The world of grim Edinburgh tenements and bedsits in which Pat is haunting himself is likewise haunted. The city is envisioned as a limbo inhabited by stunted, self-protective lives of eccentricity, cruelty and madness, rendered with grotesque surrealism and manic comedy by turns, crazily magnified and inverted through the novel's central symbol of the front-door spyholes – compound image of complacent distrust and voyeuristic loneliness – which Pat vainly tries to sell to its variously lost souls. McCabe remythologises this symbolic contemporary Scotland through his candidly realistic revision of Hogmanay as a ritual, self-inflicted national pathology – and not the cosy institution celebrating non-existent communal harmony promoted elsewhere in the Scottish novel. In this way he succeeds in showing that it is Scotland itself, perhaps, and not its hapless, hopeless anti-hero, which is the true impostor and impersonator.

This 'real' Scotland is the circle of Pat's friends who, it transpires in the climactic scene of revelation, have been too busy enjoying their long and conspiratorial laughter at Pat's supposed suicide to bother informing his mourning girlfriend that he is actually alive. A precarious balance between tragedy and comedy is the hallmark of Scottish humour, but the tension is orchestrated here with unnervingly tangible horror. This glimpse into the hellish emptiness beneath the clichéd superficiality of a much-vaunted native bonhomie – as mendacious as the tartan TV Hogmanay show from which Pat's big-break comic slot has been edited out because it is supposed to appear 'live', while Pat has been reported 'dead' – makes *The Other McCoy* a new and serious statement about Scottish life. If Scotland's 'state of mind' is determined by pastiche and imitation, what chance does Pat stand of retrieving an individual voice from his internalised chorus of mimicry and learning to imitate himself? Such is the implication of the novel's ending, an indeterminate compromise between optimistic comic closure (Pat reunited, but not reconciled, with Yvonne) and pessimistic circularity. The only comic resolution possible is the New Year variety: a cycle of self-defeating, deceitful will to change in chronic repetition.

> McCoy looked around the room and took it all in, as if to fix it in his memory, a night to remember, the New Year he had died, then he wondered what it would really be like to be nobody, nobody else, nobody not himself, as the three couples circled around each other slowly and the dawn light began to show through the curtains.
>
> It was the first day of the year. (*TOM*, 191)

In its thematic preoccupations, *The Other McCoy* traverses the familiar territory of recent Scottish fiction. Pat's internalised comic monologues, a refuge from his fear of vocalising his own thoughts, have a clear affinity with the self-inciting fantasies of Jock McLeish. Pat might even be interpreted as a comic alternative to the even more acutely self-lacerating Patrick Doyle in Kelman's *A Disaffection* (1989). Doyle's stream of consciousness, comprising much agonised parody of pseudo-Latinate diction and formal philosophical discourse, is repeatedly halted and polluted with the expletives which both mock and frustrate a chronic inability to articulate. What distinguishes McCabe's interpretation, however, is the comparatively rigorous degree of formal compression and structural elegance which his comic reading of dissociation permits, in marked distinction to the looser narrative frameworks of Gray and Galloway or the unrelenting shapeless continuums of Kelman.

Such measures of formal restraint and structural ingenuity are rare in Scottish fiction, a tradition that has been slow to learn the sensitivity to narrative experiment and formal self-awareness taken for granted in other literatures. It is all the more to be regretted, then, that one exception to this reluctance to innovate, Ron Butlin's *The Sound of My Voice*, has suffered such surprising neglect. This remarkable novella represents one of the most significant achievements in Scottish fiction in the 1980s: as conspicuous an innovatory landmark as Gray's *Lanark*, and the most ambitious rendition of all the tropes of damaged identity discussed above so far achieved by a Scottish writer.

The author's description of the work as a 'painstakingly short novel'[14] conveniently encapsulates the unique nature of its achievement: a consummate synthesis between narrative technique and thematic content. The novel is unbearably 'painful': a claustrophobic anatomy of its protagonist's struggle to escape the poisoned Scottish past which has exacerbated his increasingly destructive alcoholism. Butlin's is not, however, another booze-and-crack-up dose of Calvinist Scottish blues, nor does it rely at all upon the eccentricities of Gray or the parodic burlesques of McCabe. Instead, Butlin 'painstakingly' creates an innovative technical framework through which the clinical and psychological realities of alcoholism and its patterns of euphoria, withdrawal and delirium can be contained, examined and expressed, and also formally enacted. Developing from the experiments in narrative perspective, chronology and tense-shift which characterise his short stories, and reflecting the preoccupations of the *nouveau roman*, Butlin locates in the single and ingenious formal departure of narrating his novel in the second person as precise and apposite a vehicle as can be imagined for its delineation of dissociation and psychic damage. The reiterated and relentless 'you' of Morris Magellan's subconscious voice frighteningly combines a shocking intimacy with clinical neutrality in an obsessive monologue that is paradoxically dialogue. It is the sound of the Scottish divided self locked into a newly-deranged and disarming conflict; damaged identity skinned down to the raw of its exposed nerves.

> You were at a party when your father died – and immediately you were told, a miracle happened. A real miracle. It didn't last, of course, but was convincing enough for a few moments. Then, an hour later, you took a girl home and forced her to make love. You held on to her as she cried and pleaded with you: even now her tears are still the nearest you have come to feeling grief at your father's death. You are thirty-four years old; everything that has ever happened to you is still happening. (*SMV*, 9)

Uniting present and past tense in disorientating temporal fluidity, the narrating voice, by turns manic and monotone, becomes a suitably protean identity: not merely Morris Magellan's inner self or conscience providing commentary critical and protective on his life, but a network of transactions embracing an implied author-surrogate, character and reader who revolve around each other in perplexingly unresolvable circularity.

It is precisely the disorientating quality of this complex textual surface which provides such a disturbingly exact context for the novel's uncannily convincing recreation of the psychological disfigurement of alcoholism, and the perverse inner logic through which addiction is simultaneously denied and compounded – 'For you, there is only the fear of immortality in the pause between drinks'; 'When one drink is too much the rest are never enough. Never' (*SMV*, 30, 93). This extends into the equally complex metaphorical interchanges of the novel, in which Morris is seen only to be able to breathe *underwater* when 'drowning' in drink ('You *do* drink like a fish, for drink allows you to breathe underwater'); when the mud in which he feels engulfed during withdrawal symptoms transforms choking into 'thirst':

> Mud-streets, mud-skies, and – inside you – the mud rising. You drink to keep it down, to stop from choking. You drink to gain another breath – and so you struggle through that afternoon. Recently it has been getting hard for you to struggle through the morning as well. Sometimes you wake already choking in mud. But not always, not yet. (*SMV*, 39)

It is part of the narrative voice's purpose, of course, to supply 'unconscious' euphemistic metaphors and images for Morris's dependency. These ironically collude in the strategies of evasion and suppression which he has devised in order to drink his 'conscious' way through the banality of his job as executive in a biscuit-making firm – often rendered with keen satire – and survive a fragile web of delusion, woven in complicity with a wife and two young children who cannot bring themselves to confront his addiction fully. Morris's 'inner voice' is therefore simultaneously self-delusory and self-accusatory; it does not know whether to love or hate him. Not until Morris learns to love himself sufficiently to acknowledge his addiction, after the shock of witnessing a stranger's death 'you felt to be your own', will the voice become self-consolatory. And not until he reaches that point of inner silence will Morris be able to listen, paradoxically, to what his voice has been saying all along, and reach the point of reconciliation and healing to which it has been gently leading him.

> You have reached a moment quiet enough to hear the sound of my voice: so now, as you stare out into the darkness, accept the comfort it can give you – and the love. The love. (*TMV*, 129)

To receive 'the love' Morris must, like so many other Scottish fictional *miserables* before him, confront his past and a childhood in which all gestures of love, affection and self-respect have been 'crushed utterly' by the familiar Scottish paternal tyrant, whose cold and callous distrust of emotion has engendered in his son a crippling sense of shame and guilt – the destructive Calvinist heritage once more; alcoholic compensation so often its deadly inheritance.

The novel's dependence upon this traditional archetype is made more resonant precisely by the explicitly non-Scottish context of most of its setting; we have escaped here the urban, macho, working-class drinking grounds of the industrial West to find searing Scottish guilt positively thriving in a world of middle-class commuters, executive meetings and green-lawn suburbia which surely suggest the South of England. The disjunction makes the cathartic reunion between the 'English' Morris and the buried 'Scottish' self of twenty years ago, when the voice can finally reveal its identity and resurrect a life, infinitely more memorable as one of the most moving final gestures of redemption to be found in any Scottish novel. Paralleling the novel's opening scene of the childhood trauma of a family picnic, Morris while driving his own family back from theirs also drives back into that past to exorcise – and forgive – his father, almost fatally colliding with his apparition, the last spectre to appear in Morris's final delirious withdrawal.

> At the last moment your father seems to hear you; he begins as though to raise his arm in your direction – then abruptly he is gone.
>
> It is only *now* that you are aware of Mary clutching on to you,

> her voice screaming at you to stop. There are tears running down your face as your release the accelerator and begin to slow down. When the car comes to a halt on the hard shoulder you are weeping uncontrollably. Your tears – and mine. (*SMV*, 139)

To find the cracked and strangled Scottish voice and lend it healing speech will take the Scottish novelist on a journey through a mental landscape disfigured by all the 'horrors' of self-inflicted silences. But no matter where it is finally heard, the sound of that new-found voice will always be recognised as unmistakably ours. We must continue to listen to what it has to say, and to understand the weeping that comes with its new-found words; tears that are yours and mine must also, by grammatical and moral definition, be ours as well.

NOTES

1. Kirsty McNeill, 'Interview with James Kelman', *Chapman* 57, Summer 1989, p. 9.
2. Tom Leonard, *Intimate Voices 1965–1983* (Newcastle: Galloping Dog Press, 1984), p. 109.
3. Douglas Gifford, *The Dear Green Place? The Novel in the West of Scotland* (Glasgow: Third Eye Centre Publications, 1985), p. 10.
4. *Cencrastus* no 39, Spring 1991, p. 19.
5. Isobel Murray and Bob Tait, *Ten Modern Scottish Novels* (Aberdeen: Aberdeen University Press, 1984), 'Introduction', p. 8.
6. Peter Zenzinger, 'Contemporary Scottish Fiction' in Peter Zenzinger ed., *Scotland: Literature, Culture, Politics*, Anglistik & Englischunterricht, Band 38/9 (Heidelberg: Carl Winter, 1989), p. 228.
7. See Tom Nairn, 'Scottish Identity: A Cause Unwon', *Chapman* 67, Winter 1991–2, pp. 2–12.
8. Quoted in Zenzinger, op. cit., p. 218.
9. Gifford, op. cit., p. 11.
10. Alasdair Gray, *1982, Janine* (London: Jonathan Cape, 1984), p. 341.
11. Janice Galloway, *The Trick is to Keep Breathing* (Edinburgh: Polygon, 1989), pp. 103–4. Subsequent references are to this edition.
12. See Gavin Wallace, 'Compton Mackenzie and the Scottish Popular Novel', in Cairns Craig, ed., *The History of Scottish Literature Volume 4: The Twentieth Century* (Aberdeen: Aberdeen University Press, 1987), pp. 243–57.
13. Brian McCabe, *The Other McCoy* (Edinburgh: Mainstream Publishing, 1990; reprinted Harmondsworth: Penguin Books, 1991), p. 7. This and subsequent references are to the Penguin edition.
14. Ron Butlin, *The Sound of My Voice* (Edinburgh: Canongate Publishing Ltd, 1987; reprinted London: Paladin/Grafton Books, 1989), author's dedication. Subsequent references are to the Paladin edition.

Sixteen

The Scottish Novel since 1970: A Bibliography

Alison Lumsden

The bibliography gives details of first editions only. Collections of short stories, short story sequences and novellas are included.

ANDERSON, Freddy, *Oiney Hoi* (Edinburgh: Polygon, 1990)
BANKS, Iain, *The Wasp Factory* (London: Macmillan, 1984)
——, *Walking on Glass* (London: Macmillan, 1985)
——, *The Bridge* (London: Macmillan, 1986)
——, *Espedair Street* (London: Macmillan, 1987)
——, *The Player of Games* (London: Macmillan, 1988)
——, *Canal Dreams* (London: Macmillan, 1989)
——, *The Crow Road* (London: Scribners, 1992)
BANKS, Iain, M., *Cleaning Up* (Birmingham: Birmingham Science Fiction Group, 1987)
——, *Consider Phlebus* (London: Macmillan, 1987)
——, *The State of the Art* (Willimantic, Conn: MV Ziesling, 1989)
——, *Use of Weapons* (London: Orbit Sphere, 1991)
BARKER, Elspeth, *O Caledonia* (London: Hamish Hamilton, 1991)
BLACKHALL, Sheena, *A Nippick O' Nor' East Tales: A Doric Hairst* (Aberdeen: Keith Murray, 1989)
—— with Rosemary MACKAY and Wilma MURRAY, *Three's Company: A Collection of Stories from Aberdeen* (Aberdeen: Keith Murray, 1989)
BOLD, Alan, *The Edge of the Wood* (Barr Luath: Barr Luath Press, 1984)
——, *East is West* (Aberdeen: Keith Murray, 1991)
BOYD, William, *A Good Man in Africa* (London: Hamish Hamilton, 1981)
——, *On the Yankee Station and Other Stories* (London: Hamish Hamilton, 1982)
——, *An Ice-Cream War* (London: Hamish Hamilton, 1982)
——, *Stars and Bars* (London: Hamish Hamilton, 1984)
——, *The New Confessions* (London: Hamish Hamilton, 1987)
——, *Brazzaville Beach* (London: Sinclair-Stevenson, 1990)
BOYCE, Chris, *Catchword* (London: Gollancz, 1975)
——, *Brainfix* (London: Panther, 1980)

——, *Blooding Mister Naylor* (Glasgow: Dog and Bone, 1990)
BROOMFIELD, Janet, *A Fallen Land* (London: Bodley Head, 1990)
BROWN, George Mackay, *Greenvoe* (London: Hogarth Press, 1972)
——, *A Time to Keep* (London: Hogarth Press, 1972)
——, *Magnus: A Novel* (London: Hogarth Press, 1973)
——, *Hawkfall and Other Stories* (London: Hogarth Press, 1974)
——, *The Two Fiddlers: Tales from Orkney* (London: Chatto and Windus/The Hogarth Press, 1974)
——, *The Sun's Net and Other Stories* (London: Hogarth Press, 1976)
——, *Witch and Other Stories* (London: Longman, 1977)
——, *Andrina and Other Stories* (London: Chatto and Windus/The Hogarth Press, 1983)
——, *Time in a Red Coat* (London: Chatto and Windus, 1984)
——, *The Hooded Fisherman*, Illustrated by Charles Shearer (Pitlochry: Trumpet Press, 1985). An Edition of 205 Copies
——, *Christmas Stories*, with wood engravings by John Lawrence (Oxford: Perpetua, 1985)
——, *Keepers of the House*, illustrated by Gillian Martin (London: Old Stile Press, 1986). An Edition of 225 Copies
——, *The Golden Bird: Two Orkney Stories* (London: John Murray, 1987)
——, *The Masked Fisherman and Other Stories* (London: John Murray, 1989)
BROWN, Hamish, *Five Bird Stories* (Kington: Pettycur Publishing, 1984)
BRUCE-WATT, Jeremy, *The Captive Summer* (Edinburgh: Chambers, 1979)
BURGESS, Moira, *The Day Before Tomorrow* (London: Collins, 1971)
——, *A Rumour of Strangers* (London: Collins, 1987)
BURROWES, John, *Jamesie's People: A Gorbals Story* (Edinburgh: Mainstream Publishing, 1984)
——, *Incomers* (Edinburgh: Mainstream Publishing, 1987)
——, *Gulf* (Edinburgh: Mainstream Publishing, 1989)
BUTLIN, Ron, *The Tilting Room* (Edinburgh: Canongate Publishing, 1983)
——, *The Sound of My Voice* (Edinburgh: Canongate Publishing, 1987)
CAIRD, Janet, *The Umbrella Man's Daughter* (London: Macmillan, 1980)
CAMPSIE, Alistair, *By Law Protected* (Edinburgh: Canongate Publishing, 1976)
——, *Perfect Poison* (London: Robert Hale, 1985)
——, *The Clarinda Conspiracy* (Edinburgh: Mainstream Publishing, 1985)
CATHCART, Alex, *The Comeback* (Edinburgh: Polygon, 1986)
——, *The Missionary* (Edinburgh: Polygon, 1988)
CHANDLER, Glenn, *The Sanctuary* (London: Hamlyn Paperbacks, 1981)
——, *The Tribe* (London: Hamlyn, 1981)
——, *Killer* (Edinburgh: Scottish Television/Mainstream Publishing, 1983)
COLE, Gerald, *Gregory's Girl*, based on the screenplay by Bill Forsyth (London: Allen, 1981)
——, *Comfort and Joy*, based on the screenplay by Bill Forsyth (London: Methuen, 1984)
COWAN, Evelyn, *Portrait of Alice* (Edinburgh: Canongate Publishing, 1976)
CRAIG, David, *King Cameron* (Manchester: Carcanet, 1991)
CROW, Christine, *Miss X or the Wolf Woman* (London: Women's Press, 1990)

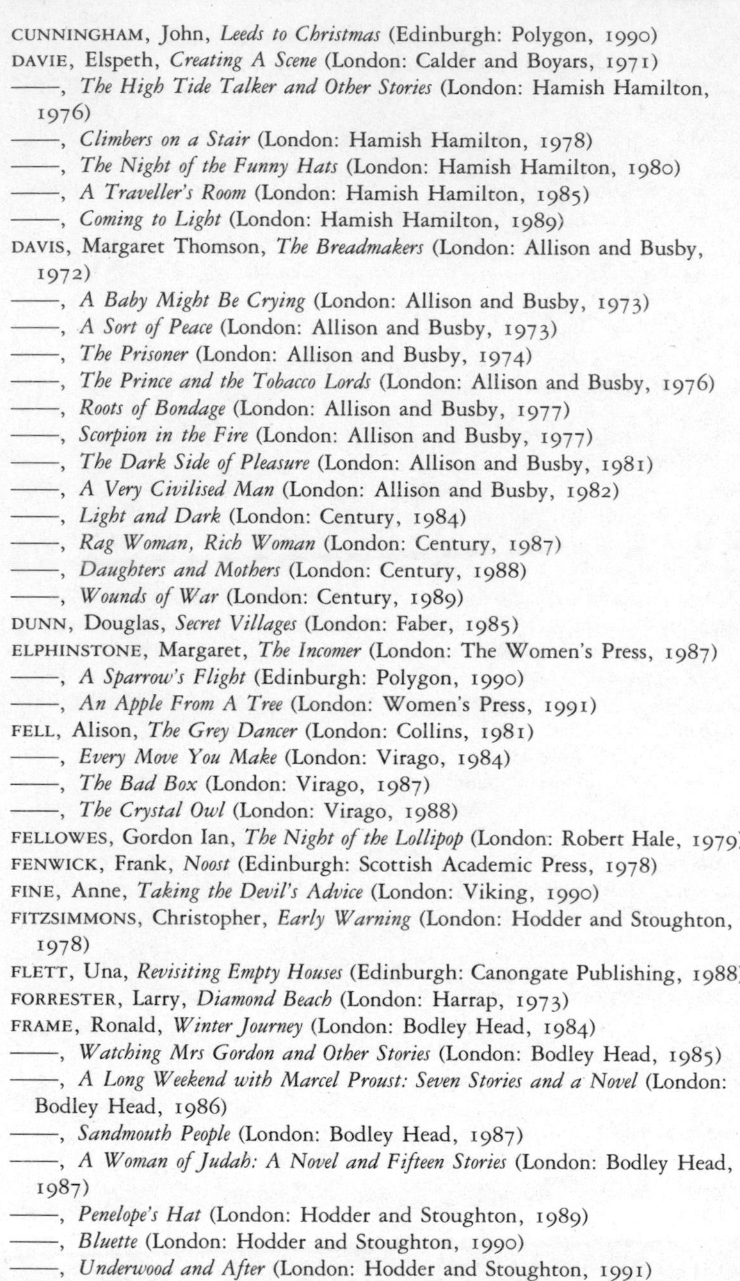

CUNNINGHAM, John, *Leeds to Christmas* (Edinburgh: Polygon, 1990)
DAVIE, Elspeth, *Creating A Scene* (London: Calder and Boyars, 1971)
——, *The High Tide Talker and Other Stories* (London: Hamish Hamilton, 1976)
——, *Climbers on a Stair* (London: Hamish Hamilton, 1978)
——, *The Night of the Funny Hats* (London: Hamish Hamilton, 1980)
——, *A Traveller's Room* (London: Hamish Hamilton, 1985)
——, *Coming to Light* (London: Hamish Hamilton, 1989)
DAVIS, Margaret Thomson, *The Breadmakers* (London: Allison and Busby, 1972)
——, *A Baby Might Be Crying* (London: Allison and Busby, 1973)
——, *A Sort of Peace* (London: Allison and Busby, 1973)
——, *The Prisoner* (London: Allison and Busby, 1974)
——, *The Prince and the Tobacco Lords* (London: Allison and Busby, 1976)
——, *Roots of Bondage* (London: Allison and Busby, 1977)
——, *Scorpion in the Fire* (London: Allison and Busby, 1977)
——, *The Dark Side of Pleasure* (London: Allison and Busby, 1981)
——, *A Very Civilised Man* (London: Allison and Busby, 1982)
——, *Light and Dark* (London: Century, 1984)
——, *Rag Woman, Rich Woman* (London: Century, 1987)
——, *Daughters and Mothers* (London: Century, 1988)
——, *Wounds of War* (London: Century, 1989)
DUNN, Douglas, *Secret Villages* (London: Faber, 1985)
ELPHINSTONE, Margaret, *The Incomer* (London: The Women's Press, 1987)
——, *A Sparrow's Flight* (Edinburgh: Polygon, 1990)
——, *An Apple From A Tree* (London: Women's Press, 1991)
FELL, Alison, *The Grey Dancer* (London: Collins, 1981)
——, *Every Move You Make* (London: Virago, 1984)
——, *The Bad Box* (London: Virago, 1987)
——, *The Crystal Owl* (London: Virago, 1988)
FELLOWES, Gordon Ian, *The Night of the Lollipop* (London: Robert Hale, 1979)
FENWICK, Frank, *Noost* (Edinburgh: Scottish Academic Press, 1978)
FINE, Anne, *Taking the Devil's Advice* (London: Viking, 1990)
FITZSIMMONS, Christopher, *Early Warning* (London: Hodder and Stoughton, 1978)
FLETT, Una, *Revisiting Empty Houses* (Edinburgh: Canongate Publishing, 1988)
FORRESTER, Larry, *Diamond Beach* (London: Harrap, 1973)
FRAME, Ronald, *Winter Journey* (London: Bodley Head, 1984)
——, *Watching Mrs Gordon and Other Stories* (London: Bodley Head, 1985)
——, *A Long Weekend with Marcel Proust: Seven Stories and a Novel* (London: Bodley Head, 1986)
——, *Sandmouth People* (London: Bodley Head, 1987)
——, *A Woman of Judah: A Novel and Fifteen Stories* (London: Bodley Head, 1987)
——, *Penelope's Hat* (London: Hodder and Stoughton, 1989)
——, *Bluette* (London: Hodder and Stoughton, 1990)
——, *Underwood and After* (London: Hodder and Stoughton, 1991)
FRIEL, George, *Mr Alfred M.A.* (London: Calder and Boyars, 1972)

——, *The Empty House* (London: Calder and Boyars, 1974)
GABRIEL, Henny, *The Inner Case* (?: Tallis Press, 1990)
GALFORD, Ellen, *Moll Cutpurse her true history: a novel* (Edinburgh: Stramullion, 1984)
——, *The Fires of Bride* (London: The Women's Press, 1986)
——, *Queendom Come* (London: Virago, 1990)
GALLACHER, Tom, *Apprentice* (London: Hamish Hamilton, 1983)
——, *Journeyman* (London: Hamish Hamilton, 1984)
——, *Survivor* (London: Hamish Hamilton, 1985)
——, *The Jewel Maker* (London: Hamish Hamilton, 1986)
——, *The Wind on the Heath* (London: Hamish Hamilton, 1987)
GALLAGHER, Paul, *A Hero of Our Time* (Glasgow?: Dorchester Press, 1986)
GALLOWAY, Janice, *The Trick is to Keep Breathing*, (Edinburgh: Polygon, 1989)
——, *Blood* (London: Secker and Warburg, 1991)
GILMOUR, David, *The Hungry Generations* (London: Sinclair-Stevenson, 1991)
GORDON, Giles, *About a Marriage: A Novel* (London: Allison and Busby, 1972)
——, *Farewell, Fond Dreams* (London: Hutchinson, 1975)
——, *100 Scenes from Married Life: A Selection* (London: Hutchinson, 1976)
——, *Enemies: A Novel About Friendship* (Brighton: Harvester Press, 1977)
——, *Couple* (London: Sceptre Press, 1978)
——, *The Illusionist and Other Fictions* (Brighton: Harvester Press, 1978)
——, *Ambrose's Vision: Sketches Towards the Creation of a Cathedral* (Brighton: Harvester Press, 1980)
GRAHAM, Barry, *Of Darkness and Light* (London: Bloomsbury, 1989)
——, *The Champion's New Clothes* (London: Bloomsbury, 1991)
GRAHAM, John J., *Shadowed Valley* (Lerwick: The Shetland Publishing Company, 1987)
GRAY, Alasdair, *The Comedy of the White Dog* (Glasgow: Glasgow Print Studio Press, 1979)
——, *Lanark: A Life in Four Books* (Edinburgh: Canongate Publishing, 1981)
——, *Unlikely Stories, Mostly* (Edinburgh: Canongate Publishing, 1983)
——, *1982, Janine* (London: Jonathan Cape, 1984)
——, *The Fall of Kelvin Walker: A Fable of the Sixties* (Edinburgh: Canongate Publishing: 1985)
——, *The Fall of Kelvin Walker, revised edition* (Harmondsworth: Penguin, 1986)
——, *McGrotty and Ludmilla, or The Harbinger Report* (Glasgow: Dog and Bone, 1990)
——, *Something Leather* (London: Jonathan Cape, 1990)
——, *Poor Things* (London: Bloomsbury Publishing, 1992)
GREIG, Andrew, *Electric Brae: A Modern Romance* (Edinburgh: Canongate, 1992)
HAMILTON, Alex, *Gallus, Did You Say? and Other Stories* (Glasgow: Ferret Press, 1982)
—— with James KELMAN and Tom LEONARD, *Three Glasgow Writers* (Glasgow: Molendinar Press, 1976)
HANLEY, Clifford, *Prissy* (London: Collins, 1978)

——, *Another Street, Another Dance* (Edinburgh: Mainstream Publishing, 1983)
HAYTON, Sian, *Cells of Knowledge* (Edinburgh: Polygon, 1989)
HEALY, Thomas, *It Might Have Been Jerusalem* (Edinburgh: Polygon, 1991)
HENDERSON, William, *King of the Gorbals* (London: New English Library, 1973)
HERDMAN, John, *Stories Short and Tall* (Thurso: John Humphries, 1979)
——, *Three Novellas: Pagan's Pilgrimage* (Edinburgh: Polygon, 1987)
HIGHLANDS, Alexander, *The Dark Horizon* (London: Jarrolds, 1971)
HOOD, Stuart, *In and Out the Windows* (London: Davis-Poynter, 1974)
——, *A Storm from Paradise* (Manchester: Carcanet, 1985)
——, *The Upper Hand* (Manchester: Carcanet, 1987)
——, *The Brutal Heart* (Manchester: Carcanet, 1990)
——, *A Den of Foxes* (London: Methuen, 1991)
HUTCHISON, Stewart, *Scully's Lugs* (Edinburgh: Chambers, 1979)
JAMIESON, Robert Alan, *Soor Hearts* (Edinburgh: Paul Harris, 1983)
——, *Thin Wealth: A Novel from an Oil Decade* (Edinburgh: Polygon, 1986)
——, *A Day at the Office* (Edinburgh: Polygon, 1991)
JENKINS, Robin, *The Expatriates* (London: Gollancz, 1971)
——, *A Toast to the Lord: A Novel* (London: Gollancz, 1972)
——, *A Far Cry from Bowmore and Other Stories* (London: Gollancz, 1973)
——, *A Figure of Fun* (London: Gollancz, 1974)
——, *A Would-be Saint* (London: Gollancz, 1978)
——, *Fergus Lamont* (Edinburgh: Canongate Publishing, 1979)
——, *The Awakening of George Darroch* (Edinburgh: Waterfront Communications, 1985)
——, *Just Duffy* (Edinburgh: Canongate Publishing, 1988)
——, *Poverty Castle* (Nairn: Balnain Books, 1991)
KELMAN, James, *An Old Pub Near the Angel and Other Stories* (Orano, Maine: Puckerbush Press, 1973)
——, *Short Tales from the Night Shift* (Glasgow: Glasgow Print Studio Press, 1978)
——, *Not Not While the Giro, and Other Stories* (Edinburgh: Polygon, 1983)
——, *The Busconductor Hines* (Edinburgh: Polygon, 1984)
——, *A Chancer* (Edinburgh: Polygon, 1985)
——, *Greyhound for Breakfast* (London: Secker and Warburg, 1987)
——, *A Disaffection* (London: Secker and Warburg, 1989)
——, *The Burn* (London: Secker and Warburg, 1991)
—— with Alasdair GRAY and Agnes OWENS, *Lean Tales* (London: Jonathan Cape, 1985)
KENNAWAY, James, *Silence* (London: Jonathan Cape, 1972)
KENNEDY, A. L., *Night Geometry and the Garscadden Trains* (Edinburgh: Polygon, 1990)
KESSON, Jessie, *Another Time, Another Place* (London: Chatto and Windus, 1983)
——, *Where the Apple Ripens and Other Stories* (London: Chatto and Windus, 1985)
——, *The Jessie Kesson Omnibus* (London: Chatto and Windus, 1991)

KUPPNER, Frank, *A Very Quiet Street* (Edinburgh: Polygon, 1989)
——, *A Concussed History of Scotland* (Edinburgh: Polygon, 1991)
KYDD, Robbie, *Auld Zimmery* (Glasgow: The Mariscat Press, 1987)
——, *The Quiet Stranger* (Edinburgh: Mainstream Publishing, 1991)
LEGGE, Gordon, *The Shoe* (Edinburgh: Polygon, 1989)
——, *In Between Talking About the Football* (Edinburgh: Polygon, 1991)
LIDDELL, Helen, *Elite* (London: Century, 1990)
LINDSAY, Frederic, *Brond* (Edinburgh: MacDonald, 1983)
——, *Jill Rips* (London: Andre Deutsch, 1987)
——, *A Charm Against Drowning* (London: Andre Deutsch, 1988)
——, *After the Stranger Came* (London: Andre Deutsch, 1992)
LINGARD, Joan, *The Prevailing Wind* (Edinburgh: Paul Harris, 1978)
——, *The Second Flowering of Emily Mountjoy* (Edinburgh: Paul Harris, 1979)
——, *Greenyard* (London: Hamish Hamilton, 1981)
——, *The Winter Visitor* (London: Hamish Hamilton, 1983)
——, *Sisters by Rite* (London: Hamish Hamilton, 1984)
——, *Reasonable Doubts* (London: Hamish Hamilton, 1986)
——, *The Women's House* (London: Hamish Hamilton, 1989)
——, *Between Two Worlds* (London: Hamish Hamilton, 1991)
LLOYD-JONES, Robin, *Lord of the Dance* (London: Gollancz, 1983)
MCALLISTER, Angus, *The Krugg Syndrome* (London: Grafton Paperback Original, 1988)
——, *The Canongate Strangler* (Glasgow: Dog and Bone, 1990)
MCCABE, Brian, *The Lipstick Circus and other Stories* (Edinburgh: Mainstream Publishing, 1985)
——, *The Other McCoy* (Edinburgh: Mainstream Publishing, 1990)
MCCONDACH, J. P., *The Channering Worm* (Edinburgh: Canongate Publishing, 1983)
MCCORMACK, Eric, *The Paradise Motel* (London: Bloomsbury, 1989)
——, *Inspecting the Vaults* (London: Bloomsbury, 1989)
MACDONALD, Colin, *All the Young Dudes* (?: Pulteney Press, 1979)
——, *Under a Northern Sky* (Edinburgh: Exiles Press, 1980)
MACDONALD, Norman Malcolm, *Calum Tod* (Inverness: Club Leabhar, 1976)
MACDONALD, Sharman, *The Beast* (London: Collins, 1986)
——, *Night Night* (London: Collins, 1988)
MCDONALD, Stuart, *The Adventures of Endill Swift* (Edinburgh: Canongate Publishing, 1990)
MACDOUGALL, Carl, *Prosepiece* (Markinch: Markinch Pavement Press, 1979)
——, *The One-Legged Tap Dancer* (Glasgow: Glasgow Print Studio Press, 1981)
——, *Elvis is Dead* (Glasgow: The Mariscat Press, 1986)
——, *Stone Over Water* (London: Secker and Warburg, 1989)
MCEWAN, Todd, *McX: A Romance of the Dour* (London: Secker and Warburg, 1990)
MCGILL, John, *That Reubens Guy* (Edinburgh: Mainstream Publishing, 1990)
MCGINN, Matt, *Fry the Little Fishes* (London: Calder and Boyars, 1975)
MCGINNESS, Ian, *Inner City* (Edinburgh: Polygon, 1987)
——, *Bannock*, (Edinburgh: Polygon, 1990)

MCGREGOR, Iona, *The Burning Hill* (London: Faber, 1970)
——, *Death Wore a Diadem* (London: Women's Press, 1989)
MCILVANNEY, William, *Docherty* (London: Allen and Unwin, 1975)
——, *Laidlaw* (London: Hodder and Stoughton, 1977)
——, *The Papers of Tony Veitch* (London: Hodder and Stoughton, 1983)
——, *The Big Man* (London: Hodder and Stoughton, 1985)
——, *Walking Wounded* (London: Hodder and Stoughton, 1989)
——, *Strange Loyalties* (London: Hodder and Stoughton, 1991)
MACKAY, Colin, *The Song of the Forest* (Edinburgh: Canongate Publishing, 1987)
——, *The Sound of the Sea* (Edinburgh: Canongate Publishing, 1989)
MACKAY, Shena, *An Advent Calendar* (London: Jonathan Cape, 1971)
——, *Babies in Rhinestones and Other Stories* (London: Heinemann, 1983)
——, *Redhill Rococo* (London: Heinemann, 1986)
——, *Dreams of Dead Women's Handbags* (London: Heinemann, 1987)
MACKENZIE, David S., *The Truth of Stone* (Edinburgh: Mainstream Publishing, 1990)
MACKENZIE, John, *City Whitelight* (Edinburgh: Mainstream Publishing, 1986)
MACLAVERTY, Bernard, *Secrets and Other Stories* (Belfast: Blackstaff Press, 1977)
——, *Lamb* (London: Jonathan Cape, 1980)
——, *A Time to Dance and Other Stories* (London: Jonathan Cape, 1982)
——, *Cal* (London: Jonathan Cape, 1983)
——, *The Great Profundo and Other Stories* (London: Jonathan Cape, 1987)
MCLEAN, Duncan, *The Druids Shite It, Fail to Show* (South Queensferry: Clocktower Press, 1991)
——, *Bucket of Tongues* (London: Secker and Warburg, 1992)
—— and James MEEK, *Safe/Lurch: Short Stories* (South Queensferry: Clocktower Press, 1990)
——, *Zoomers* (South Queensferry: Clocktower Press, 1991)
MCLELLAN, Robert, *Linmill: Short Stories in Scots* (Preston: Akros Publications, 1977)
——, *Four Linmill Stories* (Glasgow: Scotstoun, 1979)
——, *Linmill Stories* (Edinburgh: Canongate Publishing, 1990)
MACLEOD, Charles, *Devil in the Wind* (Edinburgh: Gordon Wright, 1979)
MCNAB, Tom, *Flanagan's Run* (London: Hodder and Stoughton, 1982)
——, *Rings of Sand* (London: Hodder and Stoughton, 1984)
MCWILLIAM, Candia, *A Case of Knives* (London: Bloomsbury, 1988)
——, *A Little Stranger* (London: Bloomsbury 1989)
MAITLAND, Sara, *Daughter of Jerusalem* (London: Blond and Briggs, 1978)
——, *A Book of Spells* (London: Michael Joseph, 1987)
——, *Telling Tales* (London: Journeyman, 1983)
——, *Virgin Territory* (London: Michael Joseph, 1984)
——, *Three Times Table* (London: Chatto and Windus, 1990)
MASSIE, Allan, *Change and Decay In All Around I See* (London: Bodley Head, 1978)
——, *The Last Peacock* (London: Bodley Head, 1980)
——, *The Death of Men* (London: Bodley Head, 1981)
——, *One Night in Winter* (London: Bodley Head, 1984)

——, *Augustus: A Novel* (London: Bodley Head, 1986)
——, *A Question of Loyalties* (London: Hutchinson, 1989)
——, *Tiberius* (London: Hodder and Stoughton, 1990)
——, *The Hanging Tree: A Romance of the Fifteenth Century* (London: Hodder and Stoughton, 1990)
——, *The Sins of the Father* (London: Hutchinson, 1991)
MEEK, James, *McFarlane Boils the Sea* (Edinburgh: Polygon, 1989)
——, *Last Orders* (Edinburgh: Polygon, 1992)
MILLAR, Martin, *Lux the Poet* (London: Fourth Estate, 1985)
——, *Milk, Sulphate and Alby Starvation* (London: Fourth Estate, 1987)
——, *Ruby and The Stone Age Diet* (London: Fourth Estate, 1989)
——, *The Good Fairies of New York* (London: Fourth Estate, 1992)
MILLER, James, *Dougie: Episodes in the Life of a Caithness Crofter* (Inverness: James Miller, 1985)
MILLS, Joseph, *Towards the End* (Edinburgh: Polygon, 1989)
MILSTED, David, *The Chronicles of Craigfieth* (Edinburgh: Mainstream Publishing, 1988)
——, *Market Forces* (Edinburgh: Mainstream Publishing, 1989)
MITCHISON, Naomi, *Sunrise Tomorrow: A Story of Botswana* (London: Collins, 1973)
——, *Solution Three* (London: Dobson Science Fiction, 1975)
——, *Images of Africa* (Edinburgh: Canongate Publishing, 1980)
——, *What Do You Think Yourself?* (Edinburgh: Paul Harris, 1982)
——, *Not By Bread Alone* (London: Marian Boyars, 1983)
——, *Beyond This Limit*, ed. Isobel MURRAY (Edinburgh: Scottish Academic Press, 1986)
——, *Early in Orcadia* (Glasgow: Richard Drew, 1987)
——, *A Girl Must Live* (Glasgow: Richard Drew, 1990)
——, *The Oath-Takers* (Nairn: Balnain Books, 1991)
——, *Sea-Green Ribbons* (Nairn: Balnain Books, 1991)
[illegible], [illegible], *[illegible]* (London: Secker and Warburg, 1991)
MUNRO, Hugh, *The Brain Robbers: A Clutha Tale* (London: Robert Hale, 1977)
——, *The Keelie* (London: Robert Hale, 1978)
MURRAY, Angus Wolfe, *Resurrection Shuffle* (London: Peter Owen, 1978)
NELSON, Gillian, *The Cypress Room* (London: Bodley Head, 1981)
——, *The Spare Room Cupboard* (London: Hamish Hamilton, 1984)
——, *A Secret Life* (London: Hamish Hamilton, 1985)
NYE, Robert, *Merlin* (London: Hamish Hamilton, 1978)
——, *The Memoirs of Lord Byron: A Novel* (London: Hamish Hamilton, 1989)
——, *The Life and Death of My Lord Gilles de Rais* (London: Hamish Hamilton, 1990)
OWENS, Anges, *Gentlemen of the West* (Edinburgh: Polygon, 1984)
——, *Like Birds in the Wilderness* (London: Fourth Estate, 1987)
PALLISER, Charles, *The Quincunx* (Edinburgh: Canongate Publishing, 1989)
——, *The Sensationalist* (London: Jonathan Cape, 1991)

PENNEY, Bridget, *Honeymoon with Death and Other Stories* (Edinburgh: Polygon, 1991)
PLATE, Peter, *Black Wheel of Anger* (Edinburgh: Polygon, 1990)
——, *Darkness Throws Down the Sun* (Edinburgh: Polygon, 1991)
POTTINGER, George, *Whisky Sour* (Edinburgh: Paul Harris, 1979)
RAE, Hugh C., *Kiss the Boss Goodbye* (London: Constable, 1970)
——, *The Saturday Epic* (London: Blond, 1970)
——, *The Badger's Daughter* (London: Constable, 1971)
——, *The Marksman* (London: Constable, 1971)
——, *The Shooting Gallery* (London: Constable, 1972)
——, *Whip Hand* (London: Constable, 1972)
——, *The Rock Harvest* (London: Constable, 1973)
——, *The Rookery* (London: Constable, 1974)
——, *Harkfast* (London: Constable, 1976)
——, *Sullivan* (London: Constable, 1978)
——, *The Haunting at Waverley Falls* (London: Constable, 1980)
——, *Privileged Strangers* (London: Hodder and Stoughton, 1982)
RANKIN, Ian, *The Flood* (Edinburgh: Polygon, 1986)
——, *Knots and Crosses* (London: Bodley Head, 1987)
——, *Watchman* (London: Bodley Head, 1988)
——, *Westwind* (London: Barrie and Jenkins, 1990)
——, *Hide and Seek* (London: Barrie and Jenkins, 1991)
ROSE, Dilys, *Our Lady of the Pickpockets* (London: Secker and Warburg, 1989)
ROSS, Bess, *A Bit of Crack and Car Culture and Other Stories* (Nairn: Balnain Books, 1990)
——, *Those Other Times* (Nairn: Balnain Books, 1991)
RUSH, Christopher, *Peace Comes Dropping Slow* (Edinburgh: Ramsay Head, 1983)
——, *A Twelvemonth and a Day* (Aberdeen: Aberdeen University Press, 1985)
——, *Two Christmas Stories* (Aberdeen: Aberdeen University Press, 1988)
——, *Into the Ebb* (Aberdeen: Aberdeen University Press, 1989)
SCOTT, Douglas, *The Spoils of War* (London: Secker and Warburg, 1977)
——, *The Gifts of Artemis* (London: Secker and Warburg, 1979)
——, *The Burning of the Ships* (London: Secker and Warburg, 1980)
——, *Die for the Queen* (London: Secker and Warburg, 1981)
——, *In the Face of the Enemy* (London: Secker and Warburg, 1982)
——, *The Hanged Man* (London: Secker and Warburg, 1983)
——, *Chains* (London: Secker and Warburg, 1984)
——, *Eagle's Blood* (London: Secker and Warburg, 1985)
——, *The Albatross Run* (London: Secker and Warburg, 1986)
——, *Shadows* (London: Secker and Warburg, 1987)
——, *Whirlpool* (London: Century, 1988)
——, *The Disinherited* (London: Century, 1990)
SHARP, Alan, *Night Moves: A Novel* (New York: Warner Paperback Library, 1975)
SHORT, Agnes, *The Heritors* (London: Constable, 1977)
——, *Clatter Vengeance* (London: Constable, 1979)

——, *The Crescent and the Cross* (London: Constable, 1980)
——, *Miss Jenny* (London: Constable, 1981)
——, *Gabrielle* (London: Constable, 1983)
——, *The First Fair Wind* (London: Constable, 1984)
——, *The Flowing Tide* (London: Constable, 1986)
——, *The Dragon Seas* (London: Constable, 1988)
——, *Silvercairns* (London: Constable, 1990)
——, *Rainbow Hill* (London: Constable, 1991)
SMITH, Anne, *The Magic Glass* (London: Michael Joseph, 1981)
SMITH, Iain Crichton, *Survival Without Error and Other Stories* (London: Gollancz, 1970)
——, *My Last Duchess: A Novel* (London: Gollancz, 1971)
——, *The Black and the Red and Other Stories* (London: Gollancz, 1973)
——, *Goodbye, Mr Dixon* (London: Gollancz, 1974)
——, *The Village* (Inverness: Club Leabhar, 1976)
——, *The Hermit and Other Stories* (London: Gollancz, 1977)
——, *An End to Autumn* (London: Gollancz, 1978)
——, *On the Island* (London: Gollancz, 1979)
——, *Murdo and Other Stories* (London: Gollancz, 1981)
——, *A Field Full of Folk* (London: Gollancz, 1982)
——, *The Search* (London: Gollancz, 1983)
——, *Mr Trill in Hades and Other Stories* (London: Gollancz, 1984)
——, *The Tenement* (London: Gollancz, 1985)
——, *In the Middle of the Wood* (London: Gollancz, 1987)
——, *The Dream* (London: Macmillan, 1990)
——, *Selected Short Stories* (Manchester: Carcanet, 1990)
——, *An Honourable Death* (London: Macmillan, 1992)
SOUTHMAN, Christopher, *The Principal* (London: Albyn Press, 1985)
SPARK, Muriel, *The Driver's Seat* (London: Macmillan, 1970)
——, *Not to Disturb* (London: Macmillan, 1971)
——, *The Hothouse by the East River* (London: Macmillan, 1973)
——, *The Abbess of Crewe* (London: Macmillan, 1974)
——, *The Takeover* (London: Macmillan, 1976)
——, *Territorial Rights* (London: Macmillan, 1979)
——, *Loitering with Intent* (London: Bodley Head, 1981)
——, *Bang Bang You're Dead and Other Stories* (London: Bodley Head, 1981)
——, *The Only Problem* (London: Bodley Head, 1984)
——, *The Stories of Muriel Spark* (London: Bodley Head, 1987)
——, *A Far Cry from Kensington* (London: Constable, 1988)
——, *Symposium* (London: Constable, 1990)
SPENCE, Alan, *Its Colours They Are Fine* (London: Collins, 1977)
——, *The Magic Flute* (Edinburgh: Canongate Publishing, 1990)
STEELE, Hunter, *The Wishdoctor's Song* (London: Macdonald, 1984)
——, *Chasing the Gilded Shadow* (London: Andre Deutsch, 1986)
——, *Lord Hamlet's Castle* (London: Andre Deutsch, 1987)
——, *The Lords of Montplaisir* (London: Macmillan, 1989)
STEPHEN, Ian, *Living at the Edge* (Aberdeen: Machair Books, 1982)
——, *Varying States of Grace* (Edinburgh: Polygon, 1989)

STEWART, Mary, *The Crystal Cave* (London: Hodder and Stoughton, 1970)
——, *Airs Above the Ground* (London: Hodder and Stoughton, 1972)
——, *The Hollow Hills* (London: Hodder and Stoughton, 1973)
——, *Touch Not the Cat* (London: Hodder and Stoughton, 1976)
——, *The Last Enchantment* (London: Hodder and Stoughton, 1979)
——, *The Wicked Day* (London: Hodder and Stoughton, 1983)
——, *Thornyhold* (London: Hodder and Stoughton, 1990)
TAIT, Harry, *The Ballad of Sawney Bain* (Edinburgh: Polygon, 1990)
TENNANT, Emma, *The Time of the Crack* (London: Jonathan Cape, 1973). Reprinted as *The Crack* (London: Faber, 1985)
——, *The Last of the Country House Murders* (London: Jonathan Cape, 1974)
——, *Hotel de Dream* (London: Gollancz, 1976)
——, *The Bad Sister* (London: Gollancz, 1978)
——, *Wild Nights* (London: Jonathan Cape, 1979)
——, *Alice Fell* (London: Jonathan Cape, 1980)
——, *Queen of Stones* (London: Jonathan Cape, 1982)
——, *Woman Beware Woman* (London: Jonathan Cape, 1983)
——, *Black Marina* (London: Faber, 1985)
——, *The Adventures of Robina By Herself* (London: Faber, 1986)
——, *The House of Hospitalities* (London: Viking, 1987)
——, *A Wedding of Cousins* (London: Viking, 1988)
——, *The Magic Drum: An Excursion* (London: Viking, 1989)
——, *Two Women of London: The Strange Case of Ms Jekyll and Mrs Hyde* (London: Faber, 1988)
——, *Sisters and Strangers* (London: Grafton, 1990)
——, *Faustine* (London: Faber, 1991)
TORRINGTON, Jeff, *Swing Hammer Swing!* (London: Secker and Warburg, 1992)
TOULMIN, David, *Hard Shining Corn* (Aberdeen: Impulse Books, 1972)
——, *Blown Seed* (Edinburgh: Paul Harris, 1976)
——, *Harvest Home* (Edinburgh: Paul Harris, 1978)
TRANTER, Nigel, *Robert the Bruce: The Path of the Hero King* (London: Hodder and Stoughton, 1970)
——, *Robert the Bruce: The Price of the King's Peace* (London: Hodder and Stoughton, 1971)
——, *The Young Montrose* (London: Hodder and Stoughton, 1972)
——, *Montrose the Captain General* (London: Hodder and Stoughton, 1973)
——, *The Wisest Fool* (London: Hodder and Stoughton, 1974)
——, *The Wallace* (London: Hodder and Stoughton, 1975)
——, *Lords of Misrule* (London: Hodder and Stoughton, 1976)
——, *A Folly of Princes* (London: Hodder and Stoughton, 1977)
——, *The Captive Crown* (London: Hodder and Stoughton, 1977)
——, *Macbeth the King* (London: Hodder and Stoughton, 1978)
——, *David the Prince* (London: Hodder and Stoughton, 1980)
——, *The Chosen Course* (Glasgow: Molendinar Press, 1980)
——, *True Thomas* (London: Hodder and Stoughton, 1981)
——, *The Patriot* (London: Hodder and Stoughton, 1982)
——, *Lord of the Isles* (London: Hodder and Stoughton, 1983)
——, *The Riven Realm* (London: Hodder and Stoughton, 1984)

——, *Unicorn Rampant* (London: Hodder and Stoughton, 1984)
——, *James, By The Grace of God* (London: Hodder and Stoughton, 1985)
——, *Rough Wooing* (London: Hodder and Stoughton, 1986)
——, *Columba* (London: Hodder and Stoughton, 1987)
——, *The Flowers of Chivalry* (London: Hodder and Stoughton, 1988)
——, *Mail Royal* (London: Hodder and Stoughton, 1989)
——, *Warden of the Queen's March* (London: Hodder and Stoughton, 1989)
URQUHART, Fred, *Palace of the Green Days* (London: Quartet, 1979)
——, *A Diver in China Seas* (London: Quartet, 1980)
——, *Proud Lady in a Cage* (Edinburgh: Paul Harris, 1980)
——, *Seven Ghosts in Search* (London: William Kimber, 1983)
——, *Full Score*, ed. Graeme Roberts (Aberdeen University Press, 1989)
WATSON, William, *Beltran in Exile* (London: Chatto and Windus, 1979)
——, *The Knight on the Bridge* (London: Chatto and Windus, 1982)
WILLIAMS, Gordon, *The Upper Pleasure Garden* (London: Secker and Warburg, 1970)
——, *Walk Don't Walk* (London: Allison and Busby, 1972)
——, *Big Morning Blues* (London: Hodder and Stoughton, 1974)
——, *Pomeroy* (London: Michael Joseph, 1983)
YORKES, Matthew, *The March Fence* (London: Viking, 1988)

About the Contributors

CAROL ANDERSON is a graduate of the universities of Aberdeen and Edinburgh. She has taught in Japan and Italy, and is a Lecturer in Scottish Literature at the University of Glasgow. She edited Violet Jacob's *Diaries and Letters from India 1895–1900* (1990), and is preparing an edition of Jacob's historical novel, *Flemington*, to be published in 1993 by the Association of Scottish Literary Studies.

JOHN BURNS received his PhD from the University of Edinburgh in 1982 and is a short-story writer and the author of *Celebrating the Light*, a study of Neil Gunn's interest in Zen Buddhsim. A founding editor of *Cencrastus*, he has written widely on modern Scottish literature in articles published both at home and abroad.

CAIRNS CRAIG is a lecturer in English and Scottish literature at the University of Edinburgh. He is the author of *Yeats, Eliot, Pound and the Politics of Poetry* (1982) and *Out of History* (1992). He is the editor of Polygon's *Determinations* series, and was general editor of the four-volume *History of Scottish Literature* (1987–90). He has been closely involved with the magazines *Cencrastus* and *Radical Scotland*, and is the author of many highly influential articles on Scottish literature, culture and politics.

BETH DICKSON, a graduate of the Universities of St Andrews and Strathclyde, writes mainly about twentieth-century Scottish fiction. She lives in Kilmarnock and continues with essay-writing and reviewing as the demands of children permit.

DOUGLAS DUNN is Professor of English Literature at the University of St Andrews. His most recent collections of poetry are *Elegies* (1985), *Selected Poems* (1986) and *Northlight* (1988). He has published a collection of short stories, *Secret Villages*, and has edited *Scotland: An*

Anthology (1991) and *The Faber Book of Twentieth Century Scottish Poetry* (1992).

DOUGLAS GIFFORD is Senior Lecturer in the Department of Scottish Literature at the University of Glasgow. He is the author of *Lewis Grassic Gibbon and Neil M. Gunn* (1983), and has published extensively in the field of Scottish literature, especially on nineteenth- and twentieth-century fiction. He reviews Scottish fiction regularly for *Books in Scotland* and *The Bibliotheck*.

CHRISTOPHER HARVIE is Professor of British and Irish Studies at the University of Tübingen in Germany. A regular broadcaster and commentator on European and Scottish politics, he is the author of *No Gods and Precious Few Heroes: Scotland 1914–1980* (1981), *Scotland and Nationalism: Scottish Society and Politics* (1977) and *The Centre of Things: Political Fiction in Britain from Disraeli to the Present* (1991).

ALISON LUMSDEN is a research assistant at the Centre of Scott Research at Aberdeen University. She has recently completed a PhD thesis on nineteenth-century Scottish fiction in relation to postmodern thought at the University of Edinburgh.

MARGERY METZSTEIN is a part-time lecturer in a college of further education in Glasgow and is completing her PhD thesis on Dorothy Richardson and Modernity. Previous research includes a dissertation on the novels of Catherine Carswell, since when her commitment to women's writing and feminism has rapidly increased. She is a mature student and single parent, and tutors adult learners with the Open University and in community education.

EDWIN MORGAN was born in Glasgow in 1920. He was formerly Emeritus Professor of English Literature at the University of Glasgow, and is at present a visiting professor at the University College of Wales in Aberystwyth. Recent publications include *Collected Poems* (1990), *Crossing the Border: Essays on Scottish Literature* (1990), *Nothing Not Giving Messages* (1990; interviews and lectures) and *Hold Hands Among the Atoms* (1991; poems).

THOM NAIRN is Managing Editor of *Cencrastus* and is Writer-in-Residence with Ross and Cromarty District Council. Other editorial work includes the *Scottish Literary Journal Review Supplement*, *Understanding* and *Northwords*. With Robert Crawford, he co-edited *The Arts of Alasdair Gray* (1991). He has recently completed a PhD thesis on Sydney Goodsir Smith at the University of Edinburgh, and his poetry has appeared in several magazines and anthologies.

GLENDA NORQUAY is a Senior Lecturer in Literary Studies at Liverpool Polytechnic. Her doctoral thesis at Edinburgh University focused on the relationship between Calvinism and realism in the work of nineteenth- and twentieth-century Scottish novelists, and included detailed studies of Robert Louis Stevenson, Robin Jenkins and Muriel Spark. She has published various articles in this area and on Scottish women's writing. She is currently researching fiction of the Women's Suffrage campaigns.

IAN RANKIN was born in Cardenden, Fife, in 1960, and studied English Literature at the University of Edinburgh, eventually working towards a doctoral thesis on Muriel Spark. However, he found himself writing books rather than reading them, and consequently became the author of six novels and a collection of short stories. He has been a Hawthornden Fellow, and was awarded the 1991 Chandler-Fulbright Fellowship.

IAN SPRING is a lecturer in Media and Cultural Studies at Queen Margaret College, Edinburgh, and is closely involved with its Centre for Scottish Popular Culture. He is the author of *Phantom Village: The Myth of the New Glasgow* (1990).

RANDALL STEVENSON is a lecturer in English Literature in the University of Edinburgh. He is the author of *The British Novel since the Thirties* (1986), *The British Novel in the Twentieth Century: An Introductory Bibliography* (1988), *Modernist Fiction* (1992) and several articles on modern fiction and drama, including the chapter on recent Scottish drama in *The History of Scottish Literature* (1987). He also reviews Scottish Theatre for the *Times Literary Supplement* and *The Independent*.

GAVIN WALLACE is a tutor for Edinburgh University's Centre for Continuing Education and the Open University, and has taught and lectured overseas. His PhD thesis (University of Edinburgh) was a critical reassessment of the fiction of Compton Mackenzie, and focused on relationships between twentieth-century English and Scottish literary culture. A former Assistant Editor of *Cencrastus*, he is currently Director of the Scottish Universities' International Summer School and a regular book-reviewer for *The Scotsman*.

Index